Through Spain with Wellington

Through Spain with Wellington

The Letters of Lieutenant Peter Le Mesurier of the 'Fighting Ninth'

Edited by
Adrian Greenwood

Transcribed by
Gordon Rigby

AMBERLEY

Letters reproduced courtesy of Wigan Archives & Local Studies

Maps and family tree courtesy of the author

First published 2016

Amberley Publishing
The Hill, Stroud
Gloucestershire, GL5 4EP

www.amberley-books.com

British Library Cataloguing in Publication Data.
A catalogue record for this book is available from the British Library.

ISBN 978 1 4456 5456 0 (hardback)
ISBN 978 1 4456 5457 7 (ebook)

Typesetting and Origination by Amberley Publishing.
Printed in the UK.

Contents

Maps and Genealogical Tables

The Le Mesurier Family Tree

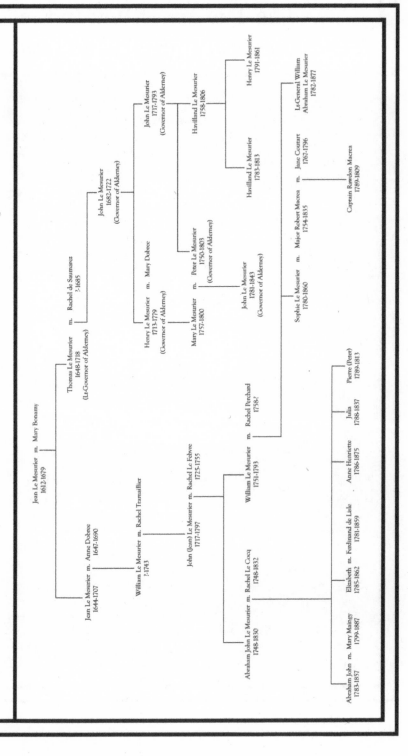

Jean Le Mesurier m. Mary Bonamy
1612-1679

Thomas Le Mesurier m. Rachel de Saumarez
1648-1718   ?-1685
(Lt-Governor of Alderney)

Jean Le Mesurier m. Anne Dobree
1644-1707   1647-1690

John Le Mesurier
1682-1722
(Governor of Alderney)

John Le Mesurier
1717-1793
(Governor of Alderney)

Henry Le Mesurier m. Mary Dobree
1713-1779
(Governor of Alderney)

Havilland Le Mesurier
1758-1806

Henry Le Mesurier
1791-1861

Havilland Le Mesurier
1783-1813

Lt-General William
Abraham Le Mesurier
1782-1877

William Le Mesurier m. Rachel Tramaillier
?-1743

Peter Le Mesurier
1750-1803
(Governor of Alderney)

Mary Le Mesurier m.
1757-1800

John Le Mesurier
1781-1843
(Governor of Alderney)

Sophie Le Mesurier m. Major Robert Macrea
1780-1860   1754-1835

Jane Coutart
1767-1796

Captain Rawdon Macrea
1789-1809

John (Jean) Le Mesurier m. Rachel Le Febvre
1717-1797   1725-1755

William Le Mesurier m. Rachel Perchand
1751-1793   1758?

Abraham John Le Mesurier m. Rachel Le Cocq
1748-1830   1748-1832

Elizabeth m. Ferdinand de Lisle
1785-1862   1781-1859

Anne Henriette
1786-1875

Julia
1788-1837

Pierre (Peter)
1789-1813

Abraham John m. Mary Maingy
1783-1857   1799-1887

The Theatre of War in the Iberian Peninsula 1808–14

FRANCE

Corunna
Betanzos
Lugo
Santander
San Sebastian
Bayonne
Vitoria
Pampeluna
Vigo
Astorga
Sahagun
Burgos
Sanabria
Castro-gonzalo
Valladolid
EBRO
Braganza
ESLA
DOURO
Oporto
Lamego
Tordesillas
TORMES
Salamanca
Viseu
Almeida
Busaco
Guarda
Ciudad Rodrigo
Madrid
Coimbra
Sabugal
Talavera
Castel Branco
TAGUS
Vimeiro
PORTUGAL
Badajoz
SPAIN
Lisbon
Malaga
Cadiz
Barrosa
Gibraltar
Tarifa
Ceuta

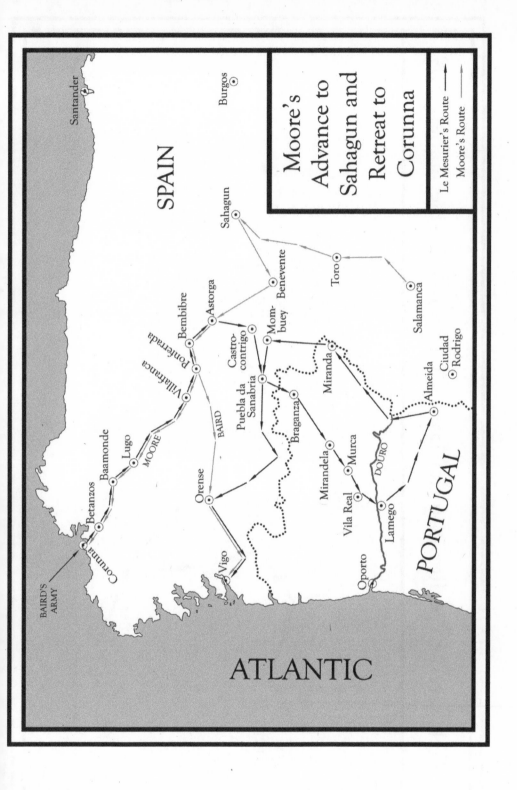

Moore's Advance to Sahagun and Retreat to Corunna

Le Mesurier's Route →
Moore's Route →

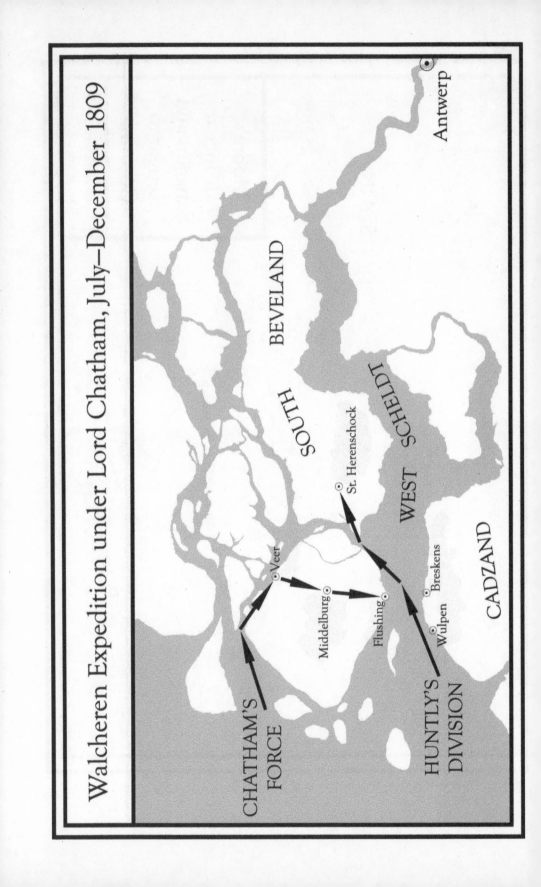

Walcheren Expedition under Lord Chatham, July–December 1809

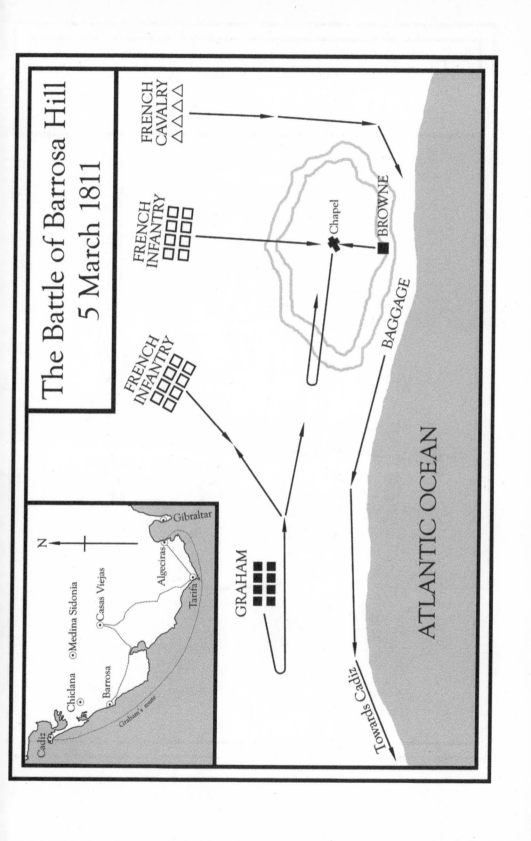

The Battle of Barrosa Hill
5 March 1811

FRENCH CAVALRY △△△△

FRENCH INFANTRY □□□□ □□□□

FRENCH INFANTRY □□□□ □□□□

Chapel

BROWNE

BAGGAGE

GRAHAM

ATLANTIC OCEAN

Towards Cadiz

N

Gibraltar

Medina Sidonia

Casas Viejas

Algeciras

Chiclana

Barrosa

Tarifa

Cadiz

Graham's route

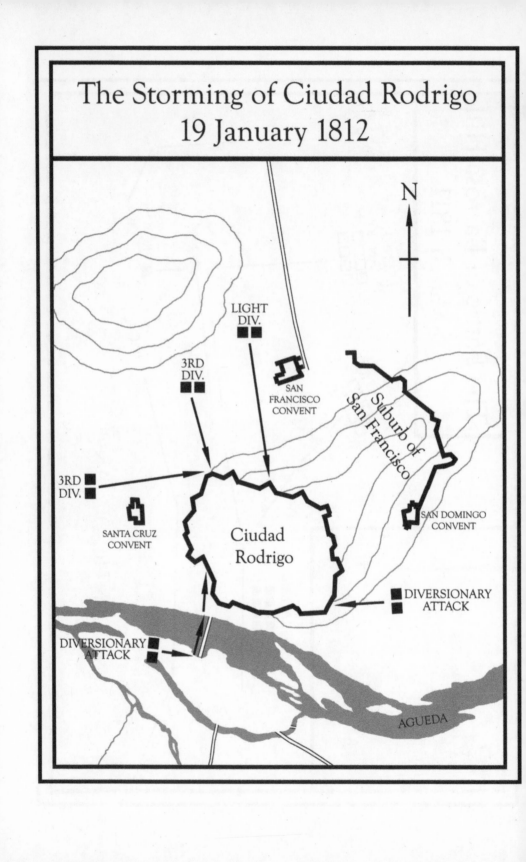

The Storming of Ciudad Rodrigo
19 January 1812

N

LIGHT
DIV.

3RD
DIV.

SAN
FRANCISCO
CONVENT

Suburb of
San Francisco

3RD
DIV.

SAN DOMINGO
CONVENT

SANTA CRUZ
CONVENT

Ciudad
Rodrigo

DIVERSIONARY
ATTACK

DIVERSIONARY
ATTACK

AGUEDA

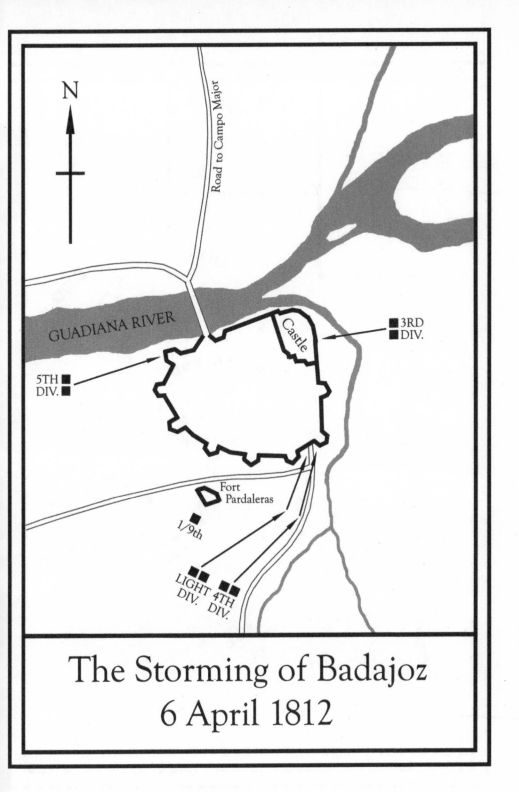

N

Road to Campo Major

GUADIANA RIVER

Castle

■ 3RD
■ DIV.

5TH ■
DIV. ■

Fort
Pardaleras

1/9th

LIGHT 4TH
DIV.   DIV.

The Storming of Badajoz
6 April 1812

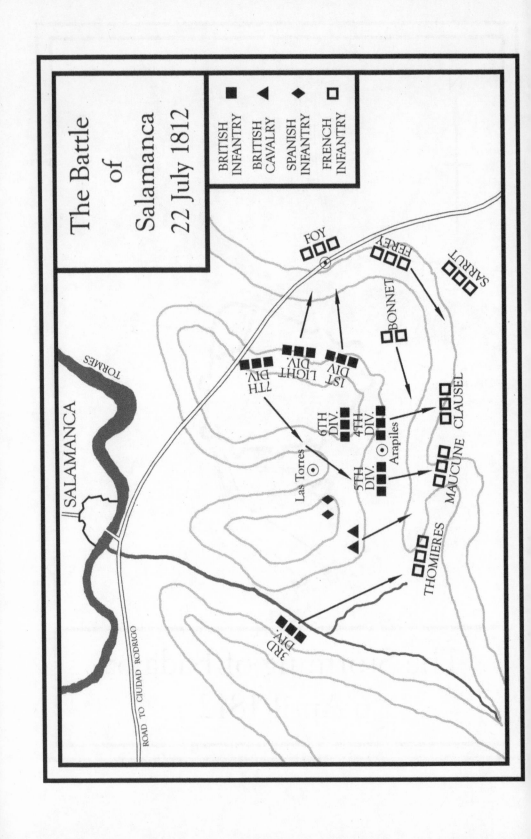

The Battle of Salamanca 22 July 1812

■ BRITISH INFANTRY
◀ BRITISH CAVALRY
◆ SPANISH INFANTRY
□ FRENCH INFANTRY

SALAMANCA

TORMES

ROAD TO CIUDAD RODRIGO

Las Torres

7TH DIV.

1ST LIGHT DIV.

6TH DIV.

4TH DIV.

5TH DIV.

Arapiles

3RD DIV.

THOMIERES

MAUCUNE

CLAUSEL

BONNET

FOY

FEREY

SARRUT

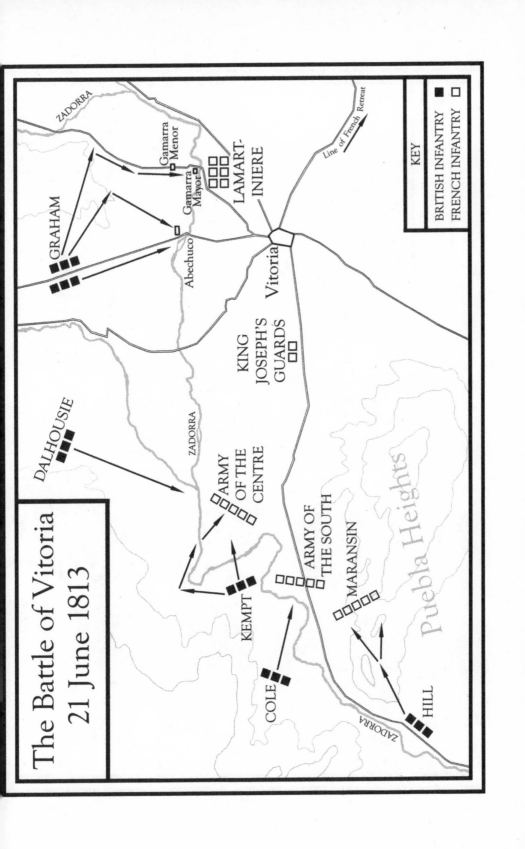

The Battle of Vitoria
21 June 1813

KEY

BRITISH INFANTRY ■
FRENCH INFANTRY □

ZADORRA

Gamarra Menor

Gamarra Mayor

Abechuco

LAMART-INIERE

Line of French Retreat

GRAHAM

Vitoria

DALHOUSIE

ZADORRA

KING JOSEPH'S GUARDS

ARMY OF THE CENTRE

KEMPT

COLE

ARMY OF THE SOUTH

MARANSIN

Puebla Heights

ZADORRA

HILL

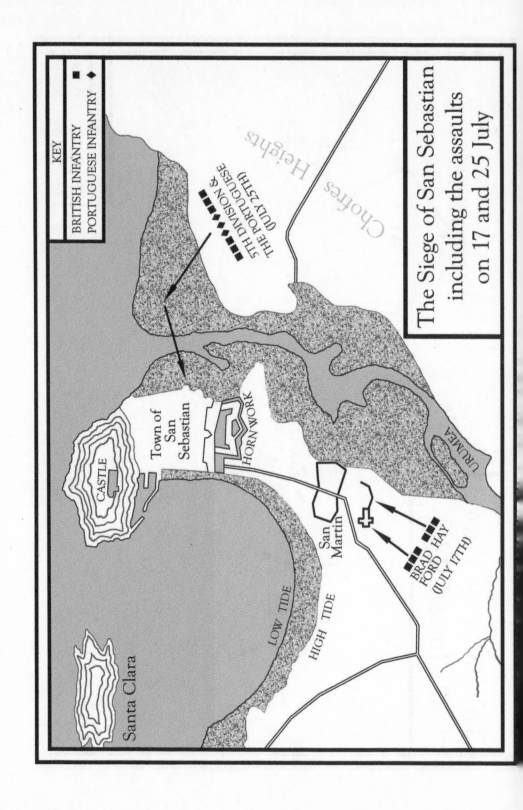

The Siege of San Sebastian including the assaults on 17 and 25 July

KEY

■ BRITISH INFANTRY
◆ PORTUGUESE INFANTRY

Choftes Heights

5TH DIVISION &
THE PORTUGUESE
(JULY 25TH)

Town of San Sebastian

CASTLE

Santa Clara

HORNWORK

San Martin

LOW TIDE

HIGH TIDE

URUMEA

BRADFORD HAY
(JULY 17TH)

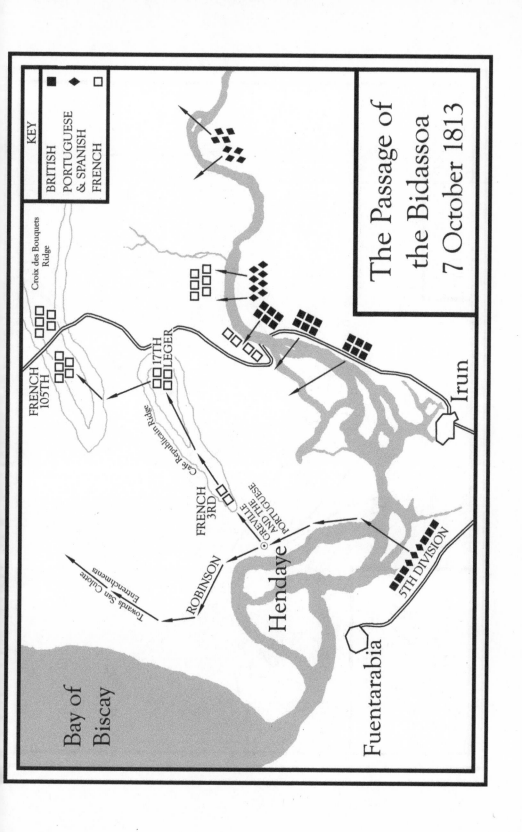

The Passage of
the Bidassoa
7 October 1813

KEY

BRITISH ■
PORTUGUESE & SPANISH ◆
FRENCH □

Croix des Bouquets Ridge

FRENCH 105TH

17TH LEGER

Café Republicain Ridge

FRENCH 3RD

GREVILLE AND THE PORTUGUESE

Hendaye

ROBINSON

Towards San Culotte Entrenchments

Irun

Fuentarabia

5TH DIVISION

Bay of Biscay

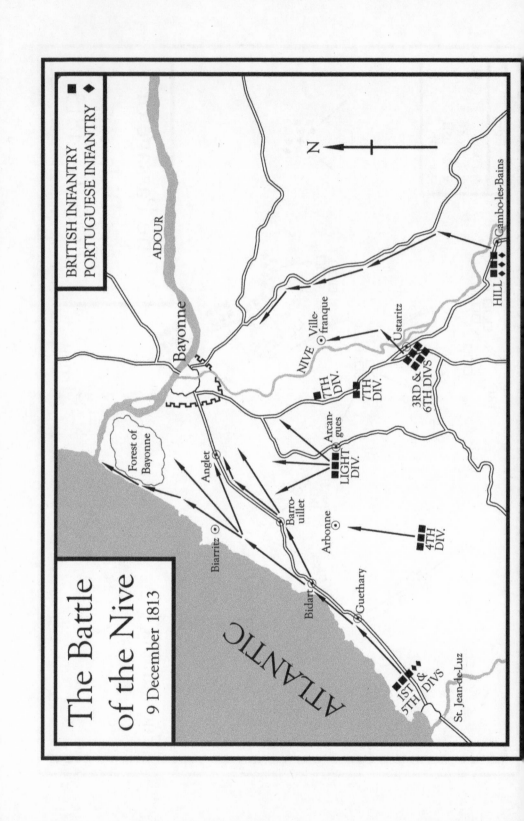

The Battle
of the Nive
9 December 1813

BRITISH INFANTRY
PORTUGUESE INFANTRY

N

ADOUR

Bayonne

ATLANTIC

Forest of
Bayonne

Biarritz

Anglet

Barro-
uillet

Arbonne

Bidart

Guethary

St. Jean-de-Luz

1ST &
5TH DIVS

4TH
DIV.

LIGHT
DIV.

Arcan-
gues

NIVE

Ville-
franque

7TH
DIV.

7TH
DIV.

Ustaritz

3RD &
6TH DIVS

HILL

Cambo-les-Bains

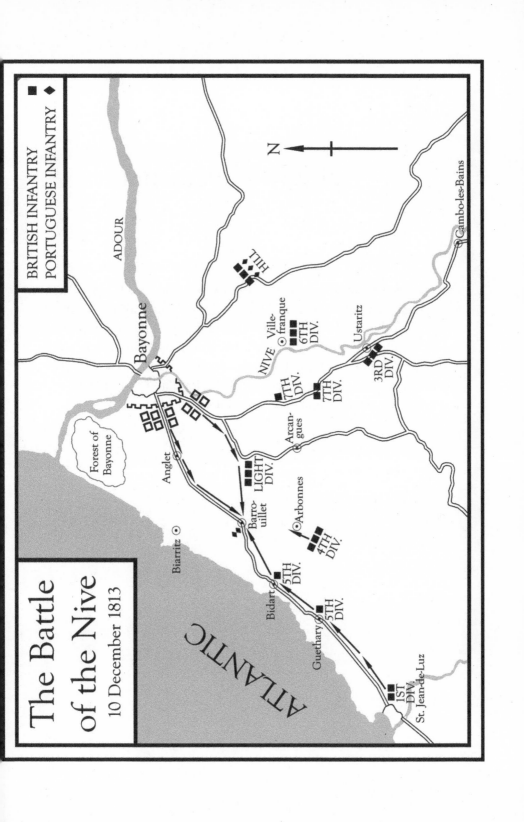

The Battle
of the Nive
10 December 1813

BRITISH INFANTRY
PORTUGUESE INFANTRY

N

ATLANTIC

ADOUR

Bayonne

Forest of
Bayonne

Biarritz

Anglet

NIVE

Ville-
franque

6TH
DIV.

HILL

Arcan-
gues

7TH
DIV.

7TH
DIV.

Ustaritz

3RD
DIV.

Cambo-les-Bains

LIGHT
DIV.

Barro-
uillet

Arbonnes

4TH
DIV.

Bidart

5TH
DIV.

Guethary

5TH
DIV.

St. Jean-de-Luz

1ST
DIV.

Acknowledgements

My sincere thanks to Stephen Knott, Alex Miller and Gordon Rigby of Wigan Archives Service, Stephen Foote and Ray Le Mesurier-Foster of the Guernsey Society, Kate Thaxton of the Royal Norfolk Regimental Museum, the staff, librarians and archivists at the Bodleian Library, the British Library and the National Archives, and the editors and designers at Amberley Publishing for all their work preparing the book for publication.

Author's Note

I have tried to keep as close to the letter book as possible, retaining the spelling, capitalisation of nouns and contractions, but as the letter book is itself an early nineteenth-century transcription, one cannot be sure they appear exactly as Le Mesurier wrote them, especially so when it comes to passages in foreign languages. It would seem that, unlike Le Mesurier, the transcriber was not multilingual, and these sections often make no sense. In places I have had to make an educated guess at the meaning, but it should not be regarded as an authoritative translation.

Where the letters were transcribed out of sequence, I have placed them in chronological order. The original transcription had virtually no punctuation so I have added it where I thought best. I have also removed the sections of the *London Gazette* quoted, and Byron's poem 'On the Death of Sir Peter Parker' which appeared at the end of the book, since these are readily available online.

In order to maintain a certain pace through the book, and for reasons of space, a small number of the letters in chapters 3–5, covering Le Mesurier's time in England, Gibraltar, Guernsey and Portugal, either recuperating or waiting for active service, have been removed where they contain information repeated in other letters or nothing of historical interest.

Introduction

Any unpublished letters from the Peninsular War are scarce, but to find such an extensive collection, covering the retreat to Corunna, the Walcheren expedition, the sieges of Ciudad Rodrigo, Badajoz, Burgos and San Sebastian, and the Battles of Salamanca, Vitoria, the Nivelle and the Nive, is rare indeed. The letters of Peter Le Mesurier include most of the key campaigns of the war – one or other battalion of the 'Fighting Ninth' saw service throughout.

As well as the big battles, Le Mesurier was involved in some fascinating sideshows. While the British Army is retreating to Corunna, he stumbles through enemy territory with a treasure convoy; sailing for Gibraltar his ship gets lost and runs into a privateer; he witnesses the murder of a French officer by the Spanish soldiers who had accepted his surrender; at San Sebastian he watches his sword shatter into 'twenty pieces' in the midst of a French sortie; and, as Badajoz is sacked, he shelters twenty women from the chaos: 'I lost a pair of Shoes in their defence, in Shewing a Portugeese Soldier the most expeditious way of retreating with an Enemy pressing hard on him.'

He suffers crafty horsedealers, light-fingered servants, a quarantine ship, rats eating his pillow, a captain stabling his horse in his kitchen and the capture by Turks of his sister and brother-in-law, but he always remains optimistic. His goal, 'Matrimony to any Lady with a decent fortune' so he might 'retire to live quietly in some little cottage,' is never far from his mind. He doesn't find a wife but he does fall in love.

The first mention I found of Le Mesurier's fascinating correspondence was in Antony Brett-James's book *Life in Wellington's Army* (Allen & Unwin, 1972). I was writing a biography of Field Marshal Colin Campbell, Lord Clyde, who served in the same regiment as Le Mesurier, the 9th Foot. Sources from the regiment were scarce, so it was exciting to hear of a new, unpublished one. But when Brett-James read the letters in the 1970s, they belonged to Edward Hall, a dealer in manuscripts. Tracking down Le Mesurier's correspondence forty years later would be hard, especially since both Hall and Brett-James were dead. Fortunately, I discovered that Edward Hall had donated numerous manuscripts to his local library in Wigan. When I visited in late 2013 I found an early nineteenth-century copybook of letters detailing Le Mesurier's service from the earliest days of the Peninsular War almost to its end.

Written in a clear, intelligible hand, they are peppered with a wry humour, some very human fears and admissions, and the casual understatement of the British officer. They begin with a touching naivety and horror at the behaviour of his fellow officers. They end with something approaching cynicism bound up with heartfelt camaraderie. Le Mesurier starts as a boy, but grows into a man.

The Le Mesurier Family

Soldiering was in the blood. The Le Mesuriers, an old Channel Islands family, provided the army with many officers. By the time Peter was gazetted, Havilland Le Mesurier (1758–1806) had been commissary-general, and his son, also called Havilland, was a captain in the 21st Fusiliers. Havilland Jnr's cousin, John Le Mesurier, had been a major but had retired on half-pay* in 1802 to become hereditary governor of Alderney. Peter's cousin, William Le Mesurier, was a lieutenant in the 24th Foot and would go on to become a lieutenant-general.

Though they had the right to bear the Le Mesurier arms,[1] Peter's branch of the family were very much poor relations. They lived on Guernsey at a house called Les Beaucamps,† built in 1608 and purchased by Peter's father, Abraham John Le Mesurier, around 1790. It was a modest home, the exterior suggesting 'a mere cottage', 'out-classed by the colonnaded Beaucamp de Haut of J. Abe Le Mesurier, and by the many storied Beaucamp de Bas'.[2]

The Le Mesuriers had five children who survived to adulthood: Abraham, Elizabeth, Anne, Julia and, born on 30 October 1789, before war with France broke out, Pierre. By the time he received his commission, he had diplomatically anglicised his name to

---

* On half-pay an officer retained his rank but received only half the normal pay. He was free to do what he liked until recalled and restored to full pay.

† Variously recorded as The Beaucamps, The Beauchamps or Les Beauchamps. By the 1950s, having had its thatch replaced by heavier tiles, the walls had developed cracks. The house was demolished in the 1960s. It stood around 300 yards from the modern school of the same name.

'Peter'. Peter's elder brother, Abraham, had established himself in trade and his eldest sister, Elizabeth, was already married. That still left Peter's sisters, Julia and Anne, to support, another reason why Peter, unlike many young officers, never received any regular additional income from his family.

Most of Peter's letters are to his siblings or his father. Remarkably few are to his mother, Rachel Le Mesurier (née le Cocq). The first appears in March 1810, and it is clear from the precis of his military career that Peter includes, that the two of them had been out of contact for over a year. As with many elements of Peter's life, this is never fully explained. That curiosity aside, it is clear they were a close and loving family.

Life in the 9th Foot

The 9th Foot, a solid, respectable infantry regiment, was first raised in 1685 by James II in response to the Duke of Monmouth's rebellion. Lacking the prestige of the cavalry or the cachet of the Foot Guards, it nevertheless had a reputation for hard fighting, a reputation not always welcomed among the men. 'Some compared it to cockfighting,' wrote one sergeant, 'for a good game cock may come off victorious in several battles but the case is, in general, that he is tried over and over again, until he is either killed or disabled: so likewise was the case with us.'[1] And so it was to prove for Peter Le Mesurier.

Though nominally the East Norfolk Regiment, the officers and men of the 9th came from every corner of Great Britain and Ireland. The 9th Foot and Guernsey had a connection through the lieutenant-colonel of the first battalion, John Cameron. While stationed on the island in 1803, Cameron had married Amelia Brock, niece of Lord Saumarez, Guernsey's great naval hero. One of Cameron's daughters went on to marry the physician Frederick Le Mesurier, and Cameron himself retired to Guernsey.

At the time of Le Mesurier's commission on 13 August 1808, the 9th Foot consisted of two battalions, each at full strength (around 1,000 men). Four ensigns had been promoted lieutenant, leaving space for four new officers. These ensigncies were available 'without purchase' i.e. without paying the £400 normally demanded by Horse Guards. The need for officers during the Peninsular War was sufficiently high that most infantry ensigncies were free. A testimonial from the Earl of Pembroke secured Le Mesurier his commission. Within a month of being gazetted, he was on a troopship bound for Portugal.

1

Corunna and Vigo

Peter Le Mesurier applied for a commission in King George's army when British prospects were at their bleakest. Napoleon's domination of Europe left the country almost friendless. Sweden and Portugal alone remained allies.

With a million or more conscript soldiers available to Napoleon, a grand continental campaign by British troops was unfeasible, yet if the French were left to consolidate their grip on the Continent and expand their navy, eventually Britain would be starved into submission or invaded. Rather than battling Napoleon head-on, the British chose to face him where conditions least favoured the emperor.

In October 1807 the Spanish government allowed French troops under General Jean-Andoche Junot to cross their territory to invade Portugal. But once Portugal was conquered, Napoleon seized power in Spain too and installed his brother as the new king in Madrid. Spain rose up in revolt leaving Junot's army of occupation cut off in Portugal. With both the Portuguese and Spanish eager to chase the French from the Iberian peninsula, it seemed the perfect theatre for a British offensive against Bonaparte.

D^r: Father   Ramsgate Sept^r: 12th: 1808

Two days after I wrote to you an order came from General Brownrigg[*] for Ensigns Luscombe, Ruse & Le Mesurier to hold

---

[*] In the 9th Foot, Lieutenant-General Robert Brownrigg (1759–1833) was colonel of the regiment. Having served with the Duke of York in the Netherlands, he

themselves in readiness to march with the Men fit for actual service to Ramsgate on the shortest notice.

The next day (Thursday) we received orders to march on the morrow at Seven in the morning. Ruse was gone to Maidstone, his native place, to get some of his things he had left behind, and Luscombe received an order to stay at Canterbury on account of L^r: Edwards being sick, so that I was obliged to march at the head of Eleven Men. On the road I was joined by another Detachment (of the 97th) of eitheen men commanded by a Sarg^t: who put himself under my command so that I came at the head of a formidable force into this Town, which was about one oclock afternoon, after which I was obliged to give in the embarkation return, and had several things to do before I coud get my Dinner which I eate with good appetite.

The distance from Canterbury to Ramsgate is 18 miles and the Roads were very heavy, it having rained all the preceding day, but I kept at the head of the party for the example, as there were some that lag'd behind. Last night I slept onboard the Transport and laid very comfortably. My pillow was my greatcoat and Boat cloak, which I can carry in my Shoulder Straps and will serve me for a Bed on the field.

There are three of the Staff corps among us. Captn Louzern,* uncle to a worthy member of the free and easy club, is one of them. Coll. Nicolay† will command the troops on board our own Ship. I suppose we shall sail this afternoon for the Downs.‡

had become military secretary at Horse Guards upon the duke's appointment as commander-in-chief in 1798, and in 1803 had been promoted to major-general and quartermaster-general.
* Captain Henry William Lauzun, Royal Staff Corps.
† Lieutenant-Colonel William Nicolay (1771–1842). Having joined the Royal Engineers he had served in the West Indies and India (including at the Battle of Seringapatam), before being appointed to the newly formed Royal Staff Corps in 1801. He went on to be governor of various British Caribbean colonies and a lieutenant-general.
‡ The stretch of sea off the coast of Kent between North and South Foreland. In the age of sail it served as a mustering point for naval ships and a safe anchorage during heavy weather, protected on the east by the Goodwin Sands and to the north and west by the Kent coast.

Le Mesurier boarded a troop ship carrying a ragbag of detachments, with just a handful of men from his own regiment. Both battalions of the 9th Foot were already in Portugal. The 1/9th had sailed from Cork on 12 July and disembarked at Mondego Bay between 1–5 August. They were part of a 9,000 strong army under the command of Lieutenant-General Sir Arthur Wellesley.* On 7–8 August Wellesley had been reinforced by 5,000 troops under General Brent Spencer.

Wellesley planned to march down the coast towards Lisbon, but Junot despatched an army north to stop him. Their first encounter was at the village of Roliça on 17 August. Here the British found a detachment of 5,000 French soldiers under General Henri Delaborde. The 1/9th were among those who engaged the enemy, forcing them to retreat and winning a technical victory, but Wellesley ended the battle with almost as many casualties as Delaborde.

Two days later, the 2/9th landed at the mouth of the Maceira River as part of Brigadier-General Anstruther's brigade. Strengthened by these troops and a second brigade under Brigadier-General Acland, Wellesley advanced to Vimeiro to face the French again. Unaware that Wellesley had been reinforced, Junot was confident of victory, but one by one the French brigades were repulsed.

Having won the first convincing British victory over Napoleon's forces in the peninsula, Wellesley was prevented from pressing home the advantage. Just as the French began to retire, Lieutenant-General Sir Harry Burrard arrived and took command. Too cautious to exploit his enemy's weakness, Burrard refused to pursue Junot.

The French offered a truce, opened negotiations and secured the Convention of Cintra. Under its generous terms Junot's troops were free to leave Portugal with their materiel and even their loot. The convention 'pared the nails of the British lion,' yet kept 'unclipped the wings of the French eagles.'[1] Wellesley was recalled to England to answer for his role in the convention.

D:F.   Falmouth Road Sept^r: 23^d: 1808

I have not been on shore leave since I embarked at Ramsgate. We

---

* Later the Duke of Wellington.

are to be joined by Sir David Baird,* expected here from Cork, and
by some Troops from Harwich. The wind is fair for both fleets. It
blows a brisk gale from the North North East.

I find myself so comfortable on board this vessel the (Peace Brig)
that I do not like the idea of stirring. I have not been sick. The first
days I had a little headach but it is gone and I feel quite at home.

We are five Subalterns on board obliged to do duty. Instead of
watching four hours alternately we watch twenty four, so that my
turn comes every five days. We are not allowed then to leave Deck
but at meals and when it rains. I begin to be used to it. I have had
the pleasure of walking the Deck a few nights. Capt[n]: Louzern kept
me company last night till past 11 o'Clock. He is a very pleasant
man. He is a married man with four Children and has left both
Wife and children behind. He has been right, for I think women
endure many hardships in transports therefore please to tell my
good Sister Ann that I do not intend to Marry before I am totally
unfit for His Majesty's service.[†]

Sept[r]: 25th: The Harwich fleet came round yeasterday. They have
the 43[d] 1st: Batt[n]: and several other Rg[ts]: They left the Spaniards in
the Downs. They are expected here soon. We shall only wait for
the Cork fleet.

Following Wellesley's recall to London, Lieutenant-General
Sir John Moore had landed in Portugal. Dynamic, intrepid
and popular, he was a striking contrast to Burrard. The
government instructed Moore be given 20,000 troops to invade
Spain, distract Napoleon's battalions and relieve pressure on
the Spanish rebels. The 1/9th would advance from Portugal
as part of Moore's army while the 2/9th would stay outside
Lisbon to help garrison Portugal and maintain a toehold in
case of a French counter-attack.

An additional 12,000 troops commanded by Sir David Baird,
including Le Mesurier, would land at the port of Corunna on
the north coast of Galicia. Corunna was selected 'partly on
account of its safe and spacious port, partly because it was

---

* Lieutenant-General Sir David Baird (1757–1829) had fought in India and
  Egypt, and in 1806 seized Cape Town from the Dutch.
† Officers were free to take their wives and children to war. A few wives of
  common soldiers were allowed to accompany their husbands. They were
  selected by ballot. They washed, cooked and plundered for the regiment.

believed that food and draught animals could be collected with comparative ease from Galicia.'[2] From there, Baird would march south-east to rendezvous with Moore.

Corrunna, October 14th: 1808

The wind being fair on Sunday last the convoy made a signal for the Fleet to weigh anchor and sail. We lay to at the mouth of Falmouth harbour till near Two o'Clock, till the whole of the Fleet, about 150 ships, were out. We then proceeded and arrived here about noon yeasterday.

A Spanish Gun Brig laying close to us told us they were to have rejoicings in the evening for the affair of Bilboa.[*] The Town was illuminated and the Bells made a noise (I can call it nothing else for I think our Câtel Bells[†] are Coelestial compared to these).

A week ago I met Tupper Carry[‡] at Falmouth. He did not know that I was there and was a little surprised to see me. He told me that Saumarez Dobrie[§] was on board of one of the Transports with him. I meant to have gone onboard to see him but it blew so hard Saturday that it was impossible for me to get a boat. I shall go as soon as I can to see both Cary and him.

As soon as we came in yesterday there was an Order from Sir D: Beard for no Officer to go on Shore, but leave has been granted for three to go at a time and to return onboard early.

We have seen some of the Spanish patriots this morning. If one judged from their appearance there woud be very little to fear from them.

October 15th: When we were in the Bay of Biscay we saw a large fleet of Transports and have since learnt that it was a part of Junots army under the convoy of the Resistance that was to see them as far as Rochefort and land them there. Whilst at Falmouth I saw a

---

[*] The Spanish army of Galicia, under General Joaquin Blake, had chased the French out of Bilbao on 11 October.

[†] The parish of St. Marie de Castel, Guernsey.

[‡] The Tuppers were an old Guernsey family. Tupper Carey (1788–1867) had joined the commissariat in 1804 (*see* Jacob, 139). A William Le Mesurier Tupper was commissioned into the 23rd Royal Welch Fusiliers in 1823.

[§] A member of another old Guernsey family.

Country paper with The Gazette* about this affair of Lisbon† on which their remarks were very severe. At the top of this paper was a Gibet with two Men hanging on it, which pleased the Officers very much.

Baird's men were prevented from disembarking by the Galician Junta, which 'assumed an attitude of very suspicious humility,' as Oman recorded, 'stating that … they thought it beyond their competence to give consent to the landing of such a large body of men.' 'Their real reason for so doing was that they wished the British troops to disembark further east, at Gihon or Santander.' 'All that they cared for was to preserve Galicia from the strain of having to make provisions for the feeding and transport of a second army.'[3]

Consequently, a messenger had to be despatched to obtain permission to disembark from the Central Junta. The Spanish officer entrusted with the request took his time, and when he did return with permission, it came with the recommendation that Baird should send his troops forward, not as one army, but in small brigades over several days. Meanwhile, Moore's troops were already well on their way into Spain.

October the 25th

I have been on shore two or three times. The Streets are very narrow but paved with very fine Stones. The Inhabitants are very dirty, particularly the women. I saw one of them hunting in the hair of her child with its head on a cake that was exposed for sales and cracking at a famous rate. After that sight I had no great wish to buy a piece of it, tho perhaps I may be very glad to meet with such a one in my Campaign.

They have small Carts drawn by two oxen. The axle tree is made fast to the wheel and goes through a hole made in a board that is fixed at each side of the cart which they are not allowed to grease so that it makes a continual creaking. This law was made on account of an old Friar, a very good man, that was run over by a Cart at night and did not hear it coming.‡

* *The London Gazette.*
† i.e. the Convention of Cintra.
‡ See also Glover, G., 46.

I went on shore yeasterday and went to see the Lighthouse about Two miles N.O. of the town of Corrunna.* It is a beautyful building about 200 feet high built of fine square stones. I went at the top from which I could see the whole of the town and harbour which had a very grand appearance. Returning from thence we went to see a place where they were making musket balls and cartridges for the Guns. We were received very civilly and permitted to walk all about the place.

A few Nights ago a Gentleman of this place who had subscribed £500 for the Patriots was attack by Two blacks and cut in the face in Eight different places. He was returning about 2 o'Clock in the morning from a visit to some officers on board of one of the transports. The villains made their escape. Some of our Officers have also been stabed at night which makes them now more cautious how they parade them in the dark.

Our detachement is attached to the 23ᵈ Regimᵗ: or Royal Welch Fusileers. We are to march with them till we join our own. We have had an allowance made for our Baggage and Forage, money amounting to £8:15: Out of this it was at first ordered that Three Subalterns together should buy a Mule which would cost 35 Guineas so that we woud have been out of Pocket. This orde caused some grumbling even among the Field Officers† and it was recall'd yeasterday, and it is understood we are to pay for them on some future day (which I hope is very distant) and at a lower rate than 11 Guineas each.

D. F.   Lugo November the 9ᵗʰ: 1808

We landed on the 29ᵗʰ: of October in the morning and marched in Barracks for that day. In the evening I went to the play. The Players dance and sing pretty well, but their acting is very bad. The Theatre is small but neatly fitted up.

On the 30ᵗʰ: we marched from Corrunna to Betanzos. The Town is small and dirty. It is four Spanish leagues from Corrunna, which

---

* The 180-foot-high Tower of Hercules, north-west of the old town of Corunna, is the oldest Roman lighthouse still in use. By N.O. Le Mesurier means 'Nord-Ouest' or north-west.
† Majors, lieutenant-colonels and colonels.

is, I suppose, 17 or 18 English miles.* The roads are almost as good as the English roads, but very dirty as the rainy season has set in and we are hardly a day without rain. I was a little tired when we came to Betanzos as I had taken hardly any exercise for a long time before.

We staid there five days. There are Three large Convents in it. The Monks are very polite. In one where troops were quartered, they gave our Officers small rooms with good beds and sent them a supply of fruit and wine. I fortunately procured myself a good Billet in a Gentlemen's house with an excellent Bed by talking a little French with an old Gentleman I met in the Convent.

From Betanzos we marched on the 6th: to Cavallotorto,† the road good but very high hills to go over. Here we encamped. We were four Officers in one tent and were comfortable till towards morning when it began to blow fresh and we found it rather cold. We were about a Mile from this village. An Officer who went there to procure Carts for our Baggage says that there are very few homes and that the best quarter he could get that night was among Cattle.

The next place we came to was Alamonda,‡ another small village. The whole of the 23d Regt:, about 600 men strong, were quartered in one house. It was intended at first that 100 men should be lodged in the house and the rest under tents, but as the Baggage Carts did not come up and it rained very hard, the men all came to shelter themselves in this house. The Officers slept in hay lofts or in every small corner, wherever they could find room.

We marched to this place yeasterday. It rained almost the whole day so that we had a complete soking and mud to our ankle the most part of the way. I do not feel tired at present after marching 16 or 18 miles. I begin to be seasoned to the marching and rain. I never leave a Town with a haversack empty. I always take bread and if I can get any kind of meat I buy it and a Small quantity of spirit to put in my Canteen to drink with water, as their wine is new and very sour. Chocolate I think is very dear. They charge us half a

---

* In fact an English league is 3 miles and a Spanish league 2.6 miles.
† Carballo Torto.
‡ Baamonde.

pistrine* for a small cup. I could take a dozen for my breakfast, but I drink Coffé and I can make a good breakfast for 1/6^d:

At dinner I have my allowance of Beef cooked at my Billet in one pinte of Wine, which is hardly fit to drink, and in the evening I have something at the Coffé house, so that I live for about Two shillings and Six pence a day, Rations included.†

Our Baggage has been carried for us as far as this place and I suppose will be carried till we join the Regim^t: which I hope will be in less than a forthnight. The Officers of the Reg^t: we are attached to are very polite.

I hope you will not be uneasy if you do not receive Letters from me for some time. We are not masters of our time. We sometimes Halt in a place where there is no post, or are on duty in one where there is a Post Office and cannot find time to write, but you may depend upon it that I will not let an opportunity pass without writing.

This morning I met one of my Guernsey Freinds, S. Dobree. I did not know he was here therefore was very agreably surprised. He looks as well as ever and desired you would be so good to tell his Parents that he had so much to do in his department that he could not write, but desired to be affectionately remembered to them. He is obliged to be up almost night and day to procure provisions and carts, &^{c}:

I belive carrying a good weight on my Shoulder has done my neck good. The swelling has very much decreased lately and I think it is owing to my carrying my Greatcoat, Sword, Canteen and haversack on that shoulder. We encamp for Three Nights. Want of better Quarters. I am &^{c}:

This last letter presaged the supply problems which lay ahead for Moore's army. 'At Betanzos we began to experience the great defectiveness of our commissariat department,' wrote

---

* 'Equal to an English shilling; five pistrines go to a Portuguese dollar, and six to a patacoon or Spanish dollar' reported the *United Service Magazine* (1835, p. 351). *The American Ship-master's Daily Assistant* (1807), however, gives the pistrine as equivalent to 10¾d, so a cup of Spanish chocolate cost the equivalent of 5–6d at a time when a pint of beer or a loaf of bread in England cost tuppence.

† Ensigns received around 4 shillings a day after deductions. The rank and file were paid 1 shilling a day before deductions.

Quartermaster William Surtees of the 95th Rifles, '... for the gentleman sent forward to provide our two battalions with food was so utterly unacquainted with his business that he was actually afraid to make an attempt to issue provisions.' The Commissariat, which provided rations and supplies, was a civil authority under the control of the Treasury, not the army; a separation which caused Wellesley much frustration. Bureaucracy and ignorance were its hallmarks. The commissaries were surprised to find the Spanish would only accept payment in specie rather than British government bills, and Baird had trouble finding enough hard currency to purchase supplies.

Quartering the troops also proved problematic. While Le Mesurier's fellow officers found billets in monks' cells, 'the men occupied only the corridors, into which straw was generally put by the authorities of the place, the men lying as close as pigs in a sty, which indeed was necessary to keep each other warm.'[4]

D^r: F.   Astorga Nov^r: 26th: 1808

We left Lugo on the 10th: and were quartered in small villages till the 12th: when we arrived at Villa Franca.[*] The Soldiers were quartered in a Convent.[†] Whilst we were there it was discovered that the Church had been broke open and the Communion Cup stolen. A strict search was made instantly in the Regiment but nothing was discovered. The Cup is said to have been of Gold ornamented with precious Stones and weighing Three pounds.

We left Villa Franca on the 14th: and arrived here on the 16th: The day we left Villa Franca we went uphill for about Eight Miles. We were a little tired when we came on top, but the weather was cold and the men kept jogging on to keep themselves warm. The mountains on every sides were covered with snow.

We encamped the night at Manzanal.[‡] The Bagage did not come up till night, and I had not my Blankets to sleep in. I borrowed one of the Soldiers' greatcoat and slept pretty well. We had a pot of soup made with our ration beef, a few cabage leaves and patatoes

---

* Villafranca del Bierzo.
† 'Monastery' and 'convent' were often used interchangeably.
‡ Manzanal del Puerto.

without either salt or pepper. A good apetite supplied seasoning. We dispatched the best part of it.

Astorga is a pretty large Town, but badly paved. You run the risk of breaking your neck at every step you take. The Cathedral is beautiful. A number of Saints are carved on the outside, and the plate inside is extremely rich.

On the 17th: a report reached us here that the French were near. In consequence Piquets were sent out and patroled all night. We learnt afterwards that it was about Six hundred light troops and 200 horse that came to Valadolia* to plunder and retreated towards Burgos afterwards. Reports are going about every day but very few prove true. The whole of the Troops (the Light Brigade excepted) have retreated towards Villa Franca. The reason we know not, unless it is for want of the Cavalry which is not come up and which we will require to cross the plains to Salamanca.[†]

You mention I must be particular about the news I give you.[‡] I cannot be more than I have been. We hear nothing but what the Spaniards are pleased to tell us, which in general proves to be untrue. They seem to care very little about who is to be their King. All their attention seems engroced to provide Tobaco and smoking it in sigars.

We must send parties to press their Mules, Carts, &[c]: to carry our Bagage. Three Subs ought to have bought one Mule to carry their Baggage but, they being very dear, Two hundred Dollars each, Government hires them at Four and Six pence each per Day which is to be paid by the Subalterns of each company, but we are told we shall get part of the money we pay for them at present returned, in order to that each Subaltern may have his Baggage carried for four pence per Day, which will be a fair price. I think the bound forage Money we get ought to go for wear and tear as we are obliged to sleep in our clothes in Camp, and in many of the small vilages we are quartered in, which wears them out very soon.

---

* Valladolid.
† 'By some stupid mismanagement at home the cavalry, the most important part of the expedition, were shipped off last and did not arrive [at Corunna] till three weeks after the rest of the troops' (Oman, I, 492).
‡ Evidently Le Mesurier's relatives had told him to be careful what he wrote. There was no official censorship, and some recipients of letters in Britain sent them to newspapers for publication. In this way, Napoleon gleaned much information from the British press.

I saw S. Dobrée this morning. He is just return'd from Monzabal where he had been ordered to retreat with the stores. His return here makes it probable we shall advance in a few days. Am &ᶜ:
P.S. We march tomorrow towards Benevente.

While Baird's column had been pushing ahead, British prospects in Spain had taken a turn for the worse: Napoleon had arrived to take personal command of the French troops in Spain, to drive the British out of the peninsula.

Moore had planned on marching to Burgos but, after hearing of Spanish General Francisco Javier Castanos' defeat at Tudela, he decided an offensive against Napoleon was beyond him. 'This renders my junction with Baird's so hazardous that I dare not attempt it,' he wrote on 30 November, 'but even were it made, what chance has this army, now that all those of Spain are beaten, to stand against the force which must be brought against it? ... As long as Castanos' army remained there was hope, but now I see none.'[5] He therefore ordered Baird to fall back on Corunna and evacuate his troops. 'This movement was not by any means liked by any of us,' complained Surtees.[6]

But before the order to retreat reached Baird, Le Mesurier was seconded to a special detachment.

Dʳ: F.   Lamego December 14ᵗʰ: 1808

In my last letter (Novʳ: 26ᵗʰ:) I mentioned that we were to March the next day. We accordingly march'd a league and a half from Astorga and there took a position commanding a bridge thrown over a small river, and return'd in the evening to Astorga. The same Evening we received orders and counter orders till the 30ᵗʰ: when we received an Order at Eight in the Morning to parade in marching order at Eleven o'Clock. When the Regiment had fallen in Colˡ: Wyatt* came up to the Detachment and made us put on our Greatcoats and told us that we were to march in disguise as we were to escort money to Sir John Moore's Army, and the French were not very far from us.

We got ready and marched at Five in the evening to Castrello.†

* Lieutenant-Colonel William Edgell Wyatt, commander of the 23rd Fusiliers.
† Probably Castrillo de los Polvazares.

The Dollars came up with us at this place. At Twelve o'Clock on the first of this Month we marched to Castrello Conrigo.[*] We arrived here at 7 o'Clock the same evening and here found an order from Col[l]: Peacock[†] (71st: Reg[t]:), who has the command of the Detachement, to proceed Three leagues further, and to march with the greatest caution. After halting here Two hours we went on to Monbuy,[‡] tho the men were so tired that many were throwing themselves down and refusing to go on. They were almost in a state of mutiny.

We got to Monbuy at 5 o'Clock in the morning of the 2[d]: and halted here one day. Col[l]: Peacock told us he had been informed that the French had advanced to Benevente, which made him give out the order for us to proceed for fear, shoud the French have had information of our march, they might have attempted to cut us off. We have Seventy Thousand Dollars with us and Three hundred Doubloons in gold.

On the 3[d]: of Dec[r]: we marched to Sanabria,[§] a Town on the frontiers of Spain. It is situated on a hill and is walled round, but there are few Soldiers and I belive not one gun to defend itself against the Enemy.

On the 4th: we entered Portugal. Our guide showed me a heap of stones and told me that was the Division between the two Kingdoms of Spain and Portugal. We came to Braganza about 5 o'Clock in the evening and were received with the greatest cordiality by the Inhabitants. I was billeted at a Gentlemans house. He gave us tea and, a little after, an excellent supper. We halted here one day. The Inhabitants wished us to stay with them a few weeks to [refresh] ourselves after our fatiguing marches. They do not like the Spaniards and belive Many of them to be Traitors and to prefer the French to the English. The inhabitants of this place gave so much wine to our Soldiers that hardly one sober was to be found in our Detachement.

On the 6th: we moved to Quintella.[¶] On the road, when we passed through some Village, the people gave us Grapes and other

---

[*] Castrocontrigo.
[†] Lieutenant-Colonel Nicholas Peacocke.
[‡] Mombuey.
[§] Puebla de Sanabria.
[¶] Quintela de Lampaças.

Fruits, and called out 'Long live the English'. In short, were ever we go, we are treated with the greatest Hospitality. We find a great deal of difference between that of the Portuguees and Spaniards. These, when ever we wished to have any thing cooked, appeared displeased and grumbled. Those always received us with politeness, and if an Officer happened to come in when at their meals, they appeared disapointed if he did not sit down to take something with them.

On the 7th: we marched to Mirandella and on the 8th: to Moursa.* We halted here one day.

On the 10th: I received an order from Coll: Peacock to stay at Moursa with the sick men and to proceed to Lamego when the men were sufficiently recovered. I applied and got leave to bring them on, on Asses or Mules and set off from Moursa the same day at 12 o'Clock and rejoined the Detachement in the evening at St: Martin's.† Next day we proceeded to a small village two Leagues from Lamego.

On the 11th: we crossed the Douro in a Ferry boat. The country on the Banks of this River is beautiful and well populated. There are a great number of Olive and Orange trees. We passed by an orange grove. The trees were loaded with fruit and looked very inviting, yet we did not touch one. We can buy them here very cheap.

After we had crossed the river we had to ascend a very high mountain and the sun was so warm that we had a great deal of trouble to go One League in Three hours. The men were halted several times. I think the sun is as warm here at this time of the year as it is in Guernsey in a hot summer day, but the nights are very Cold.

I have just now been interrupted by Robertson of the 9th:, our acting adjutant, who told me we were to March at 11 o'Clock. As I wish to write a few lines to Abram I hope you will excuse the shortness of this Letter. It was Coll: Peacock's intention to have staid here till tomorrow morning. I hope to be with my Regt: In a few days. Our Detachement consists of Men belonging to the /52d /9th/4th/2d/and 20th/ Regimts: in all about 120 Men.

* Murça.
† Probably San Martinho de Anta, east of Vila Real.

I have just now been warned for guard and I must see the Treasure loaded, therefore will not have time to write to Abram. Remember me affectionately. I am &^{c}:

It appears that when the treasure convoy got to Mombuey on 2 December, Colonel Peacock decided that getting the money to Moore was too risky, that the bullion might be seized by the French, and instead ordered the convoy south-west into Portugal. As it turned out, the French were too distant to pose a threat, and so, having marched more than 50 miles into Portugal, Le Mesurier's detachment was told to double back.

D^r: Abr^m: Almeida Dec^r: 18th: 1808
to London

We crossed the Douro at Arreguia* in a ferry and arrived the same day at Lamego. The country on the Banks of the River is most beautiful; plenty of vineyards, Orange and Olive trees, and the country well populated.

At Lamego we halted one day and a half. It was intended at first to have halted two days but we received an order from General Moore to proceed as fast as possible as the army is in want of money. We marched from Lamego at 12 o'Clock on the 14th: I wrote home from this place and I had begun a Letter for you when they came to tell me that we were to March and that I was for Guard that day. I was obliged to leave your Letter unfinish'd and go and see the Money loaded on the Mules.

The day after, we marched Six Leagues to Tarrigne.† I fortunately happened to be on the rear guard. I had the care of the Officers Baggage. In the evening, about six o'Clock, some of the baggage fell off the mules and, before it was put up, the Detachement was out of sight and I was left without a Guide. After going on for about a quarter of an hour, two Soldiers of the 52^d Reg^t: came up with a Guide they had pressed in one of the villages. I made them stop with me and went on to Torigne. When I came there I was surprised to find that the others were not come in. I got a Billet and

---

*   Peso da Régua.
†   18 miles – good going for a convoy of mules on rough roads in winter. The army expected soldiers to march about 15 miles a day.

went to bed rather tired, and next morning heard that they had lost their way and came in four hours after me.

We arrived here this morning at Eight o'Clock. All the Officers we have met who came from Spain say that the Spaniards treat them with the greatest coolness and indifference, therefore I do not expect to spend a very pleasant Christmas this year. I must own that I have often wished for a little of my good Uncle Sam's Boeufroti-poisson* whilst in Spain, and would have eaten it as a great dainty. We have been pretty well off whilst in Portugal as to eating. I have met with nothing but politeness whilst in it, except in this place where I am billeted with a surly old fellow who is greatly annoyed at my sitting up so late to write, but I pay him in his own coin by not minding what he says. I think I have written a pretty long Letter after a days march of nearly four Leagues therefore wish you &ᶜ:

P.S. My old Landlord says he wishes I was in Hell for writing so much.

While Le Mesurier and his detachment were escorting their bullion, Moore had overcome his qualms about engaging the enemy. He had been impressed at the willingness of the citizens of Madrid to defend their city from French occupation. 'There is a chance that the example may be followed and the people be roused,' he wrote on 9 December, 'in which case there is still a chance that this country may be saved. Upon this chance I have stopped Baird's retreat and have taken measures to form our junction whilst the French are wholly occupied with Madrid.' 'I am moving the troops to the Duero, and shall assemble the army at Valladolid without waiting for Sir D. Baird's corps,' he wrote in his diary. 'By this movement I shall threaten the French communications, which will make some diversion in favour of the Spaniards, if they can take advantage of it.'[7]

While Moore prepared to go on the offensive, Le Mesurier's treasure convoy had moved south-east from Lamego to Almeida, presumably to take the road via Ciudad Rodrigo to Salamanca. Upon reaching Almeida they must have heard Moore had left Salamanca and headed north, because they

* Literally 'Roast beef fish'.

retraced their steps and marched north to Miranda do Douro, at the north-east corner of the Spanish–Portuguese frontier.

Unfortunately for Le Mesurier, Moore changed his mind again. Secret despatches, found on a French officer, revealed that 20,000 troops under Marshal Jean-de-Dieu Soult, were nearby. This was an army small enough for Moore to stand a chance of beating, so he determined to attack Soult.

Once Baird's troops caught up with the main British column on 19 December, Moore had 50 per cent more men than Soult. After a successful British cavalry raid at Sahagun on 21 December, Moore deployed his troops for battle. 'Every pulse beat high, in expectation of soon congratulating each other on a victory,' recalled Surtees.[8]

Like Moore, the French had also benefitted from intelligence. Word of the British offensive had reached Madrid and Napoleon had set out with 35,000 men. As he prepared to engage Soult, Moore heard of the emperor's advance. 'Having therefore no doubt that all their disposable troops were turned against me, I had no option but to give up all idea of an attack on Soult,' explained Moore, 'and to get back to secure my communications with the Gallicias.' [9]

Moore headed for Corunna, and he wrote, 'It is not my wish to fight a battle.' 'That at present is not our game, which is rather to save this army; to protect and give time to the Spaniards to rally, if they can.'[10] 'This was most distressing information,' complained Surtees, 'for never was an army more eager to come in contact with the enemy than ours was at this moment.'[11]

Once past Astorga, Moore sent his two light brigades (approximately 4,500 men) to Vigo to embark there. 'This was done, I understand, with a view to secure a passage across the Minho,' explained Surtees, 'should Sir John, with the main army, be compelled to retreat in that direction, and probably with the view also of drawing off a part of the enemy's overwhelming force from the pursuit of that body, and to induce them to follow us into the mountains. Notwithstanding this, they continued to pursue Sir John on the great road, whilst they left us free altogether.'[12]

Though not bothered by the French, conditions for the light brigades were appalling. The roads were icy, the men had no tents and the commissariat was under-provisioned. 'The shoes and boots of our party were now mostly either destroyed or useless to us, from foul roads and long miles,' complained Harris of the 95th Rifles, 'and many of the men were entirely barefooted, with knapsacks and accoutrements altogether in a dilapidated state. The officers were also, for the most part, in as miserable a plight. They were pallid, way-worn, their feet bleeding and their faces overgrown with beards of many days' growth.'[13]

Dogged by the French, the rest of Moore's army suffered even worse as they made for Corunna. Dismayed at their general's refusal to stand and fight, the men became ungovernable and discipline fell to pieces. Looting and straggling became endemic and by the time Moore's army reached Corunna on 11 January, thousands of men had died in the snow or been taken prisoner by the French. 'Of our brigade,' wrote Ensign William Gavin of the 71st Highlanders, 'which at the commencement of the retreat consisted of 2,500 men, not more than 150 marched in with the colours, and they barefoot, covered with old blankets and many without arms.'[14]

Separated from the columns marching to Vigo and Corunna, Le Mesurier's convoy had to find its own way home.

D^r: F.   Portsmouth February 2^d: 1809

We arrived here two days ago from Vigo where we embarked on the 18th: of January and sailed from that place on the 24th: I wrote to you from Lamego on the 14th: of December and to Abr^m: from Almaida on the 18th: From this place we marched to Miranda where we halted two days, but as the post was not to go for some days I thought I should join the Regi^t: before I wrote.

We marched towards Benevente but about Six Leagues from that place we learnt that the English army had retreated to Astorga. We proceeded towards Astorga and learnt at Monbuy that the French had been there five days. Here we found an Officer which we had sent before us to let the Army know we were coming. He gave us the unwelcome intelligence that the French were at Astorga. He had been in a Village where the French piquets came every day.

We immediately struck off on the left to Sanabria, a Town we had been at before (5 leagues from Monbuy) and came here about midnight. Here we had another mortification. Those d--- scoundrels, the Spaniards, refused us admittance after keeping us One hour and a half, knee deep in the Snow, before the gates, meantime had the impertinance to send a Guard of about 60 men before us on the wall who primed and loaded before us and there remained abusing us untill we moved off. I never saw men so vexed and enraged as those of our Detatchment were.

We marched about one league further to Torries[*] where we arrived about Three o'Clock, having marched between Eight and Nine leagues without resting. The Detatchment marched from hence about noon. I was left behind to bring up the straglers and proceeded with them the next day. I had not gone above Three Leagues when I overtook the men, Stuck in the Snow on the top of a high mountain. We were nearly two hours before the Spaniards (about Thirty in number) had cleared the road sufficiently for us to go on.

We continued to march every day till we arrived, the Thirteenth of January, at Vigo in the evening and embarked immediatly. On the road, before we came to Frankira,[†] we saw Men, Women and Children dead on the road. Some of our Officers found a young woman dead with an Infant still lying in her arms. He was taken up and brought on but died in about half an hour after. We hardly walked a hundred yards without stumbling on Dead horses or mules.

I must not omit to tell you a small adventure happened to Cap^{tn} Balderson of the 4th: Reg^{t}: and myself at Villa Reino which I shall not forget in a hurry. A Spanish noble man invited us to go and sleep at his house, a Mile and a half from where the Detachment was quartered. We accepted the invitation and went there. He gave us fried Pig's liver for Diner, and then began to talk about the affairs of Spain. After about two hours conversation, in which he appeared to favour the French very much, he told us 'Charles the fourth is a fool, the Queen is a Whore and Ferdinand the 7th: is a fool also. We will have none of that family, we will have Joseph Napoleon for our King'. After this, supper was brought in – Pig's liver again. The evening concluded by his abusing the English and our quarelling with him. Next morning he sent his Servant to shew us the way out, as he did not chuse to be disturbed. Going out,

---

[*] Terroso, a small village west of Puebla de Sanabria.
[†] A Franqueirán.

we passed thro a place in which we saw a great plenty of Beef and Mutton hanging up. C'est ce que j'appelle une petite avanie,* and I think we deserved it for not taking our Servants with us, when we knew the disposition of the Spaniards in general was unfreindly towards the English.

I am almost ashamed to show myself, I am so dirty. I shall want everything new. I am not getting rich in the Army. Am &c:

Le Mesurier was lucky not to fall prisoner to the French. His detachment reached Spain to find Moore in retreat and a French army in the way. Given their circumstances, the fact that they found their way to the coast and boarded a ship for home is remarkable. They did enjoy one great advantage; because they were only a small party of soldiers it was easier for them to find sufficient food and shelter.

The light brigades, which had split off from the rest of Moore's army on 31 December, took the road via Ponferrada to Vigo. Le Mesurier's detachment used the more southerly route via Verin. These two roads met at Orense, and it was between here and Vigo that Le Mesurier saw the corpses. It was only a hint of the horrors endured by the rest of the army.

By the time Le Mesurier reached Vigo, most of the Royal Navy's men-of-war and hired transports had sailed up the coast to collect Moore's army at Corunna. Those still at Vigo, 'remained as long in the bay as it was safe, sending stragglers as they arrived on board the different ships,' explained Surtees, 'but within a few days after our arrival, the enemy entered the town, which of course precluded all hope of more escaping. We consequently weighed and stood out towards the outer bay.'[15]

The first vessels from Vigo did not reach Corunna until 14 January. Soult's troops were only a few miles south of the town. Moore evacuated the sick, the injured and most of his artillery, and then redeployed his healthy men outside the town to fend off the French. Soult attacked on the afternoon of the 16th and, after an indecisive battle, both sides were left pretty much where they started, but it kept the French at bay long enough for the British to disembark that night under the cover of darkness. Moore died a hero's death, receiving a mortal blow from a cannonball in the thick of the battle.

---

* 'That's what I call a bit of a snub'.

D^r: Abr^m: Guilford Feb^y: 13th: 1809

We received orders on the 9th: of Feby to disimbark and proceed by land to Guilford, where we should have another Route. By this we learn that we are going to our Old Quarters; Canterbury.

I saw Genl: Brownrigg at Portsmouth. He received me politely. I staid but a short time with him as he was very busy. I met him the next day and we had some little conversation.

I told you I would give you my opinion of the Army from the little I have seen. When the Officers are together the conversation is generally about the success they had the night previous to it in getting (*de bonnes aventures*).* I have heard some of those Esprits forts say the Bible was a parcel of Stupid Stuff, unintelligible to their understandings.† Plaguing young Officers, which do not exactly agree with them on these points, is their greatest delight. I had some altercation this morning with one of ours for making some observations on me because I did not go out with them on their nocturnal expeditions. I do not like their morals. They are dissolute in general yet I hope to find some in the Reg^t: with whom I shall take pleasure to associate.

Do not mention any thing of what I say about the army to my Father. He might think I wish to leave it, which is certainly not the case.

---

*   Literally 'some good adventures' but suggestive of sexual encounters.
†   Contempt for religion in the army was more common than one might think. As one soldier recalled, 'I never saw a Bible nor do I remember ever seeing anyone read the Bible' (Bell, 96).

2

Walcheren

The men of the 1/9th formed the rearguard at Corunna. They escaped before the French seized the port, by rowing out to the British transports already outside the harbour, where they found berths in many different ships. Landing in England in dribs and drabs, they took time to make their way to their barracks. On reaching Canterbury on 9 February 1809, Private Hale of the 9th found only 'about fifty men of our regiment in possession of the new barracks who had arrived several days before us from Dover; for in consequence of being a few in one ship and a few in another, some disembarked at Plymouth, some at Gosport, some at Dover and some at Liverpool. Therefore about the end of February we assembled about four hundred and fifty men, but when we disembarked in Portugal our strength was one thousand and twenty men'.[1]

After their losses in the retreat the battalion was brought back up to strength with new recruits. By the summer the 9th Foot had recovered and was ready to take part in Britain's next big military adventure. Viscount Castlereagh (Secretary of State for War and the Colonies) wanted a campaign in the Netherlands to distract Napoleon and relieve pressure on Britain's ally, Austria. British troops would land on the Dutch island of Walcheren, storm the port of Flushing, and then march inland to Antwerp to capture or destroy the French warships harboured there.

The scale of the amphibious force mustered for the expedition was vast. More than 600 ships were needed to carry the 42,000 troops across the Channel, including the 1/9th. Despite its scale, Captain Gomm* of the 9th was unimpressed; 'As to our sending a flimsy force to gain a footing in Germany ... we may as well send them to Brobdingnag.'[2]

D^r: Abr^m: Canterbury July 13th: 1809

Since my last we have had troops passing through this place every day and consequently company to dine at the Mess nearly this forthnight. All the troops have now reach'd their destination and only wait for the Transports to embark. The 9th: 38th: & 42^d Regim^{ts}: are to be in one Brigade commanded by Genl: Montresor,[†] in the 3^d: Division of the Army commanded by the Marquis of Huntley.[‡]

Sunday night I took leave of Dallas.[§] He was very low at parting and gave me a Pipe at least worth a Guinea.

D^r: F.   Brig Robert.[¶] Downs July 18th: 1809

The route came to us Sunday evening about 10 o'Clock, and on Monday morning at 4 o'Clock we marched for Ramsgate where we arrived about Noon and sailed in one hour after for this place. We have a very pleasant set of Officers on board this vessel. Col^l: Crawford** is the Commanding Officer on board.

The Fleet in the Downs is very large and Transports are joining every day. When the whole is collected together it will amount to above Four hundred sails. Some say our destination is to Flushing, others to the Baltic. However, where ever we go I hope success will attend us. &^{c}: &^{c}:

---

* Later Field Marshal Sir William Maynard Gomm (1784–1875).
† Brigadier-General Henry Tucker Montresor (1767–1837).
‡ Lieutenant-General George Gordon, Marquis of Huntly and eventually the 5th Duke of Gordon (1770–1836).
§ Ensign Robert William Dallas (1789–1849), son of judge Sir Robert Dallas, defence counsel for Warren Hastings. Though serving from 1808 to 1818, Dallas was never promoted above ensign.
¶ No brig named *Robert* is recorded in His Majesty's Navy, so this must have been a hired transport.
** Major Henry Craufurd who, due to the complex rank structure of the time, was a major in the 9th Foot but simultaneously held the army rank of lieutenant-colonel.

On arrival in Ramsgate 'we were marched down to the place of embarkation and put on board immediately,' recalled Hale, 'eight companies on board two transport ships, and the grenadier and light company on board the Thalia frigate, accompanied with the band and staff of the regiment.' Here the fleet mustered for several days until it was so large 'it appeared at a distance, or as I might say to people standing on the shore, something resembling a wood. This was the finest expedition ever known to sail from England.'[3]

The six battalions in Huntly's division would land on the Dutch mainland at Cadzand, across the Scheldt estuary from Walcheren. Their targets were the Wulpen semaphore signal station and the batteries at Breskens. Huntly expected to encounter around a thousand enemy troops, but, forewarned of the British plan, the French had reinforced their garrison.

D^r: F.   Heinkensand August 15th: 1809

On the 28th: we sailed from the Downs with a fair wind and anchored the same evening off Blankenburg, not far from Ostend. The next day we anchor'd near Cadsand, where we were to have landed, but a Storm coming on prevented us. It proved fortunate as we could only have landed 600 men at a time and the Enemy appeared the next day very numerous on the sea Shore.*

On the 2^d: of this month we could see the troops exercising on the sands and a few horse Men parading along the Shore.

The 3^d: a Schuyt† came out of Flushing and was chased by a Gun Brig and a few Men of Wars Boats. The Batteries at Flushing and Cadsand opened a very heavy fire on the Brig and boats, which was return'd by the Brig very briskly, who lost both her Topmast and had 16 men killed and wounded. The Batteries from the Shore fired a few Shells in the Fleet but did not hurt us.

---

* Huntly had only enough boats to land between 600–700 men at once. Given that Huntly expected each tranche of soldiers would take over an hour and a half to land, the first wave would have to secure the beachhead and defend it against several thousand Frenchmen while subsequent tranches of troops arrived. Faced with this prospect, Huntly decided against a landing.

† A bluff-bowed, flat-bottomed Dutch sailing boat used on canals and for coastal work.

On the 4ᵗʰ: it blew a Storm which lasted the whole day. Many Ships received some damage.

On the 5ᵗʰ: we left our very disagreable station off Cadsan and came round to Camvere where we got in a fresh stock as ours was just out that day.*

On the 8ᵗʰ: we moved up the Scheld and on the 9ᵗʰ: landed on South Beverland. We marched through a beautiful country to Heinkensand which is Six Miles from the place where we landed. The roads are good and shaded by trees on both sides. The Dutch are very clean about their houses. I dropt a little water in the room in which I was sitting and was reprimanded by the good Lady of the house rather sharply.

Eatables are very cheap here; Fowls a shilling a couple, butter 8ᵈ: a pound, wild Ducks, patriges and Pigeons are plenty hereabouts, but for want of Powder and Shot we cannot kill any. From the Steeple of one of the churches here we can see the firing at Flushing. Its a grand sight. Some of the Dutch gentry told us the Town was on fire. We can see a very heavy smoke but we are too far to distinguish from this place weither it arrises from the Town or not.

On the 18ᵗʰ: we received an order to hold ourselves in readiness to march but this order was countermanᵈ in the evening. The left wing is quartered in a Village three miles from this. We meet half way every morning and, after being inspected and a little manouvering, we march back again and arive here about 11 o'Clock.

Some of the Officers the[y] go shooting, some fishing, and when the weather is bad some play Billiard and others Cards. This is all our employment. As we were ordered to take only light Baggage we have very few books. Last Friday, after obtaining leave of the Farmers, I went over some Stubble fields. I starded above 50 brace of Partriges, but did not shoot one. I came home about 5 o'Clock with a water fowl and a wood Pigeon only. My Gun was so bad it mist fire nine times out of ten.†

* By 'stock' Le Mesurier means food brought along by officers to supplement the naval rations. They had expected to be at sea for just a few days, but by 5 August Le Mesurier had been aboard for nineteen days.
† As an officer, Le Mesurier carried only a sword in battle, so this must have been a shotgun he had brought for bagging game. It would have used the same unreliable flintlock firing mechanism as the muskets carried by the men. The standard army issue smoothbore musket 'misfired once in seven rounds in dry

This place is far from being healthy. We send a great many Men every day in the Hospitals. We have only one officer Sick. The Inhabitants tell us that it will be much worse in September. They say it is as unwholesome a place as Batavia.*

I was sorry to see that Macrea was again severely wounded at the Battle of Villa Reina.† I hope he will recover. I spoke a few days ago to Col¹ Cameron‡ and enquired if he had heard anything of my Lieut^cy: He said he had not, but that he supposed I had been Gazetted long ago.

Saturday I went out to perform some light manouvres with the light companies,§ to practice leaping ditches &^c: As I had no wish to have a dive in one of these ditches, I made every effort in my power to leap over, and succeeded, but in making a very great effort to go over a wide one my Pantaloons, which were rather tight, gave way about the Knees, which accident afforded, you may well suppose, a great deal of amusement to the numerous idle spectators present.

I am writing this Letter in a room where there is no less than 6

weather' and was 'unlikely to fire at all in heavy rain. Only an exceptional flint would fire more than thirty rounds, after which it had to be changed' (Glover. M., *Peninsular War* 31).

* Jakarta in the Dutch East Indies. Confusingly, the Netherlands at this time was called the Batavian Republic.

† The Battle of Talavera de la Reina, on 27–28 July, had been a victory for Wellesley. Captain Rawdon Macrea (87th Foot) was the son of Major Robert Macrea who had married Sophia Le Mesurier in 1804, following the death of his first wife. Rawdon had also been injured at Monte Video in 1807, but this time he died of his wounds.

‡ Lieutenant-Colonel John Cameron (1773–1844). 'Of all the colonels of the 9th, Sir John Cameron is the one most distinguished, not only by his achievements as a regimental officer, but by his long and intimate connexion with the regiment in its service in the field' (Loraine Petre, II, 344). Commissioned into the 43rd Foot aged fourteen, he spent his early years fighting in the Caribbean, and was promoted to major aged only 27. After gaining a lieutenant-colonelcy in the 7th West India Regiment in June 1807, he exchanged into the 9th Foot in September of that year. He became a lieutenant-general and received a knighthood.

§ Each battalion had a light company and a grenadier company. 'Perhaps, some will be ready to ask, what difference is there in these two companies? Why, the grenadier company consists of all the tallest and stoutest men in the regiment, and always stands on the right; but the light company is generally young men, straight and slender (who stand from about five feet seven to five feet nine inches high), and when in settled quarters, stands on the left of the regiment; but on the line of march they are placed several hundred yards in front as a sort of advance guard' (Hale, 39).

Dutch Frows* who at least make as much noise as Twenty of our Maket Ladies could do chatting all together. Probably the next Letter I write shall be dated from my old quarters. Am, &c:

The Walcheren expedition ended in humiliation for Britain. Despite being given one of the largest British armies ever amassed on the Continent, its commander, the Earl of Chatham, failed to press forward the attack with the speed required. The flooding of the dykes by the defending troops left Walcheren and the nearby islands inundated, giving rise to a malarial disease the British called 'Walcheren Fever'. 'Strong and fine young men, who had been but a short time in the service, seemed suddenly reduced in strength to infants, unable to stand upright, so great a shaking had seized upon their whole bodies from head to heel,' wrote one rifleman.[4] 'Deaths were so frequent that a general order was issued to dig large pits and bury the dead by night,' explained Ensign Gavin, 'in order that the sick and convalescent should not witness the removal of the dead.'[5]

The disease spread rapidly, crippling the British Army. That September, evacuation of the sick began. The 1/9th embarked on 4 September but due to adverse weather did not reach England until the 15th. Eleven days in a cramped transport ship helped the disease strengthen its grip, leaving the battalion prostrate. 'We took possession of the new barracks as before, but in a short time our hospital was crowded with sick,' explained Hale. 'Every day the number of the sick increased with the ague and fever, for in about one month nearly half our regiment was on the sick list, by which a great many were summoned to their last homes.'[6]

* Women.

3

Gibraltar and Malaga

D^r: Abr^m: Canterbury Sept^r: 27th: 1809

I am on a good footing with the Officers except two; Capt^ns: P & C* who are intimate friends of Miss A. The first have not spoken to me since that affair took place and has tried to get me in a scrape once with Co^l: Crawford which, however, did not succeed.

I am unhappy at the thought of spending so much, and no bright prospect before me, yet it is not possible to spend less than I do and when I am promoted my pay will hardly maintain me.

I do not enjoy the company of our Officers. Their conversation is very different from that I have been accustomed to hear. I am obliged to stay in my room the greatest part of the day or be in their company. R is nearly as bad as the Rest. He begins to follow P's example to laugh at Religion.

Sunday, I went to the Cathedral. After divine service the Archbishop ordained Three young men. The Cathedral was crowded. I stood the whole time near four hours. His Grace is a good looking man and has a good voice.

I am told Sir John Hope† has retired to his Estate in Scotland,

---

* This must have been Captain Adam Peebles and either Captain Hector Cameron or Captain Alexander Campbell. Miss A remains an enigma.

† Lieutenant-General the Hon. Sir John Hope (1765–1823) had been knighted after taking command at the Battle of Corunna following Sir John Moore's death. He commanded the reserve at Walcheren and was eventually promoted to full general. He received a peerage in his own right before succeeding to the title of Earl of Hopetoun on the death of his elder half-brother.

disgusted with our late Expedition. We have about 500 of our Men Sick at Deal, Harwhich and here. The Fever seems to be as bad as ever. Out of 19 Men which had been sent to Harwhich, Dallas writes Seven are Dead. The 42^d: have 700 Sick. The Officers belonging to the 2^d Batt^n: I am informed will go out to join it.[*] In the course of a forthnight I shall loose all my old acquaintances except Dallas.

D^r: Abr^m: Canterbury Octo^r: 3^d: 1809

I am almost constantly in my room at present as Ruse is gone to Dover to take charge of the sick men there, and, as I am not very intimate with the others (Seaward[†] excepted, who is better than most of them), I amuse myself in reading or looking over my Algebra.

I received a Letter from my D^r: F. this morning. He desires me to draw for what sum I want, however, I shall try to do without it for some time. You know my reason for not purchasing the Lieut^{cy}, yet I am not sure that my Father will be pleased with it, and I should be excessively sorry to displease him after his kindness to me. Advise me how to proceed.

I told Col^l Cameron yeasterday that I declined the purchase. He seemed to wish to have my reason. I told him that little things had happened since I gave in my name that made me decline it. He said he supposed I wish'd to remain an Ensign sometime longer. I made him a bow and retired.

The army, as you justly observe, are very Licentious and I belive all Reg^{ts}: are alike. I think if the heads were to show a good example they might check such conversations as are not fit to be heard by Gentlemen at the Mess Tables, but on the contrary they seem to encourage them. I have heard Officers go on with shocking conversations before the men. No wonder they do not pay them the respect they ought to do.[‡]

---

[*] Officers were often transferred from one battalion to the other, as were detachments of men, especially if one battalion had lost troops on campaign.

[†] Ensign William Seward. Since Ensign Colin Campbell (later Field Marshal Lord Clyde) also counted Ruse and Seward as friends long after he left the 9th Foot, Le Mesurier's judgment seems sound.

[‡] The 9th Foot's *Mess, Bet and Presentation Book* notes 'The following are long-established fines at the Mess, and are to be strictly enforced –

We have a great many Sick. We buried four men last friday.* On an average we bury Ten a week. I shall write home Thursday but will not mention the Lieut^cy till you favour me with your advice.

Nov^r: 7th: Yeasterday we were inspected by Lieut. Genl: Nichols,† in the riding School as the weather was very rainy, who was highly pleased with the appearance of the Reg^t: but wish'd to see a little more Blood in their faces.‡ The want of it is the effect of our Walcheren expedition. &^c:

D^r: Abr^m: Canterbury Nov^r: 21st: 1809

At last my destination is determined. I received orders from Col^l: Cameron yeasterday to be ready as I was going to join the 2^d: Batt^n: at Gibralter, and to day he said from a Letter he had received from the War Office he expected we shoud embark tomorrow. Therefore we are all in great bustle. I shall get the pay of a Lieut^t: from the time I embark. It appears very curious to me that after the money being paid last Monday for my Lieut^cy: I was not Gazetted last Saturday.

Le Mesurier's change of heart over his lieutenancy is a puzzle. Having put his name forward, he then seems to have withdrawn it, but by 8 November had reapplied.[1] His promotion was announced in the *London Gazette* of 20 November. It is strange that in a time of war and disease, Le Mesurier purchased his promotion. There had been a high turnover of

1) Having a Drawn Sword in Ye Mess Room
2) Speaking three words of Latin
3) Throwing across the Table
4) Taking the Newspaper or Books belonging to the Regiment out of the Mess Room
5) Tearing or otherwise defacing the Mess Books or Newspapers
6) Indecent conversation at Dinner during the time servants are in the Mess Room' (Loraine Petre, II, 422)

* This tallies with Hale who noted 'Several times, three or four in a day were carried to the burial ground' (Hale, 46).
† Lieutenant-General Oliver Nicolls (*c.* 1740–1829).
‡ The preference for rosy-cheeked soldiers encouraged the retention of the uncomfortable leather stock worn by the rank and file on parade. By half-throttling the men, it brought colour to their faces.

subalterns in the regiment and the prospects of promotion without purchase for an ensign were very good.

On 9 December he was ordered to Deal to await the transport brig Jane, which was to take him and other officers of the 1/9th to Gibraltar.

D^r: F.   Onboard (Duchess of Bedford) N°. 420 off the Needles}
                                          Jan^y: 13th: 1810

I take the opportunity of the Pilot going on shore to write a few lines. I was put on board this ship in consequence of some changes made by the Transport agents as the ships were too much crouded with our officers. We had laid in a stock for the voyage in the Jane which we divided.

I went on Shore every day at Portsmouth in hopes of having a Letter from Guernsey, but was disapointed. In one of my excursions on shore I met with M. T. DeLisle who told me he was going out again to the West Indies. I think he is thinner than when I saw him in Guernsey.

The wind came round to the Eastward last night and the signal was made to weigh early in the Morning. It blows pretty fresh and we may expect to be in the Bay of Biscay tomorrow. This ship is much larger than the Jane and has very good accomodations for Six Officers which is our Number, all Lieut^{ts}: We are very comfortable (315 tons). I think I shall be pretty well this trip. I do not feel any inclination to be sea sick. A year ago today we embarked at Vigo.

D^r: F.   Gibralter Jany 30th: 1810

As soon as the Pilot had left us on the 13th: it came to blow hard. The Fleet was so large that we were unable to see the Comodore's light at night. Next morning we saw about Thirty sails of Transports & Merchantmen without the Convoy, which made us suppose he was a head. In consequence we made more sail but saw nothing of him and by dark could only see two Ships, which kept company with us for two days more.

On the 17th: we saw a strange sail to windward. We shewed our colours & fired a Gun. She passed under our Stern without shewing hers. Fortunately for her, our caronade* asterne was in bad order or else the Captⁿ: would have fired into her as she appeared to be a Privateer. On hailing her she proved to be a Spanish vessel from Gijon to Cadiz. We sent our boat onboard. She informed us we were to the Southward of Cape Finistere. About Ten o'Clock at night we made the Rock of Lisbon, the first land we had seen since we left Portland.

On the 20th: we made Cape Trefalgar. The wind at East, we were obliged to beat up† as far as the Rock, when it fell Calm and we were drawn in by the current, Seven or Eight leagues to the Eastward of it. On the 22^d: a breeze sprung up and we anchored about Nine o'Clock at night close to Gibralter. On the 23^d: we Landed and were received very civilly by the Officers who were glad to receive so strong a reinforcement.

I had heard at Portsmouth that the Reg^t: was in disgrace.‡ On our arrival we expected to have found them employed in working parties, but were agreably surprised to find they were considered the best Reg^t: in the Garison by Genl: Campbell,§ that they had been drilling the other Regim^{ts}:

Our Messing is very dear, even more so than at Canterbury. It cost us about one Guinea a week. Besides our wine, we are expected to drink one allowance which amounts to about Eightpence. Bread is bad & dear. We are allowed Ten or Eleven pence a day for our rations, which will reduce our Expenses a little, our expensive Dinners. Every little article we want is very dear except Tea and Sugar. A Sack of Patatoes has no price; we almost pay the weight in silver.

We are quartered in the south, about one Mile from Europa-point. The Officers' rooms are about one Mile from the Barracks where the 9th: are, so that we have to trott up a steep hill & bad

---

* A carronade was a short, smooth-bore cannon.
† Tacking or zig-zagging, so a ship can sail towards the wind.
‡ The 1/9th Foot had been one of the worst behaved corps in the retreat to Corunna and the extent of the Walcheren fever in the regiment meant Wellington viewed them as a diseased battalion, not to be used in the front line, but quite why the 2/9th were in the doghouse is unclear.
§ Lieutenant-General Colin Campbell (1754–1814), appointed lieutenant-governor of Gibraltar on 12 November 1809.

Road once or twice a day, which will reduce my poor body a great deal in the summer.

We expect to be cooped up in this place in the course of a few days, as the French are advancing rapidly into Spain. I am affraid they will be at Malaga before any enquires can be made about the wines. All the Spaniards capable, who were in Gibralter, have been turned out and sent to join the Army.

It is reported the Spanish lines are to be blown up in a few days to prevent the French from anoying us for some time. Col^l: Doyle* has been here for some resting after his fatigues. He dressed in Spanish Brig. Genl:'s uniform with long mustachoes. I hear he is very unwell. Our duty is not very severe. Our Col^l: is not so strict as the one of the 1st: Batt^n:

By the time Le Mesurier landed in Gibraltar, the French had subdued most of Spain, but Andalucia, including the central Spanish junta at Cadiz and the British rock fortress of Gibraltar, remained outside their control. Marshal Soult was anxious to invade and conquer this last rebellious tract.

With a French attack imminent, the Spanish, now Britain's allies, removed the guns which they had formerly trained on Gibraltar and allowed the British to blow up the nearby forts of St. Philip and St. Barbara which had so recently opposed them.

D^r: F.   Gibralter Febr^y 7th: 1810

We have all been in a bustle lately at this place. Two Reg^{ts}: have been embarked and ordered to Cadiz. It is supposed they go in order to bring off the Fleet. A Batt^n: of the Veterans sailed for Ceuta† yeasterday morning. The Spaniards refused to let them land. They are now on their way way back.

All the men that could be spared from the Garrison duty, after these Three Reg^{ts}: embarked, have been employed in working on the Spanish lines. We are preparing to blow up their forts before the French take possession of them. About two hundred men

---

*   Major John Milley Doyle (1781–1856), lieutenant-colonel in the Portuguese army, had been inspector general of the Guernsey militia.
†   The spit of land sticking out from the North African coast opposite Gibraltar.

are employed every day. In two days more Fort St. Philip, that mounted 28 Guns, and Fort Barbara will be ready. The guns and mortars that were on them are safe in this place. The explosion will be very great. It will require about Eleven thousand pounds of powder for each fort.

Spaniards have been flocking into Algesiras and Sᵗ: Roche lately. They are not allowed to come in here without a pass from the Town Major, Officers excepted. The latter are dressed very gay; plenty of silver lace about their dress and Hats.

Our Regᵗ: has changed Quarters. We are now in Town. The English Counsul from Malaga arrived here a few days ago. The news he brought were the French were expected every minute in that place when he left it. A Spanish General arrived here on Saturday from Cadiz with dispatches. His Aid de Camp told me that the French were within ten Leagues of Cadiz and were making a bold push for the Fleet. If this intelligence is true they will be there before our troops can get there, as the wind continues to blow from the westward.

The 47ᵗʰ: & 30ᵗʰ: Regᵗˢ: are ordered to hold themselves in readiness to embark in the Transports (that bring out the 4ᵗʰ: & 28ᵗʰ:) which are to carry them to Cape de Verd's Island, where they are to wait the arrival of the India fleet which will carry them to India.

The 8ᵗʰ: Some Spanish soldiers embarked for Cadiz. We were ordered to hold ourselves in readiness to be under arms at one moment's warning, whilst the Spaniards were embarking in casse of any disturbance. The greater part of those that embarked were Officers, who I suppose had better means of running than the soldiers. Horses sold for 5 or 6 Cobs* that at any other time would have fetched Eighty or Ninety, but these gentlemen had no means of carrying them to Cadiz.

The General who landed here on Saturday (I was informed) had attempted to make his escape to America. All the Guards have orders not to let him pass out of the Garrison. His name is said to be Conte Lee, a Lieuᵗ: Genˡ: None of the supreme junta who are here are allowed to go out. The reason assigned for this is that, till

* Spanish dollars.

it is known for certain they have not been guilty of Treachery, they will be kept here.

Malaga was seized by the French last Tuesday. All the principal passes in the Sierra Morena are in their hands. We have very little to hope for from the Spaniards. They say now that the French come quietly into their country, therefore why should they ill use them?

The 9th: Four thousand Spaniards embark'd to day for Cadiz from this place and one Thousand from Algeziras.

The 12th: The Batteries on an Island near Algeziras, which annoyed Sir James Saumarez[*] so much when he attacked the Fleet there, have all been destroyed and the Barracks burnt, also the forts at Algeziras.

The 16th: The French (about 50 Dragoons) entered the above place on the 14th: and, after raising a contribution of 3000 Dollars, retreated. At that time no less than 1000 Spanish Dragoons were outside the Barriers begging admittance.

The Forts were blown up the 14th: in the Evening. The explosion was not so great as I expected, considering the quantity of powder employed. The men are employed levelling a small part that was not knocked down. Our Reg[t]: was under arms during the time of the explosion in casse any disturbance had happened. I am &[c]:

D[r]: F.   Gibralter 27th: Febr[y] 1810

I have some satisfaction in being in a place like this where I now and then see some of my Guernsey Freinds who have occasion to call here. Besides those I mentioned in my last Letter, a gentleman, I was told on Friday, called on me when I was away from home without leaving his name. I saw Price who told me he had seen this Gent and directed me to the Inn where I was most agreably surprised with meeting W: Metivier.[†] Had I not been informed he was there I most probably would have past him in the Streets without knowing him. He is very Stout but not so tall as I expected

[*] Admiral Lord Saumarez (1757–1836). He was Nelson's second in command at the Battle of the Nile, and repulsed the French from Algeciras on 6 and 12 July 1801.

[†] William Métivier, brother of poet George Métivier.

he was. He was dressed after the Spanish Fashion with a greatcoat on. He was just arrived from Cadiz.

We passed the evening much to our satisfaction, relating our adventures since we last met. I was on Guard the day after, where he came to see me & promised to Breakfast with me the Sunday, which Engagement I am sorry to say he could not keep as he was obliged to sail with the Convoy for Port Mahon. In a Note he sent me just before to sail, he desired me to remember him affectionately to Mr Metivier and all his Friends in Guernsey, in which place he hopes we shall meet shortly. He observed that I had too much baggage for a Soldier. I offered him part, which he positively refused, tho I think he was short as he had travelled from Taragona to Cadiz. He said he had plenty whenever he could get at Taragona, therefore would take nothing.

It is now Spring with us. A few trees thinly scattered here and there in a few small gardens are the only places where we can see a little Green. I do not like to read Thomsons Seasons now. A person who has lived on this Rock for some time can hardly suppose such scenes as he paints could exist, yet this place n'est pas sans agrément. Je jouis d'un concert sous mes fenêtres tous les matins,* or rather of a Trio as the concert is only composed of Three performers; Two Jack Asses and a Parrot.

I have been very Lazy since I came here. I have not yet engaged a Spanish Master. I look now and then in my Grammar and can now decline the Pronouns & Verbs. When I am studying, my attention is frequently drawn off by a discharge of Cannon from the Gun boats who are annoying the French Cavalry round the Bay.

On the 25th: Forty Spanish Dragoons were sent out to attack a French Piquet at a small village, between this place and St Roque, called Campo.† I was on guard and could not see the sport. Several of our Officers went to look on. The French had 20 Men. The Spaniards charged, had their commander (a Sicilian Captⁿ:) kill'd, faced to the right about, and made off. However, they rallied and had another brush about dusk. The French retreated but their commander's horse took it in his head to stand still, on which [h]is master dismounted and surrendered himself to Cap^m: Cowley

* '[I]s not without cheer. I enjoy a concert under my windows every morning'.
† Campamento.

(Military Secretary of this place). The Spaniards rode up to him. One presented his carbine at Cap^tn: C. and two or three more butchered the unfortunate French officer and here ended this great Battle.

The Sicilian Captn: was buried last night with all the honours of war. It was reported he was Drunck when he went out, as were the greatest part of his Dragoons. The Lines were covered with spectators on that Day.

I have a beautiful view of the Bay from my window and can see from it the Gunboats amusing themselves, firing on the French Dragoons as they go along the coast from Algesiras to St Roque. H^y. Le Mesurier, H^d:'s son,* called on me a few days ago. I did not know him. He thought I was the brother of the Govr: of Alderney. I could do no less than than invite him to Dinner, which I did twice: the first he was engaged, and he sailed the day after for England.

D^r: M^r: Gibralter March 24th: 1810

I shall begin by answering your questions and then tell you the news we can pick up at this place. I was Gazetted the 13th: August 1808, Ensign; joined the Detachement at Canterbury 2^d: September; embarked for Spain the 11th; disimbarked at Corunna October the 29th; embarked at Vigo Jany the 13th; 1809; disimbarked at Portsmouth February the 1st; Embarked for Zealand July 17th: Disimbarked at Slow, South Beverland the 9th: of August; Embarked at Borselen the 4th: of September; Disimbarked at Deal the 16th; Marched to Canterbury and lastly Embarked again at Deal the 19th: of December and Disimbarked here the 23^d: January 1810.†

Thus far pretty well. I think it is probable my next trip will be to Cueta. The 4th: Reg^t: embark'd for that place yeasterday and a salute has just been fired there. I suppose on their landing another Reg^t: is to be sent there shortly. It is a place of too much consequence to the English ever to give it up again as no ship can pass without being seen from Cueta or this place. The French, we

* Henry Le Mesurier (1791–1861), son of Commissary-General Havilland Le Mesurier (1758–1806), was not gazetted ensign in the 48th Foot until 13 May 1812, so quite what he was doing on Gibraltar is a mystery.

† Yet in his letter of 2 February 1809, Le Mesurier wrote that he embarked from Vigo on 18 January and disembarked at Portsmouth on 9 February.

are informed, were preparing boats at Malaga to send troops over to Cueta. For once we have been before hand with them, tho we were a long time in settling that business.

I have not yet taken a survey of the whole Rock as there is nothing very interesting to be seen but a great quantity of Monkeys. I am in so retired a place on this Rock that I seldom hear any news but at Dinner. The Town is not very healthy in Summer from the number of Inhabitants. In the Streets your nose is regaled by a compound of sweet scents – Oil, Garlick, Fish &c: &c: &c: The French have not had the civility to come in the environs of this place lately, which diminishes something from the amusement we used to derive at seeing the Gunboats fire at them.

I cannot, for once, agree with my D^r. Mother in her choice of Quarters. I most certainly woud prefer being on Active Service than cooped up on this Rock, or be in a Country where I might take a ride or a walk without the same prospect always in view. I woud not enjoy returning to England as I am not partial to the Quarters we had there. After actual service I shoud like to see America or the East Indies but as I cannot chuse, I must even rest contented with this place.

Dobrie, Price and myself Dine with one another now and then. The former has been rather unwell but is getting better. My other countrymen and I are very distant and only make a bow when we pass each other. However, as it was their own choice, I see no reason why I should not indulge them.

I have the Hat I first bought when I came into the Army. After my Spanish expedition I had it covered with Oilskin and wore it in Zealand. Since that I had the Oilskin taken off and had it turned. It is rather shabby now and Messrs: D & P crack some jokes on it, but it must see the Summer out, and then I may lay by the Veteran. Those Gentlemen do not consider that a Sub must be a good oeconomist to live decently &, like Uncle John, I like to have old Cloths on my back. All my red coats go once, sometimes twice, to the Rightabout,* but I always keep one for les Dimanches & les jours de Fetes,† &c:

---

* i.e. to be cleaned and repaired.
† 'for Sundays and festivals'.

D[r]: F.   Gibralter April 12th: 1810
                                                                    do 14th:

About a week ago one of our Officers received a Letter from the Military Secretary to inform him that a list of Officers was making out of those who chuse to serve with the Spaniards, and offered to put down his name, which he accepted, and I requested at the same time to have mine put on the List, but other changes have since taken place and we have been dissapointed. The Light companies of the different Reg[ts]: in the Garison embarked for Tarriffa at day light this morning onboard a Sloop of War, to prevent, we suppose, the French from taking possession of it as they woud cut off our supplies from thence and other parts.[*]

Nine of our Officers have been ordered to join the 1st: Batt[n]: in Portugal[†] and Col[l]: Cameron says probably a couple of hundred men will receive the same orders in a short time, in which casse we should see our Old Quarters at Canterbury, to take charge of the Sick and to recruit. In case that happens I shall apply to go in the Portuguese Army rather than return to England.

There was a report here a few days ago that a reduction was about to take place in the Lieut[ts]: 24 were to be allocated to a 1st: Batt[n]: and 12 to the 2[d]: Batt[n]: If that takes place I must turn a patatoe merchant.[‡]

I am now accustomed to the Gibralter living and find every thing good. I always compare our living here to that we had in Spain and find the ballance so much in favour of this place that I am contented. I take a great deal of exercise. I am always on foot in the course of the Day, either climbing up the Rock or Fishing.

P. D. Dobrée called here a few days ago and brought a Gentleman with him. I was reading the papers in my own room. They appeared

---

[*] Early in 1810 the governor of Gibraltar learned of French plans to assault Tarifa, a small port just along the coast at the very southernmost tip of Spain. He decided to garrison it with a detachment of 360 men comprising the light companies of the 2/9th, 2/30th and 2/47th Foot, a battalion company from the 28th Foot, some thirty artillerymen and two small guns. In command was Major Browne of the 28th Foot.

[†] The 1/9th were now in Portugal, having anchored off Lisbon on 27 March.

[‡] The Army List of 1810 lists forty-six lieutenants in the 9th Foot. Since Le Mesurier was one of the most junior, had they been reduced to thirty-six he might have been required to exchange or go on half-pay.

a little astonish'd at the size of my appartment which is about 12 feet long and 8 broad & pretty well filled with my Baggage and Bed. On my offering Dobrée a share, in case of a Siege, he very soon accepted my offer. I dined with him and his Freind, a M^r: Maitland, the same day at one of the Inns. We were rather annoyed during our dinner by a gentleman playing on a Flute. On enquiring from M^r: M, he told us it was a M^r: Lee, brother-in-law to a Mrs Lee who ran away some years ago with the Gordons, and who is out of his right senses in consequence of Mrs Lee's Husband shooting himself when he heard of their elopement.*

15th: The wind came round to the East this morning. An Immense Fleet of Transports sailed for Lisbon & the Offi^{rs}: ordered to join the 1st: Batt^n: went off with them. Our Mess is now reduced to a Dozen.

16th: I have just received a visit from P. B. D. He brought me your kind Letter of the 23^d: Ult^o: together with the Papers and Belts, which I find much better and stronger than any I could have purchased here, though they cost us more than double the Sum.

I think Genl: Beckwith pays the York Rangers the greatest complim^t: that can be. Martineau was fortunate in being in such a Reg^t: as that, and, after having seen pretty much service, made his exit in a way all Military men must wish to end this Life.†

I certainly would wish to be in the 1st: Batt^n: at present as they have some hopes of seeing Service, instead of being cooped up and only have the reading of what is done by such a Reg^t: in such an action. &^{c}: &^{c}:

D^r: Abr^m: Gibralter May the 19th: 1810
London

I have been unwell for the last week but am now much better. I

---

* Mrs. Rachel Fanny Antonina Lee (1774?–1829) was a Georgian celebrity. Having eloped with Matthew Lee in about 1794, the couple soon separated. In January 1804 she eloped again with Loudon Gordon, accompanied by Gordon's brother, a married clergyman. The two men were tried at Oxford assizes, suspected of abduction, but the trial collapsed. See De Quincey's *Autobiographic Sketches*.

† Lieutenant-General Sir George Beckwith had used the York Rangers in his invasion of Martinique in 1809 and his capture of Guadeloupe early in 1810. Lieutenant Martineau of that regiment was killed in the fighting.

belive it was a little fever. I have received Letters from Guern^y: up to the 21st: Ult°: and papers to the 16th: by which I see you have had fine doing in London. I hope you were not one of those who dirtied their hands by taking up mud to throw in the faces of the Military. I think the Military behaved well and with great moderation.*

On the 4th: Ins^t: Three Algerine Frigates & a Brig passed the Straits. The Portugees had been on the lookout for them for a long time with a superior force, one Seventy four and Three Frigates, but, through their stupidity or cowardice, they suffered them to go so far before they began to chasse, that at night they had not come up to them, though it was early in the morning when the Algerines made their appearence in the entrance of the Strait and continued going up under easy sail the whole of the time.

We have been in Camp about a forthnight at Europa point. A little misunderstanding has arisen between two of our Capt^ns: and two Subs. In the first instance it was a triffle, but mark the end – the First was a Sub who wrote a Note to a Captn: to have a Table, rather in high terms. The Captn: shewed it to the Col^l: who, after hearing both parties, dismissed them with a little admonition. The next Sub (your Brother) who wrote a very civil note to a Captn: to desire him to take his horse out of the Stable (a Kitchen), where he was obliged to have his victuals cooked. The Captn: sent the note back unanswered, upon which he was obliged to have recourse to the Col^l: who ordered the Captn: to take his Horse out. This is the same Man who had the dispute on board Ship.

Two Spanish Three Deckers and a Fifty Gun Ship are riding in the Bay under the Protection of our Batteries. Some of our Men of War were at Carthagena when the French were marching towards it, upon which the English sent to the Junta to allow them to take these Ships away – at the same time sent Seamen on board each to get them under weigh. As they were moving off, the Junta sent back word that they could not allow the Ships to be taken away. Alas! It was too late, as Jack will not part with them and allow them to fall in the hands of the Enemy.

I suppose you have seen the late regulations by which I am

---

* Le Mesurier is probably referring to the arrest of Sir Francis Burdett, critic of the government and 'Man of the People', whose imprisonment in the Tower caused riots in London that April.

become a supernumarary L^t: however, it will make no difference as we are continued on the list. This will hurt the Ensigns whose promotion will be very slow till the Lieut^{ts}: are effective. We have now seven supernumararies at present.[*]

I have lost at least ten pounds of flesh during the last fortnight. I am getting on by degrees, and in the course of a few days will be able to take my Duty. The last Letter I receiv'd from you was dated 25th: of March. I should write oftener, by merchant vessels if I was nearer Town, but it is so far and so warm that I seldom go, besides not over and above healthy. I write when I can. I have been obliged to write at different times from a counfounded headache. I hope to hear from you soon. Belive me &^{c}:

D^r: F.   June the 6th:

Since I wrote I have had an attack of the ague, which has now left me about a week. I have taken Bark in pretty good quantities.[†] I have joined the Mess to make up for time lost. I get a little stouter; I have a pretty good appetite. I have nearly demolish'd a fowl for my Dinner to Day.

The Portugeese Men of War, which had sail'd after the Algerines, came in three days ago. They fired a Salute which was not returned. I think they must look rather ashamed of themselves.

[*] Seven 'supernumerary' lieutenants meant the regiment had seven more lieutenants than it really needed and when they were promoted captain, no ensigns would take their place, hence the slow promotion prospects for the ensigns.

[†] Bark infusions were the standard treatment for malarial fevers.

4

Guernsey and Canterbury

Dʳ: Abrᵐ: Gibralter June 15ᵗʰ:1810
London.

I have a companion, an Offʳ: of ours who is rather light-headed.*
I am [h]is acting agent. I have had an attack of the Ague which has
weakened me pretty much, but it is over now, thank God.

You say in your Letter of the 14ᵗʰ: you are surprised at my
appearing so unhappy; I should think having nothing to do would
be a sufficient cause, however, I have engaged a Spanish Master
who will attend every day for One hour. As to Algebra, it has been
left off recently for this reason; that when I was in Camp we were
three in one Tent and it was impossible to work with those Gentᵐ:
in the place, and since I have been unwell I have done nothing. As
to [blank], if ever I mentioned it, it must have been in joke as I
hope I have a little more fortitude than not to be able to bear with
my lot.

The last Packet brought us an augmentation to the Battⁿ: of one
Captⁿ: and three Subs, which brings me the Senior Supernumerary
Lieutᶜʸ:

Manly† of the 44ᵗʰ: came over a few days ago from Cadiz and
married Genˡ: Fraser's‡ daughter.

We are in dayly expectation of hearing of a Battle between Lord

---

*   i.e. delirious from fever.
†   Probably Lieutenant William Manby.
‡   Major-General John Fraser, commander of the small British force at Ceuta.

Wellington and the French.* They were within three days march of each other. Our First Batt^n: are in the environs of Lisbon in a very sickly state, many of the Officers sick.

22^d: A pretty Job – the Regiment is gone on an Expedition between Malaga and Ronda and I am left behind with the Sick & baggage, not till after grumbling pretty much at it. However, un Tout se mele de Docteur† had more weight with the Col^l: than I had, and here I am, not very happy as you may suppose at being left for the first time behind. The Col^l: was very civil and has been kind enough to lend me a horse he leaves behind to ride, which makes two I have at command, as I had already one from one of our Capt^ns: The Expedition is command'd by Genl: Bowes‡ & consists of the 9th: and 47th: Reg^ts: It is supposed to be some coup de main on Malaga or its environs. &^c:
Les Dames minvite au Thé.§

The 2/9th (minus the flank companies which were still at Tarifa) left Gibraltar on 22 June 1810 as part of the amphibious force under Major-General Bowes sent to assault Malaga. Finding the strength of the enemy too great, Bowes decided against a landing and instead returned to Gibraltar.

D^r: Abr^m: Mother Bank¶ August the 4th: 1810
London.

You no doubt will be surprised to find me here. Our Surgeon, finding I was getting worse & worse, thought fit to send me home. I am reduced to a skeleton but find myself better since I have

---

* Sir Arthur Wellesley was now Viscount Wellington following his victory over the French at the Battle of Talavera in July 1809.
    In early 1810 Napoleon sent Marshal André Masséna (1758–1817) to invade Portugal. For the French the obvious routes were either along the road leading south-west from Salamanca through Ciudad Rodrigo, over the frontier and on to Guarda, or via the road west from Merida past Badajoz. As a result, the two fortified Spanish towns of Ciudad Rodrigo and Badajoz became strategically vital.
† Oddly phrased, but seems to mean either a little meddling doctor, or one who meddles with the doctor.
‡ Major-General Barnard Foord Bowes (1769–1812).
§ 'The ladies invite me to tea'.
¶ A sandbank off Ryde, Isle of Wight.

been embark'd. In my sick certificate the cause of my sickness is mention'd; Discease of the Liver & Debility. Since I wrote I had two attacks of the Ague which, however, did not last any time.

I only received my leave of absence when the Fleet was under way and two leagues at Sea. Fortunately a Ship bound to Cadiz remained. I embarked onboard and got to this vessel by Eight at night without any stock whatever, so that I have been living on salt provisions for nearly three weeks. I had the whole of my Cloths wet, as the sea was rough when I was put on board this Ship. I am encumbered with Lieu^r: Ford of ours, who is light headed, so that I must stop at Portsmouth or Lymington, wherever we land, till his Freinds come for him. We have had 3 weeks papers. My leave of absence ends 15th: October. I shall write again soon. &^{c}:

D^r: F.   Yarmouth August the 14th: 1810

After sending Ford home, I went to Southampton and there found Cp^m: Denis who told me he woud sail Thursday evening but, according to custom, put it off till Sunday morning when we made him sail and got as far as Cowes by dinner time, and in the evening weighed again, but after getting as far as the Needles were obliged to put back to this place on account of the wind blowing rather fresh and a heavy sea.

I wrote to you last Friday, a week from the Mother Bank, but am doubtful if the Letter went as it was put in the Quarantine boat. I think I am better onboard Ship than on shore. I shall want a little of the Doctor's attendance to reastablish me completely. As I am afraid I shall be late for the post, I must conclude.

D^r: Abr^m: Guernsey Sep^r: 5th: 1810
London.

I was unable to write, as I had promised last week, as my left side was very painful. However, my Father, I suppose, gave a description of the parting. Your advice to my Sister had the desired effect; that of making them appear cheerful.

We have had company almost every day since they went, which has done us some good. I suppose your journey from Weymouth to London was pleasant as the weather was beautiful. Nothing would have pleased me more than to have been in your company. If you have not sent the things you were to buy for the Family, send me a set of Reg^l: Buttons and place them to my a/c^t: If you would get my Commission from Greenwood and Cox* I should thank you to send it also with the Parcel.

If I am to join at Canterbury, I suppose I shall receive my orders very soon. I receiv'd a Letter from O'Neil who told me 'Some time previous to your leave expiring you should proceed to Portsmouth or solicit leave to join at Canterbury as circumstances may require'. If I do not hear from Major Cambell before 15th: I shall write to him for leave to join his Detachment.

My Father introduced me some days ago to Col^l: Le Marchant† who told me, as soon as the application for my going to Wycomb was forwarded to Lord Harcourt,‡ if I would write a few lines privately to him he would take care that the application should be granted immediately. Otherwise I might be Eighteen months or two years before I could be admitted.

I called on the Governor the day you embarked but did not find him at home. I have had some invitations to Dinner but I honnor no body yet with my Presence. Todo Rogamos que v m d viva muchos y dichosos Anos.

Su aficionado Hermano§

Dr. P. L. M.

Despite Le Marchant's offer, Le Mesurier opted for a posting with Major David Campbell at the 9th Foot barracks at Canterbury. While Peter was recuperating in Kent, the war in the peninsula once again erupted. Having taken Ciudad Rodrigo on 9 July, Marshal André Masséna soon occupied the Portuguese garrison town of Almeida. Wellington pulled his men back into Portugal, south-west towards Coimbra.

The French followed and the two armies eventually joined

---

* Regimental agents and often regarded as the bankers of the British Army.
† Colonel John Le Marchant (1766–1812). Descended from an old landed Guernsey family, Le Marchant opened the first British Army staff training college, the Royal Military College, at High Wycombe in 1799. He was still in charge in 1810.
‡ The 3rd Earl Harcourt ran the junior branch of the college, founded at Great Marlow in 1802 in order to train gentleman cadets as junior officers.
§ 'We ask that all v m d [?] live for many happy years. Your affectionate brother'.

battle at Busaco on 27 September. The 1/9th, who had been in Portugal since March of that year, acquitted themselves well. 'Several columns made their appearance on the top of the hill, and commenced firing on us very sharply, before we were hardly within musket shot,' recalled Hale. 'We were then ordered to load, but not to fire a shot till ordered.' At about a hundred yards they gave the French a volley but 'the enemy stood their ground till we got within twenty yards of them; but seeing that it was our intention to use the bayonet, they took to their heels and made off as well as they could.'[1]

Though victorious, Wellington was worried the French might cut off his line of retreat, so he abandoned the ridge the next day and fell back to the lines of Torres Vedras, a series of fortifications he had constructed outside Lisbon. There the 9th 'remained very comfortable and peaceable till after Christmas,' reported Hale, 'for the enemy never made an attack on our brigade during the time we remained at that place'.[2]

D^r: Abr^m   Canterbury Dec the 13th: 1810
London

We only arrived at this place a quarter before seven yeasterday morning. I was fagged and tired as the Coach was full and I could not sleep comfortably. On my arrival at the Rose, I immediately ordered a warm bed in hopes of getting rest but there again I was disapointed for the cursed Waggons and Carts kept me awake till half past Eight, when I got up with a counfounded headach and came up to the Barracks.

I found Major Campbell, Captⁿ: Sankey and two of our Ens^{ns}: at the Depot with about 100 men.* A party of about thirty is under orders for Portugal with clothing for the Reg^t: which it seems they want very much. There is very little chance of my going out to Gibralter this winter. I shall be wanted here to do the duty for the detachm^t: which is but little; visiting the Barracks every day, see the Men are clean on Parade & going to church every Sunday. I should find it very tiresome had I not books to amuse myself. I

---

* While a regiment was overseas a depot was maintained in England to continue the work of recruitment. Such depots were often commanded by a major.

read and study the whole day and pass the evening with some of our Gentlemen.

I met with a very freindly reception from Major Campbell. I arrived about 9 o'Clock at the Barracks and immediately reported myself. He made me stop to Breakfast and in the Evening I smoked a pipe with him. We smoked some of my Segars which he found excellent. He wished me to take supper with him. I refused as I wished to go to Bed. He tried to tempt me with Oisters but my supper on them last week was too fresh on my memory to allow another trial. I go there now and then in the evening and pass a few hours with him.

I saw a Letter from the surgeon of the 1st: Batt^{n}: who mentions that, the Day previous to the Battle of Busaco, Coll^{l}: Cameron was very ill of the Dissentery, but the moment he heard the Enemy were advancing he said he was better and, contrary to the advice of the Surgeon, mounted his horse and went out. His Horse was killed under him (the same his Brother rode when he was killed at [blank]) and, though much bruised in the fall, continued fighting on foot till quite exhausted, when he was carried off the field by two Serg^{ts}: He has three months leave of absence and, if sufficiently well when he arrives, is, I understand, to take the command of the Detachment here, in which case Major Cambell will go to join the 1st: Batt^{n}: in Portugal.

Ford has sent a Certificate for a Six months leave. I understand he is rather better since he has been home. Since I have been here we have had a continual South westerly wind and Rain. The Surgeon who attends the Sick gave me a little piece of advice; 'To take care not to get wet feet, not to Drink wine, and to only eat plain meat, and that I need no more Medecines'. I spoke to him for this reason; that, should I have been ordered to Gibralter soon, it would not have looked well to have reported myself sick, though going out might have done me a great deal of harm, tho, if I am allowed, which is Major Campbell's opinion, to winter here I need fear nothing as I am getting Stout every day.

Government, as you will have seen by the Papers, are sending great quantities of Stores to Portugal, and yet the Gents of the army seem to think that Lord Wellington will not be able to retain the small part of Portugal he has got for any considerable time. I, for my part, am more sanguine in my hopes & expect that, ere long, those worthy Folks may think so too.

Lindsay* lost his arm at the Battle of Busaco which I suppose will oblige him to leave the army or retire on full pay. Gordon, one of our Senior Lieut^{ts}:, will, I am told, be suspended in the next Gazette for being absent without leave.[†]

I have not felt the pain in my side today or yeasterday. Am &^{c}:

D^r: Abr^m Canterbury Jany 27th: 1811
London.

I received a Letter from Guernsey last Thursday from my Father & Julia. They meant to have sent it by Guilband with one for you, but as he was detained longer than they expected, they sent mine. My Father desires me to inform you that M^{rs}: Maingy[‡] had received a Letter from John dated Naples 27th: November, in which he says (Tous sont en bonnes santé)[§] without mentioning anything particularly of Betsy or Ferdinand, so that they suppose at home that their Letters have miscarried or have been taken in a vessel near the Caskets.[¶] John Maingy had met with a cordial reception from his old freinds. Whilst under Quarantine they had some very rough weather and parted one of their cables, but after being landed the weather grew worse and the ship was wrecked in the very place where they had performed quarantine. They landed on 24th: Nov^r: 1810. Such is the substance of my Father's letter. I meant to have written to you on the same day, but I shall allow you to judge if I have delayed.**

---

* Lieutenant George Lindsay (9th Foot).

† Lieutenant Thomas Gordon exchanged into the 3rd West India Regiment in February 1811.

‡ Peter's brother Abraham went on to marry Mary (or Maria) Maingy in 1832. The Maingys (or Maingays, or Mainguys) were an old Guernsey family who had prospered as Neapolitan merchants.

§ 'All are in good health'.

¶ Les Casquets, a group of rocks west of Alderney, were the cause of many shipwrecks.

** According to Hubert Le Mesurier, Peter's sister Elizabeth (Betsy), 'having set out with her husband [Ferdinand] on a voyage to the Mediterranean about the year 1811, reached Naples in safety. Afterwards, the ship they were in was captured by the Turks and they were taken to Constantinople where, owing to the immense efforts made on their behalf by the British Consul, they were eventually liberated, otherwise they might have been sold as slaves!' (Hubert Le Mesurier, *Stories about Les Beaucamps* 44).

At ten on Thursday we were mustered, being the 24th: Immediately after, Major Campbell ordered a Court Martial to sit which kept us Three hours & a half. I wrote home after that & attended Parade. So much for Thursday.

Friday I was put in orders to take the Acting Adjutancy and Quartermastership, with orders to Overhaul the Regimental stores, which took up an imense time, after which I went to walk, as I found myself unwell from so much confinement. I have not been so well these last three or four days. I attribute it to the Damp & cold weather we have had. Do not mention this to my Father or any of the Family when you write or I shall cease to give you any account of my health, as it is nothing of consequence & would serve to make them uneasy. It may also be attributed to eating some stew'd hare soup that was spiced. You may depend upon my abstaining from anything of the kind since I suspect it does not agree with me. Do not mention it to your London freinds as they are apt to blab & it woud go to Guernsey.

Was I Commander in Chief, I would warn G.t: B: ears the 1st: Batt.n: have had their Clothing on their backs two years. You may suppose what kind of a Coat that must be a Man wears constantly for two years, not only in the day but are often obliged to sleep in it. Such is the state of the 1st: Batt.n: at present, and through mere avarice this detachment, that might have marched to Portsmouth and been off by this time, is here waiting for a ship to take them from Dover by which G.t: B. save a few L: and the Reg.t: is left naked, for naked they absolutely are if we are to belive some men that are come home sick.

I do not receive the allowance of A.A. and Q:M till the Detachment is off. I secured the post as Sterling* would have had the first refusal, had he been here. I give Luscombe the whole allowance till he goes. Was that a good manouvre?

Major Campbell dragg'd me to see Horsemanship and Tumbling the other night. There was no refusing him. When we came to the Door I flung my coin over the receiver's box. The old Gentleman was just behind me. 'Tut. Tut. Tut. Take that again. You must not pay'. I pretended not to hear him & went in. As soon as we were seated he began to ask the reason I payed and wanted to repay me,

---

* Lieutenant George Stirling (9th Foot).

which I positively refused, and after a long altercation I came off victorious. Such is his disposition.

Sterling was ordered to join from Scotland the 31st December & has not made his appearance yet. The Major has been obliged to send in a return since that, in which he returns him ordered to join, whilst another would have said absent without leave.

Extracts of Several Letters he wrote from
To his Sister A.   Canterbury Feby 11th: 1811

A periodical paper has lately been publish'd here called the Whim. The authors are said to be Officers which does but little Credit either to their heads or hearts. It ridicules Religion, the Clergy, in short it attacks every body. The Chief composer of this stuff is a young man of the 23^d Light Dragoons who is vain enough to compare himself to some of our best authors. I do not think it will continue long as I belive the Author will be brought to an account if he does not employ his talents to some better use.*

I heard a very plain good Sermon yeasterday in the Cathedral in consequence of this Publication, which went to shew what punishment attended those who scoff at Religion.

I have not read so much lately as I used to do. My Eyes have been weak. I shewed them to the Surgeon who said it would go off in a short time and attributed it to cold.

D^r: Mother   Feb^y: 25th: 1811

I had heardly finish'd reading your Letter when L^t: Sterling came in and told me he was going to Portsmouth to take charge of the Detachment that left us some time ago, as a melancholy accident had deprived them of their Officers; Ens^gn Luscombe & Ass^t: Surgeon

---

* *The Whim* ran to only twelve issues between December 1810 and June 1811. Its prose style was a mixture of Swift and Sheridan pastiche. Although satirical in nature, and critical of public figures in Canterbury in particular, it was nowhere near as vicious as, say, the contemporary cartoons of Gillray. It poked fun at the army, but was staunchly patriotic. Its editors claimed 'they never wantonly injured any feeling; their satire has never been applied but where it was loudly called for'. They believed that the main objection to their periodical from fellow officers was simply that 'it is very ungentlemanlike for Gentlemen to publish' at all.

Gray, who were both drowned last Thursday by a Boat upsetting as they were coming on shore. We have had no further particulars of this dreadful accident. Luscombe was a freind to Edwards. He was on the eve of promotion. Through a little negligence he lost his life. About Eighteen months ago he was put in orders to mount Guard the next day. He refused to do it, alledging a previous order which said that Offic^{rs}: at Drill were not to mount guard as the reason for his refusal. In consequence of this his Promotion was stopped and he was kept here (after the Reg^t: marched from this for Service) to take charge of the sick men. Had it not been for that unfortunate guard he would have been promoted long ago and probably have been sent to the 2^d: Battⁿ:

Gray's casse is of another nature. He came home with a severe attack of the Liver complaint. He got pretty well in London and waited on the Medical Board, who thought from his appearance he was sufficiently recovered to go out to Portugal again. When he had been here some time he got much worse and obtained three or four certificates of the Medical Staff here, stating his incapacity of going on service. They required his presence in London to examine him. He was unable to go, but, rather than be persecuted in that manner, he resolved to go out, firmly persuaded of never returning to England. This is a short sketch of the life of these unfortunate young Men. It has cast a gloom over all of us.

I have not been quite so well as I had been. I have a few symptoms of my old complaint which I attribute to anxiety, but which I hope will soon be removed. I must beg of you or some of my sisters, when they see my newly married cousin, to congratulate her on my part & to wish her many happy years as M^{rs}: Thomson. I am affraid, however, a soldier's life will not be the hapiest she could have chosen. I must own, it would not give me much pleasure to hear of my Dear Sisters being engaged to an Off^r: From what I have seen & heard it would by no means suit them. It makes both the Husband & Wife wretched. When the Regiment is under orders for Service she is affraid of loosing him & he dreads the consequences, should he have the misfortune to lose his life, of leaving a beloved wife and family with perhaps a wretched pitance of Forty or Fifty pounds a year. These are my reasons against a Soldier's marrying, which I hope will be approved of by my Dr Sisters.

I must conclude as I have a disagreable task to perform ex officio, that of informing an Off^r: that he is reported absent without leave which, however, I hope will not hurt him as he has a chance of getting over it quietly by sending a Certificate of ill health. With prayers for your health, &^c:

While Le Mesurier remained in England, the 2/9th's sojourn on Gibraltar was interrupted. Cadiz, the seat of the independent Spanish government, had been besieged by the French. In an attempt to raise the siege Lieutenant-General Sir Thomas Graham sailed a contingent of British troops from Cadiz down the coast to Algeciras. From there he marched to Tarifa where he collected the British garrison, including the two flank companies of the 2nd/9th, and in alliance with a large force under Spanish General La Pena, advanced on Cadiz.

As the allies approached their target, the two flank companies (part of a battalion of flank companies under the command of Major Browne) were left as a rearguard at Barrosa Hill. Here they were set upon by the French. Heavily outnumbered, Browne retreated, only to be ordered by Graham to retake the hill. The 2/9th flank companies suffered grievous casualties. Only 90 of 160 soldiers were fit for duty a few days later. One captain and three lieutenants from the regiment were injured, including Lieutenant Seward, in command of the light company.

Browne's battalion occupied the French on Barrosa Hill long enough for Graham's main force to turn back and beat them. Unfortunately La Pena refused to help, so Graham could not capitalise on the victory and the enemy escaped. The battle 'was as honourable to the English as it was disgraceful to the Spaniards, who behaved shamefully', wrote Surgeon Dent of the 9th Foot. 'They were not even brought into action, but remained in a Wood till the business was over.'[3]

D^r: Sister A.   March 28th: 1811

I received my Dear Ann's Letter last Saturday week with the greatest pleasure, tho she seems to doubt the veracity of my Bulletins respecting my health. I must assure her that, to the best of my knowledge, they are always true. This, I am happy to say, will be the most favourable you have had for some time. My health is mending fast. I have been released by the Surgeon from my confinement & from taking Physick. I walk Three or four Miles every day and my appetite is getting much better, so that you see I am in a fair way of being perfectly well in a short time. My stomach is rather weak from confinement & medecine but I find walking does me a great deal of good and the more I walk the stronger it gets. This, I give you my word, is the exact state of play of my health at present. I therefore hope all your uneasiness will now cease on my account. The Symptoms I felt were a pain in my right side which the blister completely removed, and a poor appetite.

Last Sunday a week we received a visit from Col[l]: Cameron. I was astonish'd to see him look so well as he did. From his own account he was in a most dreadful state after the Battle of Busaco, so bad that at one time he had an idea of stopping behind the Army, but, thinking the French might not take so good a care of him as the English, he kept up with the Army and got to Lisbon.

You will no doubt have seen in the Papers the business of Barrosa. Our flank companies of the 2[d]: Batt[n]: have suffered very severely. I am extreemly sorry to see that my old mess mate Seaward has come in for his share. It no doubt will hasten the departure of the 2[d]: Batt[n]: Gib: as many of their Off[rs]: will be obliged to join the 1st: Batt[n]: as all the wounded are coming to England. What think you of the Spanish Patriots in this affair? If I was a member of a Court Martial on the Commander in Chief, La Pena, I would hang and quarter him & go on in the like manner among all the Off[rs]: who did not do their duty. You may think I am too violent but when you consider the loss we have suffer'd in this business, occasioned by their cowardice or treachery, I think it is the least than can be done. Our first Batt[n]: are with Lord Wellington in pursuit of Massena.

Whitley and Watson are the Off[rs]: that attempted to convert the men.[*] Col[l]: Cameron told us it was quite laughable to hear the latter groaning. He tells the Men and Off[rs]: that he has cast the Devil from him, and, by so doing, that he is completely happy, but formerly the Old Gentleman tormented him constantly walking,

---

[*] These two evangelising Methodist officers, Lieutenant James Whitley and Ensign Watson, were considered a sufficiently destabilising influence for Wellington to express concern in February 1811. (Brett-James, *Wellington at War* 213).

sitting, sleeping &ᶜ: They have attempted to make converts among the Offʳˢ: but unfortunately their understandᵍˢ: are so confined, or the Offʳˢ: so hardened, that they have not succeeded and have drawn the contempt of all the Regᵗ: on themselves. At the arrival of the Colˡ: the Gentlemen will not be allowed to hold two situations at once, both Preacher & Offʳ:, but the choice will be given them of resigning one or the Other.

My Dear Father mentioned my selling out of the Army in the postscript he added to your letter, but I think it would not answer at present. I am getting a great deal better and likely to get up rapidly in the Regᵗ: If I left the Army I shoud have nothing to do nor any likelywood of getting anything for a considerable lenth of time. I am therefore inclined to try at least a year longer and, if I should not enjoy my health in the Army at that time, then I may think of leaving it. A bien. &ᶜ:

According to the 9th Foot's official regimental history, a recruitment company had been established in England on 23 February 1808 comprising one captain, two lieutenants, one ensign, eight sergeants, eight corporals and four drummers. The preferred source of new recruits was the militia, since its members already had a basic military training. The mode of recruitment was through a bounty. The amount of this bounty varied according to the demand for soldiers and the availability of recruits. To tempt him from the Royal North Gloucester Militia into the 9th Foot in August 1807, James Hale was promised ten guineas – more than six months' pay. The officers then arranged to separate the recruits from their money as quickly as possible. 'To prevent all irregularity that might have taken place in the garrison during the volunteering it was thought most proper to send such men as had volunteered to some place by themselves till they had spent their money,' wrote Hale. 'Therefore ... we were all marched off to Tavistock.' Here they received half their bounty. 'Drinking and gaming was all that was thought about as long as the money lasted. However, it did not hold long: for in about five or six days many had not the price of one pint of beer.'[4]

Dr: J.   April the 11th: 1811

As the weather is not fine enough to go out today, it being wet and cold, I have been looking over the Letters I have received from Guernsey, & the consequence is that I resolved to sit down and write a scolding letter to my Dear Julia, who I am almost sure has forgot her Brother for I could not find a little scrap of her own writing in any of the Letters I have lately received from home. I shall, however, forgive her the moment I hear from her and I dare say she will not be sorry to hear that I am doing very well. I am getting stronger every day and flatter myself my complaint is completely removed.

We are in expectation of getting many Militia Gentlemen. We have therefore been busy lately sending Soldiers to the different Regts: to try to induce their Men to come to the 9th: and, if our accounts are correct, we may expect to have a small Battn: here in the course of a Short time.

If I had not learned Patience when I was Ill I should, in my present situation as Adjt:, soon know what it is. We have a parcel of Recruits at drill and it requires no small share of it to bring them on, for some of them are uncommonly slow of comprehension and I am obliged to superintend their drill for two or three hours every day. However, it's more an amusement than a toil. I shall have more occupation when the Volunteers come in.

You have seen in the Papers that an Allowance of £250 has been made to the Messes of Regts: at home. We have applied to the Secratary at War* to know if any part of that Allowance will be given to the Depot. He has not vouchsafe[d] to return an Answer yet, so we know not if we shall get any part thereof.

Do you know, I shall be inclined to join the Oppn: shortly if Ministers do not releive our wants. You see that our pay has only been encreased 3d or 4d since the year 1614, two hundred years ago, and they will not encrease our Pay, tho the necessaries of Life have more than trebled, ay, even are Ten times dearer than they were then. I think we certainly are entitled to some increase, else how is an unfortunate Sub to live on his pay & keep clear of

---

* Responsible for the administration of the British Army but not its strategic direction: that lay with the Secretary for War.

debt? Now, for instance, Myself, I am ordered by the Surgeon to Drink a third part of a Bottle of Wine every day which costs me 1/8ᵈ, besides my Diner 2/6ᵈ; altogether 4/2ᵈ for diner. I must now get my Breakfast, Washing, &ᶜ: &ᶜ: &ᶜ: on the remainder of my dayly pay and, after the greatest oeconomy, hardly save 4ᵈ: a day to supply myself with Clothes, or run into debt (or hurt myself by discontinueing the wine necessary to reastablish my health). Can those who Govern expect we shall be able to distinguish ourselves when our minds are Labouring under Pecuniary Embarassments? I ask[ed] the Surgeon, who attended me when I was Ill, to dine with me some Days ago, which was a twelve or fourteen Shilling Job, got over. You see, a Poor Sub cannot afford to see freinds often at mess.

Tho I began my Letter in high tone, I must now beg of my Dear Julia that, if She is not too angry with me for presuming to make use of such a language, she will have the kindness to buy a few Black silk (neck) handkerchiefs for me, as my stock is getting low. &ᶜ: &ᶜ:

☞(Note by his stile you find some alteration in his health for the Better)*

Dʳ: A.   Blossom Inn Canterbury April 23ᵈ:1811
London.

Genˡ: Brownrigg has ordered an Offʳ: to go to Dover and Ramsgate, & as I am the only fit for duty, I am the Sufferer. Have the goodness to order Parkinson to send me a Blue Coat by Saturday at latest, as I shall begin my expedition on Monday and I am ordered to appear in plain clothes. It is a D-- foolish business as I shall not receive a farthing of my expenses and, what vexes me most, I am obliged to put on a Cheerful Countenance. How my finances will hold out, I cannot tell, but that this will throw me considerably back I have no doubt, and to acquit myself to my Credit I must lay out Money on the Rogues,† which you may depend upon will be <u>little</u>. I shall follow my Collonel example.

Write to me by return of Post. Old Bob does not spare trouble

* It is not clear whether this is an addition by the recipient or the transcriber.
† Contemporary meanings include 'horses', 'servants', or 'wanderings'.

when [h]is Purse is not concerned. Give my Direction to Parkinson and tell him to be sure not to fail to get it made by that time. Your coat nearly fits me.

P. S. my Pantaloons are shabby. If Parkinson has cheap & fashionable stuff, let him send me a pair. If not – not.

D^r: A.   Canterbury May 9th: 1811
Guernsey

As the weather is so bad that it prevents my stirring out today, I have taken up my pen with the determination of lecturing you for disobedience of Orders. I thought I had desired you, in the last letter you received from me before you left London, to write the moment you arrived in Guernsey. It is now a fortnight and I have no news of your arrival or from any of the Family. Unless you are very punctual in writing and answering my Letters, I shall follow your plan & not be very exact. You have plenty to say in your Letters that will interest me about the Family, the Estate and the Guern^y: news. I therefore hope
you will be more exact for the future.

I returned this day a week from Chatham, not in the very best of humour as I had no success. It was some Consolation to one, though I was sorry to hear it, that our Gentⁿ: had had no better success than myself, either at Dover or Ramsgate, as perhaps G^l: Brownrigg might have taken it into his head that I had not exerted myself as much as I could. Major Campbell was satisfied that I returned at the time I did. I left a party there who return'd a few days ago and say that, since I left Chatham, not one man has volunteered.In other Quarters our Success has been better and we have now about 220 Men sworn in for the 9th: We expect to get about 300 altogether, which is much more than our proportion of Ten Thousand. Some of them will be here this week, and next Saturday a week, a party of 140 will come in this place. The moment the clothing can be altered and the men are completed in Arms, &^c, we shall be packed off to our respective Battalions in the course of Six weeks or Two months.

The 91st: Reg^t: have received some of their volunteers and, as they are priviledged for a few days, we have constant Rows in the Barracks at Night. A few nights ago they attacked our poor Detachm^t: The Major and I sallied out with our canes and, after Marking a few of the Rogues, drove them to their Barracks. They fight with Bayonets or anything that comes in their way.

We are pretty busy getting the Barracks ready. Bustling and Exercise are good for me. I feel perfectly well at present and if I have a relapse it will not be for want of exercise whilst I remain in this place.

I read Coll^l: Wyatt's acquital yeasterday morning to the Men with a great deal of pleasure. He always behaved like a Gentleman to our Detachment in Spain. Perkins I knew very little about, but from the proceedings it appears as if he had acted a very shabby part and got what he deserved.*

I shall want a small supply of Cash. If I was certain of remaining here much longer I would not draw, as my savings from my extra allowance would bring me up again, but as there is every probability of our moving soon I must be ready for a Start, and those things I want I cannot do without. Ferdinand's Militia Jacket is of use to me for as soon as Parade is over I have it on my Back.

Do not forget when you write to Betsy to remember me most affectionately to her and all her Dear Family.

D^r: F.   Canterbury May 23^d: 1811

I have received the Shirts you sent me. They fit me perfectly. I beg you will thank my Sisters.

We have had a busy time of it since I wrote last. We have now about Two hundred and Twenty as drunken Fellows as I ever saw to deal with, that have joined from the Militia, and, when the Volunteering is over, we expect about Eighty more. The Reg^t: that was the cause of my going to Chatham, not having given the 9th: any men, has been removed and another Reg^t:, from whom we expect some Volonteers, has been sent there, and one of our Off^rs: (Captn: Perceval) sent there to Try his fortune. These Fellows had better

---

* Lieutenant-Colonel William Edgell Wyatt of the 23rd Royal Welch Fusiliers had been court-martialled over his command during the retreat to Corunna and Vigo. He was honourably discharged and his acquittal was ordered to be read to every regiment.

not triffle with the Quarter Master Genl: or else they may expect long Marches and bad Quarters. Such has been the case with those from whom we expected Men and who have dissapointed us (but this only in the Family).

As my Duty as Quarter Master obliges me to have Rooms for Off^rs: who join us, I have been sent by Major Campbell to warn them that, in all probability, all the spare rooms in the Barracks would be filled by Off^rs: and that those the Ladies occupied would be wanted.* Since that, the Ladies have taken a great dislike to me for enforcing my Orders on them, but I have now adopted the plan of sending my Serg^t: to them, as I was not received with common civility and I was afraid they would proceed to extremities and scratch my Face.

I rode Capt: Perceval's Horse the other day, as I had his permission. The Major and I rode about Eight or ten miles, & in coming home were going through a small River. My Horse got frightened at the depth of the water (it had rained a great deal the day before), turned round & began prancing till, getting his foot on a round stone, it fell and laid me snug on the Mud without hurting me in the least. The Horse, in getting up, scratch'd his head and knee a little which I hope will be nothing. I wrote to Perc^l: yeasterday and mentioned it to him, in case the Horse had received any damage, that I of course would be answerable. To day it appears very well and I am in hopes the Marks will be off in the course of a few days.

These are all my Misfortunes, but as I enjoy my health perfectly I can bear them. I bustle about from Morning till night and Sleep well. &^c:

D^r: F.   Canterbury June 6th: 1811

I have to acknowledge the receit of Ab^ms: & Julia's Letters of the 21st: May and yours of the 28th: which I received last Sunday. Though they all gave me much pleasure, yours certainly gave me most, as I learnt by it that our good Folks at Naples were in good

---

* 'Ladies' normally referred to officers' wives. However, Le Mesurier may mean the wives and children of the rank and file who usually lived in the same barrack rooms as their husbands.

health. I hope they will pass their time more pleasantly in a short time, for I think if we continue to be successful in Portugal, Master Bony will not be able to tyranize over Europe much longer, and, when once the different Nations find how he gets on in Spain & Portugal, I hope they will follow the Example set them and send him to receive the Reward for his good Works in this World.

I was sorry to find by your Letter that it was inconvenient for you to advance any money at present. However, I shall try to remit it in the course of one or two months. I wish you had told me so before, as I would have done the best way I could, without putting you to any inconvenience on my acc^t: I was not aware that you could not draw your interest from the American Bank, though I know they had refused to renew the Charter, as I supposed some arrangements had been made by their Government for the payment of the Shares.[*]

The Volunteers have been pouring in since I wrote. In all, we have received from the Militia Two hundred and fifty six, which is a very fair Number for us. All the stout young Men are picked out for Portugal. The Boys and those not fit for very active service will be sent to the 2^d: Batt^n: Major, now L^t: Col^l:, Campbell says there is no chance of their moving for some time. I shoud not be surprised if I was obliged to stop here longer than I have any Idea of at present. Some Sub^s: must stay here with the Depot, and as I am Adj^t:, &c^c:, I may be obliged to stop. If there is any chance of my being sent to Portugal, I shall resign everything immediately,[†] but if there is no likelyhood of the 2^d: Batt^n: being sent there, I am affraid I shall not go to the first, and in that case will not make any great effort to be cooped up at Gib. but take it cooly here.

In consequence of the Duke of York's reinstatement as Com^r: in Chief,[‡] it has given great & general pleasure throughout the Army. He is beloved as Com^r: in Chief and I am sure there would be a

---

* The First Bank of the United States (1791–1811) was a private company with the responsibilities of a national bank. In 1811 Congress did not renew its charter, ending its federal role and destroying its value as a going concern. As a shareholder, Peter's father evidently lost money.

† By which he means resigning the additional roles of adjutant and quartermaster, not his commission.

‡ The duke had been forced to resign in March 1809 following accusations that his mistress had been taking bribes in exchange for promotions. He was reappointed in May 1811.

general Cry in the Army if he was to be removed again. I think he has been punished enough for his former behaviour & I doubt not it will be a warning how he goes on in the future.

As I have many Queries from Ab^m: to answer I shall answer them on the other side this sheet. Am &^c:

Canterbury June the 17th 1811

As my Dear Mother might think it unkind if I delayed any longer writing to her, I rose on purpose at six this morning because we are so employed during the Day that it would have hardly been possible for me to write a long Letter. The cause of all this bustle is a Detachment having been ordered to hold themselves in Readiness to embark at the shortest Notice for Portugal, among whom I am extreemly happy to inform you I am included.

On Saturday the Coll^l: received a Letter from Cap^m: Oneil* saying that a Detachment under the command of Lt^ts: Ford, Le Mesurier, & the Two Senior Ens^ns: would be ordered off immediately & yeasterday we received the order to hold ourselves in readiness from the Adj^t: Gene^l: We shall take about Two hundred fine Fellows to the Reg^t: The Men are not ready yet, but by the latter end of this week I suppose they will be complete in everything, and most probably in the course of a fortnight we shall be embarked. I have provided myself with plenty of Stout shoes and good, stout Blue Cloth Trowsers, which our Gents wear in Portugal.^† Such are the news of the Day.

Please do tell Abr^m: that I have purchassed another Mordente's Spanish Grammer & I shall order both my Bedstead & Grammar, which I left at Gib, to be sold as soon as I get to Lisbon, for it is not likely that I shall ever join the 2^d: Batt^n: unless as Captn: I shall thank him to send me Letters of recommendation for Lisbon as soon as he possibly can. I shall now have an opportunity of seeing the Spaniards fight. I am of oppinion the only proper place to place them is in the rear, for when English and Spanish Troops

---

* Captain Thomas O'Neil (9th Foot).

† Wellington was notably lax about uniforms and so variety flourished. 'Provided we brought our men into the field well appointed, and with sixty rounds of good ammunition each, he never looked to see whether their trousers were black, blue, or grey,' wrote one subaltern, 'and as to ourselves, we might be rigged out in all the colours of the rainbow if we fancied it' (Grattan, 50).

fight together against the French, it is not likely that they would attack the former in preference to the latter, who are not so well disciplined as the former.

A Gentleman of the 23^d Light Dragoons has had no less than Three field days (Duels) within the the last two days. He winged (wounded) one of his adversaries in the side. The other Two escaped unhurt.* These Three Gents were the supposed authors of a Periodical Paper called The Whim which attacked every Body, Right and Left, and they took it in their heads to abuse this man, which has been the cause of all this business.

I give up my Adj^{ts}: & Qu^r: Mastership on Monday to Lieut^t Luscombe, brother to that unfortunate fellow that was drown'd at Spithead. I do not think I ever resigned any thing with half the pleasure I do this, as Portugal is the Cause. I had very little expectation of going to the 1st: Battⁿ: though I wished it much. I shall write to my Sisters before I go.

Parson Watson has resigned his commission in the 9th: and devotes himself wholly to preaching. I wish his Brother Parson Whitley would take it in his head to follow his example as it would give me a Step.†

Col^l: Campbell has applied to go out with this Detachment, but I am affraid will not be allowed. We shall be a most pleasant party. Ford's Brother paid him a visit the other Day & returned me many thanks for the trouble I had had, besides an invitation to go to Oxford.

My Dear Ann   Canterbury June 27th: 1811

Yeasterday morning's Post brought me all the kind and affectionate wishes of the Family. You, my Dear Ann, I must commission to thank them all for me. What will chiefly contribute to my Happyness wherever I go will be to hear that all the Family continue to enjoy health and happiness, then I shall cheerfully endure any little hardships I may meet with.

---

* Given the inaccuracy of nineteenth-century duelling pistols, missing an opponent was common. When deliberately done, to indicate the contest was beneath one, it was called deloping.

† A 'step' was moving one place up the list of officers of your rank in your regiment, ordered by seniority.

I remember once, when last in Guernsey, having caused you some little displeasure, by calling you down to give you some apples my Uncle Saml: had sent you. You expected a Letter & were disapointed. I have not been able to forgive myself for that. I felt the same as you did then.

This day a week, Col^l: Campbell sent for me. When I came in his Room I saw by his Countenance he had something to tell me which was not agreable. Judge what I felt when he told me Luscombe was Senior to me & that he was to proceed to Portugal in my place, as the order for me to go arose in a Mistake made by Captn: Oneil. I had been at a loss to guess why Luscombe was not sent and expected something of this. I had therefore resolved on the following Plan; which was to get every thing ready without delay, and on Genl: Brownrigg finding out his mistake, to remonstrate with him on the Expence incurred to me from it.

My Plan has been crowned with Success. On Friday Genl: Brownrigg's Letter arrived and mentioned to Col^l: Campbell that he would allow me to proceed on account of expence I had been put to. Luscombe will also go out. I act still as Adj^t:, &c:, untill I embark. I do this at Col^l: Campbell's request and will of course receive the emolument of the place. My Successor is Henry, who has a contraction in the Hip from the fatigue he endured in Sir John More's Retreat. He is very well off with respect to money, and I act, though he is in orders as Adj^t:, that it may cause no broken periods in the Accounts.

10 o'Clock. The arms have just made their appearence for the Men, to the great joy of the Detachement. We shall touch at Portsmouth to take in a useful piece of furniture in Portugal, i.e. a Doctor.

I must attend parade therefore am &c:

D^r: F.   Canterbury July 4th: 1811

In consequence of Lieu^t: Luscombe being unwell and unable to proceed to Portugal, the command of the left wing devolved on me & I have been obliged to purchass Sixty pairs of Strong shoes for the Gentl^n: of the said wing by order of Col^l: Campbell, which will amount to £30. I am therefore under the necessity of drawing again on you for £20, but shoud we be detained at Portsmouth about a fortnight, or Three weeks, I shall remit the money. If not, shoud we proceed to Portugal immediately, I shall remit it through M^r: Higgs.

The Lord Eldon is the name of the Ship we go in and is a very fine Vessel; 373 tons.* We expect to embark tomorrow or Saturday, as the ship left Portsmouth for the Downs two days ago. I received Mr Morgan's letter of Recommendation to Mr Higgs last Saturday, and on Monday returned my thanks for his civil Letter.

Cap^tm: Percival's Brother is going to Guernsey to join his Reg^t, the 63rd. As P. has been very civil to me here I should be much obliged to you to show him some attention.

D^r: F.   Spithead July 19th: 1811

Yours of the 9th: found me at this place last Sunday. I had almost given up every hope of hearing from you before I left England. On my return to the Transport, after writing to you, the Signal was made to prepare to Sail. Ford and I, who were in the Boat, took turn about at an Oar, as we were afraid the Fleet would get under weigh ere we reached the ship. The wind and Tide were against us and favourable for the Fleet. We had hardly been half an hour on board when the wind return'd to the old Quarter, the Westward, and we have had it from that Quarter ever since. It is now more to the southward at present and, shoud it come round a little more, we may expect to sail shortly.

We have continued busy with the men, getting them a little in order. They are all young Lads that were never embarked. It therefore requires some trouble and Patience to make them keep themselves Clean and keep regular hours. They are coming on well.

We have been unfortunate in our Meat, having laid in a Stock when we expected to sail. Part of it has been spoiled & obliged to throw it away. We have therefore laid in a stock of Ducks and a Pig. Great many Detachements have embarked and are dayly embarking at this place for Portugal. I was in hopes of seeing W^m:

---

* The *Lord Eldon* was an East Indiaman, the best class of privately hired military transport. Its crew was experienced and tough. When boarded by the men of a privateer, the *Eldon's* captain found a French sailor at the wheel and sliced his head off with one stroke of his sword (Chatterton, 178–9).

Le Mesurier,* but I have not been able to find out if a Detachement of the 24ᵗʰ: have embarked or not.

I seldom go on Shore but on business. When at Portsmouth I saw a Curiosity: a Black and White Negro Boy. I intend, if the wind continues to the westward, to go on shore at the Isle of Wight this week.Please to rember me &ᶜ:

---

* Captain William Le Mesurier of the 24th Foot, Peter's cousin. Though placed on half-pay after the Napoleonic Wars, he enjoyed a highly successful, if chequered, career. He moved back to full pay in December 1820, half-pay in April 1822, full pay in the 88th Foot in September 1823, half-pay in the Newfoundland Fencibles in December 1823, full pay in the 22nd Foot in April 1825, half-pay (unattached) in November 1829, full pay in the 45th Foot in August 1848, then immediately onto half-pay in the 95th Foot, and on the same day got a brevet promotion to major (backdated to 22 July 1832) and lieutenant-colonel (backdated to 9 November 1846), just before taking up the post of Town Major in Alderney (*see* Warren, 20). While still on half-pay he was promoted to full colonel in June 1854, ready to greet Queen Victoria when she visited the island in August that year (*see* Bonnard), then major-general in April 1861 and lieutenant-general in 1877, an astonishing progession for an officer who saw minimal active service after Waterloo.

5

Portugal

My D^r: F.   Lisbon August 24th: 1811

After a fine passage of Thirteen days we landed here on the 22^d: inst: We are to remain here till the Men are completed in Shoes, Shirts, &^c: They never leave this place without Three pair of shoes.*

Our Batt^n: is in the 5th: Division of the Army, or Genl: Dunlop's, and in Genl: Hay's Brigade.† They are at present at Head Quarters, somewhere about Salamanca, so that we have a long march before us. We are obliged to purchase Mules for the carriage of our Baggage. They are at present very dear.

I have seen four Off^rs: of the 9th: Reg^t: who have left the Army on account of Ill health. They say the Country is completely laid waste and nothing to be purchassed. They were advising me to take a Tent‡ and purchase a Horse to ride myself, but I think if a Soldier can march with his Knapsack & carry 60 rounds of Amunition, besides his Arms, I shall be able to keep up with them. My intention

---

* Before the march each soldier was issued with one pair of shoes, two spare pairs to keep in his pack and a pair of half soles. They wore out with remarkable rapidity; when manhandling artillery over rough roads, they lasted barely a day. The quality of the shoes was so poor the soldiers were advised to swap them over regularly, from left to right, to equalise the wear. They had no eyelets – a soldier had to punch his own – and needed constant maintenance. The tendency among the men to slit the leather where it caused blisters hastened their end (Davies 70; Glover, M., *Wellington's Army* 64; Wood 54).

† Major-General James Dunlop (1759–1832) and Colonel Andrew Hay (1762–1814).

‡ Tents were not issued to officers or men on the march until later in the war.

73

at present is to join with another Officer for buying a Mule, and to walk as far as the Army, then, shoud I find myself too much fagged, buy a Poney, which I am confident will not be the case.

As to this place, I think it is abominable. What makes one particularly dislike it is the Noise those infer[l]: Curs, with which this place swarms, make continualy at night, which prevent my sleeping till I am a little more accustomed to their music, and an immense number of Vermin in my Bed.[*] I am in the best part of the Town and my room is very decent. I called on M[r]: Higgs a few days ago. He acknowledge[d] the receit of Abr[m's]: Letter, but said, in consequence of having a great Deal to do, he was prevented from answering it sooner. He told me if he could be of any service he shoud be happy to do anything for me.

My freind Dallas, who is on Sick leave here, has just brought me your Letter of 5th: Ins[t]: which has given me a great deal of pleasure. I am happy to find our Dear Betsy is well. God grant her and her Family a continuance of their Health.

Some of our Off[rs]:, who have been here sometime, seem to think that the Portugeese are getting tired of this War, and that they do not behave so well to them as they used to do.

I do not know which way we are to proceed to join the Army; weither embark and go round to Figuera in Transports or up the River in Boats to Villa Franca. If we had landed at Opporto we shoud have been nearer our Army by about Two hundred miles. We do not know anything for certain about our moving from this place or how our Mules are to go, should we be ordered to Figuera. I should have thought that Govern[t]: ought to provide Carts or Mules and not put Individuals to such an expense on Service, and it will be money thrown away in the End because we shall either loose them or be obliged to leave them without selling.

I never saw so many Beggars as there are in this place; at every corner, at every Door; in short, the place is filled with them. The weather is very Hot. I am almost melted when I stir out in day time.

---

[*] 'It was the most filthy town I had ever seen,' confirmed Bell. 'It was dangerous to walk the streets by night. No end to the slops coming from the top windows, whop! into the gutters below. The dogs were ever on the alert at night, prowling and fighting – a community of scavengers without owners, rejected and kicked about; existing in mangy wretchedness, and dying in the streets. As for beggars, they were as plenty as paving stones' (Bell 43).

I Dined yeasterday with our Sick Gents at Belem* and walk'd back in the evening. Am &c:

Welllington had decided to take Ciudad Rodrigo and began blockading the town in early September. The 1/9th were posted to El Payo, a village a few miles south. It was to there that Le Mesurier marched the new detachment of recruits.

Dr: F.   Coimbra Septr: 9th: 1811

After refreshing ourselves at Lisbon for Nine days, we embarked on the first of this month for Figuera, w[h]ere we arrived on 6th: From thence we marched for Montemore Velho† on 7th:, with a Detachement of the 74th: Regt: under the comand of Major Shawe. The Inhabitants of these vilages have been cruelly plundered by the French. At an old Gentleman's house, where the Offrs: of the Detachment messed, Our Landlord told us the French had plundered him of 200 head of Cattle, besides an imense number of Fowles.‡

The roads from Figuera to Montemore Velho are very bad and our Recruits appeared tired. From Montemore we marched to Fentugal,§ a poor vilage that has been plundered like the former. A great number of the Inhabitants have left their houses so that those places apear almost deserted.

We marched this morning into this place which appears to be a good Town. Here I met Fraser,¶ one of my Old Messmates at Canterbury. He is here with a Detachment of Sick Men, and, as he informed me the Post would go out to night, I set about writing,

---

* A suburb of Lisbon.
† Montemor-o-Velho.
‡ On campaign, the French 'paid no respect to persons, they plundered every thing they came near to' (Hale 56), but by relying on what they found it was difficult for them to remain in one place for long, 'always on the trot, like locusts, eating up all before them', as Bell put it. 'They paid for nothing, and it was always an unlucky time for us when we got in their wake, for they cleared out the whole country as they went along' (Bell 47). In contrast, Wellington bought supplies from the Portuguese and and had materiel shipped in from England.
§ Tentugal.
¶ Either Lieutenant Erskine Fraser (9th Foot) or Lieutenant Alexander Fraser (9th Foot).

though I am rather fagged. The Road we came over to day was abominable; Sand and Gravel more than half the way. We had a view of the Heights of Busaco. Little did I think a year ago, when I was with you, that I shoud have had a view of the place so soon. I only saw them at a Distance to day. They appear to be very high & Lord Wellington must have had a very strong position. We shall have a nearer view of them in the course of a few days, on our way to join the Army. We shall be about a fortnight more before we can join the Reg^t:

I have joined with one of our Off^rs: in the purchase of a Mule for our Baggage & Provisions, which we are under the necessity of taking up the Country as Nothing is to be had where the French Army has been. We have taken Tea, Sugar, Ham, Tongue, Tobacco and a small Keg of Brandy. Our Mule, tho not over and above good, cost us One hundred Dollars, owing to the scarcity of every thing in this unfortunate country.

I met W^m: Le Mesurier at Figuera and met with a much more Freindly welcome than at Portsmouth. He begged I would take pot luck with him,* which I did. I have been very well since I have been in Portugal, with the exception of one day which I suspect was caused by some shrimps I eat at my Breakfast and which disagreed with me. I have followed Abram['s] advice of taking Medecine, & have had a bleeding which I think is of use coming to this warm Climate. Since our Marches have commenced I have felt particularly well and March better; that is, do not feel so tired as I formerly did in the Commencement of a March.

I got a Billet to day. When I went to the House an old Lady shewed me in a Room where she and a parcel of little Bratts slept, and told me I might have a corner of the Room which, however, I declined & took my abode with Fraser for the few days we may remain here.

I was unable to refund the £20 I had drawn from you when at Lisbon on account of the Purchassing a Mule. So many things are recommended to take up to the Army by different Off^rs: I hardly know whose advice to follow, but will take nothing but what I suppose to be absolutely necessary. Our Marches have hither to been very comfortable. We start about 5 o'Clock in the Morning,

* To create a meal from everything available.

after having taken a light Breakfast. We get in our Quarters about 9 or 10 & have the whole day before us. I have seldome got up later than half past Three o'Clock since our Marching began, therefore take a nap in day time.

You most probably will not hear from me again till I have joined the Army. I have left a small trunk onboard the storeship of the Reg^t: at Belem, with a change in case I should be unfortunate enough to lose my Baggage to have recourse to it. Am &^c:

During the weeks it had taken Le Mesurier to reach Portugal and join up with the rest of the 1/9th, the military advantage had again switched to the French. Napoleon had despatched Marshal Auguste de Marmont to take over from Masséna. Advancing with 50,000 troops, Marmont compelled Wellington to abandon his siege of Ciudad Rodrigo and retreat south-west to Alfaiates, just over the Portuguese border. The 5th Division, including the 1/9th, pulled back a few miles further to Guarda.

D^r: M^m: Guarda October 1st: 1811

On the 11th: Ult^o we left Coimbra on our way to Celorica.* The first day's march was so bad that it near knocked up two of our Gent^s: from Coimbra. I did the duty of Quartermaster for the Detachment. The whole of the Villages we passed through have suffered from the French Army. The stories the unfortunate People told us were nearly the same; the murder of some of their relatives, the destruction of their Houses and Cattle.

We expected to have a halt at Celorica, one Day, but when I reported the Detachment to the English Commandant he desired us to proceed to a village a League further, as he said there was no room in the Town for us on acc^t: of the number of Sick men in it, about Two Thousand in number. From Celorico we directed our March towards Castle Born. At this place the Scarcity of Provisions was very great. We paid here One Shilling per pound for Bread.

The first day's March from this we passed over the Plane where the Battle of Fuente de Honor was fought.† We saw an imense number of Peices of Shells, &^c: and the Breast works, and Trou

---

* Celorica da Beira.
† Fuentes de Oñoro.

77

de Loup* made by our Army to prevent the Enemy's Cavalry from acting. A number of Horses' bones and graves were spread on the Place.

On the 24th:, the Detachment having arrived about Two Leagues from Payo where our Route directed us, Ford lent me his Horse and I rode on and Reported the Detachm^t: to Col^l: Cameron, whom I found Quartered in a place that resembled the Fosse,† but the inside of the House was not near so good. I met with a very Freindly reception from the Off^rs: but what gave me the greatest pleasure was the Letter I received from my Dear Elizabeth, and that crossed by Abram, acquainting me all her familly enjoyed a good state of health.

I received the other day a Letter from Danl: Hardy acquainting me he was in the Commissariat's department and that he was to leave Lisbon immediately for head Quarters.

You may perhaps wish to know how we came to this place on the 25th: We understood that the French had received a considerable reinforcement and a Skirmish took place at El Bourbon.‡ The result we do not know exactly, it was reported in so many ways.

On the 26th:, the Division having concentrated itself at Payo, we marched about Two Leagues towards Villa Velho and took our Station on the Top of a height from whence we could see the 4th: Division at some distance, Skirmishing. Here we stoped the night; not in Tents, no, that would have been a luxury too great. We built a wigwarm and got five of us as close as possible and slept as well as we could; rather cold, I assure you.

We Started at two in the morning of the 27th: and marched about Three Leagues, about half a League from any Town. Here we passed a miserable night with very little to eat and very Cold as we had marched all day in the Rain.

On the 28th: we marched Four Leagues to Pigo. Here we got some Rice and a good Irish Stew, only it was a little Burnt, and slept like Princes under a fine Chesnut Tree, and marched here on the 29th: Our Baggage was sent off the day before we marched from

* 'Wolf hole': a conical pit with a stake in the middle.
† There are several La Fosses on Guernsey. The fields adjacent to Les Beaucamps were called Courtil de la Fosse au Courlieu (*see* Moullin, *The Old House of Les Beaucamps*, 17), so he may have meant a house on that land.
‡ El Bodon.

Payo, and we saw nothing of it till we arrived here. I had nothing to sleep in but Straw and Roll myself in my Regimental Coat, which I assure you I will not do again as I think I am perfectly able to carry my Boat Cloak on my Shoulders, and I find it very dissagreable to have nothing to sleep in at night.

We have had a rough begining but we shall do very well in future. I continue to enjoy good health & I assure you my spirits were never better, though it appears to me we are retreating. However, do not call it a retreat till you can see what Lord Wellington himself calls it. We understood we were to remain here into winter Quarters. However, the Tune is changed to day and it seems our stay here will be but short. W[h]ere we go to, I cannot say, however I shall not be sorry to leave as we have but poor Quarters here on account of the number of Troops in the place, as all the 5th: Divis^n: are quartered in it. The Portugeese have taken good care of themselves, having all the best houses in the place whilst we are left to shift for ourselves.

The number of Sick in the Army is very great. The number of Men belonging to our Reg^t: in Portugal is about One Thousand, and the actual strenth of the Batt^n: at present is not above 650. We shall soon here w[h]ere our destination may be. However, I must beg of you not to be anxious on my account as it will be impossible for me to write regularly and you may be sometimes pretty long without hearing from me, yet you may depend upon my writing when ever time and opportunity offers. From the report in Circulation, most probably the North of Portugal may be our destination.

D^r: Anne   Para de Mouca* Octo^r: 21st: 1811

A painfull Duty being over, one which agrees much better with my feelings now calls me; that which I doubt not will give pleasure to my Dear Anne. My first Duty was to write to the freinds of one to the Ensigns who came out with our Detachment, who Died on the 17th: of this month; Scatcherd. He was a worthy young man of a very delicate constitution and I belive the hardships we endured from Payo to Guarda accelerated his end considerably. Another of our Ensig^s: who also came out with us has left the Reg^t: & is gone to Lisbon in a very bad state of health. Your Brother, though you

---

* Pera do Moco.

may suppose his constitution injured from his illness last Year, is proof against everything except the misfortunes of his neighbours. His health and spirits are as good as ever. He takes plenty of exercise and Eats and sleeps like a Prince, therefore you need have no fear on his account.

I have received no Letter from Guer^y: or indeed from any of my Freinds since I left Payo, though two Packets have arrived.

On the 8th: of this Month we received Orders to March the next day to this Village, which lies about Six Miles to the Northw^d: and Eastw^d: of Guarda. You may fancy a HHouse, compared to which la Fosse is a Palace, in a fine, Airy situation, rather too much so at times, without a Window, and with two good old People in it making every thing as comfortable for us as they can.

On the 12th: we were obliged to march to a place near Guarda. On our return to this place Genl: Le Marchant passed throug.* I was talking to some of the country people. Though he had only seen me once, he recollected my Face. I had no conversation with him, a Salute passing by. He had scarcely left the Village when Lord Wellington passed through. I was much pleased to have had a sight of his Lordship, as he goes generally in a great Coat, without any Mark by which he can be known, so that you may suppose I took a survey of his Lordship, such a one as I think I shall never forget him. He spoke to Col^l: Cameron but kept going all the time. I understand he seldom stops on those occasions, not like your great Beaus who detain you half an hour without having anything to say.

I have been desired to make the following enquiries by one of our Capt^ns: but which my Father will better be able to answer than my Dear Sister: what will Bishop De Jersey & Co.† be able to pay in the pound, and if any Person in the Island would be willing to give a fair Rate for a Bill on them? Such are the enquiries I am desired to make and which I shall thank my Father to answer.

I now Smoke two or Three Sigars a day, which I think are most excellent things for health. I have about one pound of Tobaco and my Messmate has 150 Sigars which will last us till another

---

* Colonel Le Marchant of the Royal Military College, having been promoted to major-general, had left for Portugal that August to command the heavy cavalry.

† Guernsey bankers.

supply arives from Lisbon. My Messmate (Morant)* is a good sportsman. He brought home a Hare he had shot a few days ago, which afforded us an excellent Dinner. We fried it with a little fat Pork and then Stewed it with half a pinte of Wine. We require good living for the exercise we take, and to live well requires Money and I belive just now we are equally rich in the Division. They are Three months' pay in arrears. I am one, but without a farthing in my Pockets. Les Puches n'ont pas de Mercy sur nous, ils vont par Douzaine & nous echardes terriblement.†

If it was possible to send a few flannel waistcoats for me, I shoud be much obliged to you to do it, as they will be of the greatest use to me in Spring when the Campaining commences, as we have seldom an opportunity of getting under cover, therefore warm Clothing is necessary.

We are here on the direct road from Guarda to Frenada, the Head Quarters, and though Expresses pass often, we seldom hear any news. We have a very good Character in the Division. The other day a Lecture was given in Order to the Division for Plundering at Guarda, but the 9th:, with the Royal Artillery & Portugeese, were not included in it, though, to tell the Truth, I belive there are not a greater set of Plunderers than our Gents, but they are old hands at the business and are seldom Caught. Rember me &c:

Dr: Abrm: Travanca Decemr: 8th: 1811

The place I date my Letter from will be a sufficient excuse for not writing since the 4th: Novr: as you will find we have been moving. Know then, my Dr: Abraham, that on Sunday 24th:, as I was laying snug in my bed about Seven o' Clock in the morning, I was roused up in double quick time by an order to have the Baggage packed up and be ready to March off in One hour's time.

At about Nine we marched from Para de Mouca to Repoulia de Coa, a distance of Five Leagues, and on the 25th: to Alfayates. There we understood we had advanced to intercept a Convoy going to Ciudad Rodrigo, but in consequence of our movement

---

* Ensign Robert Morrant (9th Foot).
† 'The fleas give us no mercy. They appear by the dozen and teach us a terrible lesson.'

the Convoy had halted and, of course, would not move any further unless they advanced.

Alfayates is a frontier Town of Portugal, formerly fortified but now in ruins. Our Quarters there were abominable, yet I suppose you will think me very nice when I tell you we had a Hall, a Kitchen & Bedchamber without any Partition, being like three very broad steps for Eight human Creatures to sleep in, the whole house being ten feet broad by twenty long.

On the 29th: we measured back our steps to Repoulia de Coa, 2½ leagues, and on the 30th: to Guarda. We halted there on Sunday Decr: the 1st and had a Church parade. With whatever little money we could borrow, we provided ourselves with a little stock and recommenced our March to the rear on the 2d: We had a most fatiguing march on that day. We passed through Miseralia, a Village in the valey of the Mondego. The Scenery about this place is without exception the finest and most Romantick I ever saw.

After passing that village we had to ascend a Hill which, I assure you, would soon ascertain if a Person was sound, wind and Limb. The pleasure I felt reaching the Top was equal to the trouble I had had in climbing up. After leaving that Beautiful (but to me not at all pleasant) place, we passed through Lignares,‡ a good looking place, and arrived about Dusk at Villa Cortes§ w[h]ere we went into as bad Quarters as at Alfayates. I slept sound that night having marched, I suppose, 25 miles. From Villa Cortes we marched next day to St Martin, a small village near Cea.¶ I knew almost every part of the road, this day's march, having passed the same way on going to join the Regt: with the Detachment. On the 4th: we Marched to Sampiao, where we expected to have remained some time, but the Coll:, not liking the Village, we moved to this place on the 6th: This place is five Leagues from Viseur and 10 from Coimbre.

This morning an order was received to send all the Sick to the rear, which in General indicates a movement, so that God only knows how long we may stop here. We have not drawn pay since September which will oblige me to draw again on my Father as I

‡ Linhares da Beira.
§ Vila Cortez da Serra.
¶ Seia.

am in great want of a few things, Blankets in particular as I have only a Boat Cloak at present and I am almost frozen at night.

I see by some of the Papers the 50th: Regt: is gone to Guernsey. As Woodhouse* is gone to join them, I desired him to call on you, that you would be happy to see him. I shall recommend you to my acquaintance in the Army and shall not require more than 10 Pr Ct for such recommendations. What a lucky Bird you are to have such a Brother. With such interest you cannot fail making a fortune in a few years.

Tell my Dear Sister Ann I would willingly exchange my present Quarters pour une place dans l'étable aux vaches.† My Letter would be written more intelligibly, as I am so cold I can hardly hold my Pen and form my Letters.

I am now in a Mess with my Old Freind Dallas. He has had the kindness to lend me a Blanket so that I now sleep more comfortably. There is a report here of the 2d: Battn: Offrs: being likely to join their Battn: in a short time. What will become of me, I know not or do not much care. I am in good health at present and can undergo much more fatigue than in Hot weather.

I should like to be in Guernsey to hear the news between the Court and the Constables. In fact, I should have no great objection to be in the latter's places at present; a good Birth I shoud consider it. I suppose no Others ever got so much by being Constables as the present Gents.‡ With health &c: I am so cold I can hardly hold my pen. &c:

Dr: F: Travanca Decemr: 23d: 1811

I was greatly dissapointed this morning, on the arrival of an English Mail, when the Drum Major came and told me he had a Letter for me, and on readg: the address found it was not from the Family but from Canterbury, relative to the Men who came out with me. I had determined to write to day, thinking a Letter even from me would not be unacceptable to the Family as a Christmass

---

* Lieutenant Nicholas Wodehouse (9th Foot) had gained a captaincy in the 50th Foot.
† 'for a place in a byre, among the cows.'
‡ Constables in Guernsey were elected parish officials.

Box. I took my Pen with a view to give pleasure to my Friends, who so greatly contribute to my Happiness, to wish them many new and Happy returns of the Season, and that you all may continue to enjoy Health and Happiness for many Years to come.

Since my Letter to Abr^m: of the 8th: Ins^t: nothing very particular has happened. For want of Real Fighting we go out Sham fighting, which is not very pleasant. Last week we had to March about two Leagues from this Place for a Sham fight. We were out from half after Eight till Six in the Evening for Genl: Hay's amusement, and came home with a voracious appetite. We do not require very nice Bits after a day's work of that kind; a tough Beef Steak with a Musty loaf & a little Grog* satisfies our appetites. Everything here is getting dearrer & dearrer every day. Eggs, which we got at half a penny a piece, have now trebled in Price. A loaf, which in England would cost one penny, we pay 4½^d for. Patatoes – 1½^d per pound.

To day my Messmate is gone to a Fair about two Leagues from this place, to try to get something for our Christmass Dinner, as we intend to regale ourselves on that Day with something extraordinary. Our Dinners are almost always the same, Beef and Patatoes.

So many changes have lately taken place in the Reg^t: that it is very probable the 2^d: Batt^n: Off^rs: will be sent to Gibralter in the Spring, as soon as those which are effective in the 1st: Batt^n: have arrived here. Two Capt^ns: from this Batt^n: have been sent to join them, as they were greatly in want of them. I am in hopes they will leave Gib before we are ordered to join them. As you know, I have no great love for that Station. I think I have no chance of remaining with this Batt^n: if any Subs: are sent, as I am still too low on the List† to stay here.

Last week the pay master was ordered to go to Malha da Sorda (for pay for the Reg^t: to the 24th: Sept^r:), a distance of 16 Leagues there and 16 back. He had the misfortune to lose his Mule (an ill wind that blows no body good). He was obliged to buy another, and ours, that is M^r: Morant & mine, being for Sale, he bought it. I had determined to sell my half as I found it would soon come to

---

* Rather than a general term for alcohol, grog meant half-and-half water and spirits (usually rum).
† i.e. the Army List which listed officers in each regiment by seniority.

my turn to be sent on Detachment. I shall therefore buy a Bouro,* the first good and cheap one I come across. Shoud we be ordered to move suddenly, I make use of one of my Messmate['s] Animals to carry my Baggage.

We have but a bad Quarter here, having but one Room for cooking, Dining, &c:, and two little places to sleep which are filled with Mice. I awoke a few Mornings since & found something working very hard about my neck, and on turning saw a Rat scampering off. Dallas had slept there before me & had a Bag of Corn for his Pillow, which they had contrived to make a hole in & eat the Corn &, not finding their hole, would soon have worked one in my Boat Cloak. Not finding my Bed comfortable, it being only India corn straw,† I was extravagant enough to buy two bundles of Wheat Straw & borrow two Biscuit Bags of the Quarter Master, which I sowed together and now sleep as comfortable on my Palliasse of Straw, with my Blanket and Boat cloak, as I could on a Bed of Down.

A few nights ago, Dallas being out Dining, I amused myself in the Evening look^g: over my old Letters & destroying them afterwards. The latter part did not amuse me, but after reading them I thought it would be better to do it then to give them even a remote chance of falling into the hands of Strangers, which might be the case in this country where we are not Sure of a Moment.

My spirits are much better than when I wrote last. I had then about 8 Dollars to pay to Different persons which I was unable to pay from the scarcity of money. I have therefore availed myself of your kindness and drawn £10 which has enabled me to clear myself and to procure little triffles which I wanted. I shall give you a sample of our way of living; Breakfast: Coffé, Bread and butter and a few Pilchards or, if we expect any extra Drilling, eggs. Dinner: Soup, Beef & Patatoes or Rice, after which we smoke a Pipe and take a glass of Grogg, or some time a Glass of Mulled Wine. We seldom have any extra articles for Dinner except a Heart which cost us One Shilling. The ballance of pay due to me at this moment is about £13, and since I joined the Reg^t: my Expences for

---

* Burro (donkey).
† Maize straw.

Washing, Shoe Mending, &c:, have amounted to £10, including my Mess Expences which have been considerably less than the others.

Dallas, who is greatly altered for the Better since I first knew him, he being a Wild extravagant fellow, is now resolved to pull up and reduce his expences, so that we agree very well on that point. We always have Sufficient to eat, but none to waste.

One of our new made Capt^{ns}: has joined us from Lisbon. If a Company makes me as ridiculous as it has made him, I hope it will be very, very long before I get it. Poor Man hardly knows where he stands and does not deign to look upon some of his most intimate freinds. The Man's name is Robertson* (not my old Freind).

I find every body about me Stirring their Interest for Promotion, but to little effect. I must own, I should not dislike to have some Person to look up to for their Interest, for if I wait for the common course of Promotion I need not look forward for a Company these Five years.

If my Couz. F would speak a few words for me, it would go a great way in doing the business to my satisfaction. I have the Comfort of having it in my Power to get a character from the Off^{rs}: I have served under, whenever I may require it, which I shall avail myself of at some future time, should an opportunity of pushing myself forward offer itself. At present my Standing in the Army is not sufficiently long to expect any thing of the kind without the help of Freinds who have good interest and who chuse to exert it in my favour.† Please do remember me most affectionately, &c:

In early January 1812 Wellington prepared once more to besiege Ciudad Rodrigo, this time using the 1st, 3rd, 4th and Light Divisions. The town stood 'upon an eminence, on the right bank of the river Agueda', explained Grattan, 'and is difficult of access; it had been, since its occupation by the French, much strengthened by the construction of a redoubt

---

* Captain Joseph Low Robertson (9th Foot).

† Promotion from lieutenant to captain was critical for an officer. 'The period generally reckoned on by a subaltern to get his company in a good fighting regiment – that is to say, one that had the good luck to be in the thick and thin of what was going on, for all regiments fight alike for that matter – was from five to six years,' explained Grattan. 'The "extra shilling" [given to lieutenants who had been stuck at that rank for more than seven years] was rarely heard of, and never thought of but with disgust' (Grattan 55).

on the hill above St. Francisco; some old convents in the suburbs were also turned into defences, and these places no longer presented their original peaceful appearance, but were, in fact, very respectable outworks and tended much to our annoyance and loss at the commencement of the siege.'[1]

Because of the risk that the French might again arrive in strength and raise the siege, Wellington decided on a rapid, powerful barrage, followed by an infantry assault. Storming Ciudad Rodrigo was likely to cost many lives given the heavily fortified nature of the town.

D[r]: F: Travanca Jan[y]: 12th: 1812

Your kind Letter of the 4th: Dec[r]: reached me a few days after I had written to you the 23[d]: Ult[o]: I am well convinced that keeping up the esprit de Corps is the only way to keep a Reg[t]: in good order, but at the same time it is very dissagreable for the time you are undergoing the Punishment, as our's was intirely taken up drilling those Gentlemen.

I have since been removed to another Company who are not such great Blackguards as that I left. A number of those fellows are Irishmen, which accounts for their Conduct, for I really do believe that if the whole of the Irishmen in the Reg[t]: were picked out and sent about their business we should have a very decent set of Men in the Reg[t]: I have had two or Three of them as Servants and have always missed some of my Clothes before they left me. I have therefore resolved never to take another.

I trust that my conduct has been such that it is out of any Commanding Offi[rs]: power to find fault with it. I am on very good terms with Col[l]: Cameron and I attribute to that my being removed from that Comp[y]:

We expected last week to have received orders to move from this place as we understood that Lord Wellington intended breaking ground before Ciudad Rodrigo on or about the 14th: inst[t]: However, as we have received none, I should think we shall not move this time. We have been making ourselves Comfortable in our Huts,*

---

* On campaign officers and men often slept in small huts made from branches. Where the army stopped for any time these huts became more elaborate, wattle and daub structures sometimes with brick or clay chimneys.

building Chimneys, &c: I am now writing by the light of a window of our own making. We cut holes in the Shutters & put oil'd paper in them. The Portugeese are not very partial to our improvements, not even of our Fire places. Whilst we were building a very elegant one in the place, the Landlord came in and did not appear greatly pleased. On our enquiring the cause, he said it was not the custom to have chimneys in their houses and that he would have the trouble of pulling it down when we were gone, or people would laugh at him for having two Kitchins. This house smokes so much that it is almost impossible to stay in it at times. We thought of building a chimney in the Kitchin but the report of a move prevented us from so doing, as the expence is considerable (Three Dollars).

In the Genl: Orders which reached us Friday, the men at work at Almeida were ordered to join their respective Divisions Immediately, and a return of the Miners in the First, Third, Fourth & Light Divisions was to be sent to the Adj^t:Gen^ls: Office. What caused these orders, it is impossible for me to conjecture, unless to destroy what they have been doing at Almeida, in which case I suppose we should move back, or perhaps to carry on the Works before Ciudad Rodrigo.

The weather is fine but excessively cold and I should not enjoy Bivouaccing at this time of the Year. The Frost here is as severe as in England. The Estrella Mountains are Covered with snow, which appears to be very deep. Fortunately, we have plenty of wood in this Country, chiefly Pine. The Men go every day for some. Three hundred and sometimes double that number are employed on this duty, so that you may imagine the Quantity consumed by our Reg^t: alone.

I sometime think, if a Portugueese army was in England, how sour an English Farmer would look at a Party of this kind going out to cut down his Trees. God grant we may never see that day. It requires to be an Eye witness to have any Idea of a Country like this, destroy'd by the hands of most inveterate Ennemies, the Inhabitants starving & without any prospect of an end to this War, which might alleviate their distress. At present they are affraid of cultivating their grounds for fear of the French driving us back and reaping their Harvest.

Most of our Offi^rs: who were absent on account of Sickness have lately joined us. Percival & Luscombe have also arrived from

England, so that we are pretty strong in Offi^{rs}: at present. Our Men are sickly. Last week we sent 24 in the Rear, chiefly Fever cases; most of those are Volunteers who came out with us and who are not yet seasoned.

I have purchassed a fine Boura to carry my Baggage, about 4 Years Old & in high spirits. We take a Run in the Field every day. She plays like a young pup. This, I intend, shall be my Stud unless any thing should happen in which I could get a Horse or Mule gratis. As my Baggage is light it will answer my purpose well.

12 o'Clock: We have just received an order to march tomorrow morning towards Ciudad Rodrigo. We march to Manguelda tomorrow; 5 Leagues & bad roads. Weither we go further or not, is not known to us. An advanced work of Ciudad Ro^{go}: has been surprised by us. It is the only Hill that commands the place. It is called St: Francisco. The French are reported to have lost many Men. I hope we shall come in for a share of the Business and not keep in the Rear as we have hitherto done.

I must now begin to pack up my Baggage. We have a pretty good stock of eatables, which is of great consequence on a March. We leave this place with much pleasure; any thing by way of a change, and I hope some little glory may be gained. The weather continues fine though cold. I care but little about that, as I have a good Blanket. I hope the next Letter you have from me will be dated from Ciudad Rodrigo. I shall be greatly dissapointed if we do not go up as far as that place. I have a great curiosity to see it. We send off 29 men to the rear Tomorrow – a great number in one week, <u>55</u> Men.

If Abr^m: cannot find a convenient opportunity of sending the Flanel Shirts, he need not be uneasy as I have bought Two which will last me some time. Je gagnerai quelque chose par la marche – quelque P au moins.* Please do remember me to, &^c:

---

* 'I gain something by walking – several P[ounds] at least.'

6

Ciudad Rodrigo and Badajoz

Wellington persevered with his siege of Ciudad Rodrigo. As Hale explained, the 1/9th provided 'a party of different trades, such as masons, carpenters and miners, to go on a working party, ... together with a party of engineers, as there was a number from each regiment in the army to go and assist the engineers in making batteries and breastworks against the town.'[1] The rest of the battalion remained unengaged.

By 19 January two breaches had been blasted in the walls and Wellington was ready to launch his assault.

Ciudad Rodrigo Jan[y]: 26th: 1812

As I most probably would get a lecture, did I not answer my Dear Mother's Letter of the 10th: Ult[o]:, I have taken up my pen for that purpose, though the news I have to tell her will not be of a description to agree with her kind feelings.

On the 13th: we commenced our March, as mine of the 12th: will have informed you. When we had gone about half way to Mangualda we were ordered to change our direction and proceed towards Guarda, where we arrived on the 15th: almost knocked up. We left an immense number of Men behind & one of the Ens[ns]: who came out with me from England (Brooks).[*] We had marched at the rate of 5 Leagues a day. We started at Day Break & did not once get in till sun Set.

On the 16th: we continued our March, having provided ourselves

* Ensign Robert Brookes (9th Foot).

with a few little articles the evening preceeding, to Albergaria*
where we arrived on the 17th: This is a frontier Town of Spain. We
Halted here on the 18th:, which refreshed us a little, and on the 19th:
marched to Fuente Ginaldo.[†] These were short marches (compared
to those we had before we arrived at Guarda) & on good Roads.

On the morning of the 20th: an order was received to move to
Ciudad Rodrigo, & we learnt at the same time that it had fallen
on the preceeding evening. We marched about Seven and arrived at
Two; a distance of Four Leagues.[‡] We were halted outside the Town
with a strict order not to go in till the Reg[t]: marched in, which was
about One hour and a half after. A few dead Bodies lay about the
Breaches, But on entering the Town a dreadful scene presented
itself; the Town on Fire in one or Two places, which appears
to have been accidental. From Magazines blowing up, Some
unfortunate wretches were buried under the Ruins and a few of
them taken up alive with their Faces burnt, Arms & Legs broken. I,
with another Off[r]:, was ordered to patrole the streets. Immediately
on our arrival, going round a corner, I was almost horrer struck at
the scene that discovered itself – about Twenty Men laying dead,
Five or Six wounded that had not been yet taken to the Hospital,
& a house on fire from a mine which had blown up.

The Storming party mounted the Breaches at Nine o'Clock on
Sunday evening, and after the most serious part of the Business was
over, a circumstance took place which will certainly add no credit
to those who had the management of the Business; I mean that of
Sacking the Town, which was most completely done by our Troops.
This the Inhabitants, however, deserved in some degree, for Don
Carlos de Hispania[§] warned them before the French entered this
place that it would be given up to the Soldiers when retaken, if the
Inhabitants remained in it.[¶]

---

* La Albergueria de Argañán.
† Fuenteguinaldo.
‡ However, according to Hale, on the 19th, 'about eight o'clock in the evening,
  just as we thinking about taking a little rest, a dragoon came galloping into the
  village with an order for us to proceed to Ciudad Rodrigo without any delay
  whatever; therefore we assembled as quick as possible and made all speed for
  that place' (Hale 71).
§ Spanish General Roger-Bernard-Charles Espagnac de Ramefort (1775–1839),
  known as Carlos de Espana.
¶ Plundering a town which had resisted a siege was regarded as lawful, so

Our Loss has been very severe; 60 Off^rs: Killed & wounded, among which are Three Generals & One Thousand Men. Genl: Crawfurd* was buried in the Breach on Saturday with Military Honors. The space between the house he occupied and the Breach was lined by our Division. Lord Wellington attended as Chief Mourner besides an immense number of Gen^ls: and other Off^rs:

Several Deserters from the Light Division were in this place. About Twenty were taken alive and marched off to be executed† by their respective Reg^ts: A string of Spaniards, about Fourteen, were sent to Galiegos, previous to execution, for having been taken in the French service.

Such, my Dear Mother, are the scenes we have witnessed this last week. You may then judge how requisite it is to have the common feelings of nature blunted to bare these Scenes. I must confess mine are so far blunted that I have borne them like a Philosopher.

We begin to have a Market. Of course, everything is at an enormous price; Bread One shilling a lb and every thing else in proportion.

We have been hard at work repairing the Breaches, level^g: the Trenches, and about Twelve hundred Men are employed Dayly at this work. We have acquired the most honourable name of Pioneers to the Army, having always been employed in cleaning Quarters, &c:, in the rear of the Army. I am now in hopes there may be an end put to that kind of work.

Genl: Leith‡ has joined us and taken the command of the Division to the great satisfaction of all the Division. We are in expectation of moving every minute. It is supposed we shall make a Dash at Salamanca and get possession of the Stores. A circular Letter

---

Wellington's troops began looting almost immediately. The 5th Division was called in to restore order and save what had not already been destroyed. 'We were immediately set to work to extinguish the fire,' recalled Hale, 'and fortunately, by great exertion, we got the upper hand of it in a short time. The next thing that was thought most necessary for us to do was to put the dead bodies under ground and clear the streets, that the market people might be able to come in with their goods as soon as possible for at that time there was not a thing of any description to be got in the town except a few bags of French biscuits, and those our commissary seized' (Hale 73).

* Major-General Robert Craufurd (1764–1812) was mortally wounded while leading the attack on the smaller breach on 19 January and died five days later.

† For a vivid description of their court martial and execution, *see* Surtees 133–6.

‡ Major-General James Leith (1763–1816) had been ill and had temporarily handed command to Hay.

was received from head Quarters for all the Army to hold itself in readiness to move at a moment's notice. Three days Provisions are issuing at the Commissarys. I am very well satisfied to move, though we have good Quarters here.

I am in good health and in marching order. I belive I never felt better in bodily health. I was lame at Guarda from the long Marches & having my feet wet for a long time together, which made them blister. They are now perfectly well.

We hear that the French attack'd Tarifa & have been repulsed with loss. Four Companies of our 2^d: Battⁿ: were there & Six Off^{rs}: We have not heard the particulars, only that the French were double their Force.[*]

Hardyman[†] of the 45th:, who Abram must recollect from hearing me often talk of him as one of my companions in Peacock's Roving expedition,[‡] was Shot on the Breach at the storming of this place. He was waving his Hat and getting his Men on when the little messenger of Death ended his carreer.

I have just got my Rations of Beef for this day. I wish you could have a sight of them. Ils sont pire que de la charogne.[§] These were brought from the Slaughtering place to the Quarter Master on the same cart that carried many of the Poor fellows to their Grave. The rations require at least Six hours constant boiling before we can venture to touch them. The meat that is killed at present is the worst we have had yet; they are poor Old Bullocks that have followed the Army so long that they are lame, lean and tough. Such is the meat that I am doomed to grow Fat upon.

Most of the Volonteers that came out with me have taken their

---

[*] Marshal Claude Victor-Perrin had besieged Tarifa and on 29 December had opened fire with siege guns. Two days later the French launched a concerted offensive, but their grenadiers took a wrong turn, came under a withering fire from the garrison, and retired with the loss of 207 soldiers. Allied casualties were just thirty-six. Victor pressed on with the siege, but French resolve was eroded by disease and bad weather. In order to strengthen the garrison, the governor of Gibraltar sent a flotilla of gunboats on 3 January with reinforcements, including the flank companies of the 2/9th. The next day the French started to pull out their guns and at 3 a.m. on 5 January began a full retreat. The siege cost Victor three guns, 500 men, and more than 300 horses and mules. British casualties were fewer than seventy.

[†] Captain Robert Hardyman.

[‡] The bullion detachment in which Le Mesurier served in late 1808.

[§] 'They are worse than carrion'.

departure for the other world; at least 2/3ᵈ of them. Our Regᵗ: looks one of the strongest & I suppose we could not bring 500 in the field. Some people suppose we shall move to the Alentayo* to recommence the siege of Badajoz. If so, I expect our number will decrease considerably.

27ᵗʰ: The 3ᵈ Division of the Army started last night, without Packs or Baggage. It is supposed they are going to attempt to surprize the French's advanced Guard, which is about 3 Leagues in front of them. They are about 4600 [infantry] & 600 cavalry. It appears the French are retiring. The report of this day is that the Army will certainly move towards Badajoz shortly.

It appears the People of this place are not great freinds to the cause. They delivered up some Guerilas to the French, who had come to see their Freinds in this place in disguise. Some Offʳˢ: representing to Lᵈ: Wellington, on the Night of the assault, that the Soldiers were committing great enormities on the Inhabitants, he replied 'Let them, the Inhabitants richly deserve it'. This is a report, but from circumstances I am inclined to belive it.

I have seen Marshˡ: Beresford here and Don Julian Sanchez.† He is tall with a fierce countenance. Il donne l'ordre pour l'execution d'un homme avec autant de sang froid qu'il avalerois un verre de Vin.‡

With love to &ᶜ:

Dʳ: Abrᵐ: Ciudad Rodrigo Febʳʸ: 17ᵗʰ: 1812

I had the pleasure of receiving my Dʳ: Father's Letter of the 7ᵗʰ: this morning. We have been all very busy here lately, working like Negroes from morning till night at the Redoubts and Breaches. Our duty, you may suppose, is not triffling when we give from 9 to 12 Subs a day for Duty. I have not been off duty for this last week. When we go out to work we get 4/ a day. We are employed for half a day at a time.

Four Redoubts are building at present on the Hill Sᵗ Francisco,

---

* Alentejo, the region of Portugal stretching from the Tagus River to the Algarve.
† Sanchez commanded a band of guerrillas in the Ciudad Rodrigo region called the Lanceros de Castilla (The Lancers of Castile). See Chartrand 26.
‡ 'He gives the order to execute a man with as much composure as if he was asking for a glass of wine'.

which lies to the N.W. of this place. On the S. & W. the Agueda*
runs close to the Walls. On the E. the ground is very low so that
the only place the French could attack this place from is almost
rendered impregnable, unless they chuse to sacrifice an immense
number of Men.

Eleven hundred men are constantly at work & their work is not
likely to be ended for Six weeks. The Spaniards who are to garrison
the place do not make their appearance yet, though the Royals† &
38th: have left the Town to make room for them and gone to the
Suburds. We are the only Regt: at present in the Town, kept here as
Genl: Leith's body Guards.

Genl: Castanos & his staff are also in this place. When there is
no likelyhood of any thing being done, I understand the Spanish
Troops go on Furlough & the Officers place themselves on the
Staff, so that this Staff is very considerable at this time. Of course,
the Spaniards can never have very good Soldiers when at their
homes perhaps two thirds of the year.

The Place is much livelier than when we first came to it. We begin
to have a considerable Market & a few Shops are now opened, but
every single article is sold at a most enormous price; an Onion for
6d: & a pound of Patatoes 4½d. If the necessities of life were at a
moderate price we should enjoy ourselves very much here. If we
happen to be a day off Duty we go Coursing or Shooting Hares and
every kind of game is very plentyful about the Town. One of our
Gentn: killed two brace of Hares a few days ago.

We have been particularly gay lately. Three or four days ago
Genl: Leith gave a Ball & Masquerade at which, being a Curious
Bird, I went. Lord Wellington & the Prince of Orange‡ were there
and appeared to enjoy the sport very much. Refreshments were
very scarce and an Uglier collection of Ladies I never saw. Partners
were not to be had except for the staff Gentlemen, therefore I was
obliged to perch on a Chair and be a looker-on, and was amused
at some gentlemen who appeared in mask. One of our Captns:, as
an old wounded Soldier, hobbled before his Lordship and presented

---

* The river running through Ciudad Rodrigo.
† 1st Regiment of Foot (Royal Scots).
‡ The Prince of Orange had been exiled to England after his father, King William
I, lost his territories to Napoleon. The prince served as aide-de-camp to
Wellington and became King of the Netherlands in 1840.

a Petition, which I belive was a Memorial to get a Majority in the Portugeese Service; the answer I have not heard.

The Governor of this Town gave a Ball on Shrove Tuesday which was numerously attended &, though I belive he is not Rich, an elegant cold supper was paraded. I was not invited and had not the impudence to go without an invitation.

I have now a pair of Blankets & am ready for the March. There is not the least doubt but Badajoz will be the next place where we shall have an opportunity of distinguishing ourselves. The Mortars and Artillary are gone towards that place. There is a report that Lord Wellington is made Duke of Ciudad Rodrigo by the Spaniards.

I had some conversation with a French Surgeon some time ago. He thinks that, ere a Year has elapsed, there will not be a French Soldier in the Peninsula, that Bony begins to open his Eyes and sees the folly of carrying on this destructive War. Il est le Directeur General des Hôpitaux* and was left here with the French Prisoners that were wounded.

A few Spaniards arrived last night, I understand about 150 Artillery Men, part of the garrison of this place. They will not be employed at the works as they are not esteemed good workmen.

It will soon come to my turn for Detachement. I am next but one for that Duty, which is sometimes not very agreable. Remember me affectionately to &c:

Le Mesurier's guess that Badajoz was Wellington's next target was correct. The 5th Division left Ciudad Rodrigo to join the offensive. 'Badajoz, besieged for the third time, will hardly withstand the insolence of our attack, so lately crowned with complete and rapid success,' wrote Gomm, 'and its impetuosity will be increased by recollection of the double disappointment it has already experienced before her own wall.'[2]

Dr: Anne   Sabugal 14th: March 1812

Though I have not an opportunity of sending this, the Regt: being by this time at Castle Branco, yet, as I may not have another of

* 'He is the Director-General of Hospitals.'

writing for a long time, I avail myself of this to let you know that I am in the Land of the Living.

We left Ciudad Rodrigo on the first of March, since which we have been quite unsettled, staying two days in one place, four in another, and on our arrival here on the 10th: I saw an order in the Book for sending the Sick to the Rear, and on turning the leaf over 'Lt: Le Mesurier will accompany the Detachment to Castanhiares', which is Five leagues from this place.

On the 11th: I started with my Charge and went half way to that place, and on the 12th: arrived and reported myself. I was put in Dirty Quarters for the night, which of course prevented my enjoying my accostomed rest. Besides, I had an order to call on the Commandant for Orders next morning, when I expected to be ordered to Celorico, but to my infinite satisfaction the Bullocks that draged the Sick Carts here had made their escape, with the assistance of their Masters who bet the Sentry and took them off, in consequence of which I was told I might depart in peace, which order was not repeated twice.

At Eleven o'Clock yeasterday morning I departed and arrived here at Seven in the evening. I have met with a few Offrs: bound to Badajoz, and will keep them company as long as I can, if they do not delay too much, for though I am resolved not to join the Regt: till their march is over, yet I will not keep in the rear in case of any thing happening. The reason I do not wish to join is on account of the difficulty I find in getting Quarters on the march. I have sometimes been Three or Four hours standing in the Street before I could put my head under cover. Instead of which, marching by myself like a Gentleman, I walk into a house where I see a Gentleman's name Chalked on the Door,* and make myself as comfortable as I can. In a week or Ten days I shall join the Regt:

On our march from Rodrigo to El Boden we saw the 1st: Provincial Regt: of Estramadura. They had new Clothing & were well equiped altogether. They form part of the Garrison of Rodrigo. The works

---

*. The quartermasters went ahead of a column, negotiated quarters with the locals, decided which soldiers got which billets, and chalked the relevant name on the door. 'The best of the houses were marked for the officers,' explained Bell, 'one or more in each house, as there was room. The commanding officer had the best quarters, of course' (Bell 48).

have got on rapidly, tho not so much as when the English were there. The Spaniards do not work so hard as our Gentlemen.

We have had very changeable weather lately; one day as warm as Summer, the next obliges us to wear Cloaks, which has been the cause of many Men being sent to the rear with Agues. I have escaped uncomonly well, thank God, but I strongly suspect if I had been detained at Castanhiares I shoud not have done so, for if once my spirits fail, my health suffers, and the melancholy prospect of being kept for Two or Three months among Doctors & Sick Men might have had that effect completely, particularly at this time, when we expect to have some employment shortly. Had I the misfortune to fall Sick at present, or till the business of Badajoz is over, I should in all probability leave the Army altogether, for I have heard remarks made on Off^{rs}: in that situation that would drive them from the Army or fight Twenty or Thirty Duels had they heard of it. However, my Spirits are so good now that I have no fear of sickness at present. The more exercise I take, provided I can be comfortable when I come in, seems to improve my Health. I enjoy marching more than being in Quarters because I am too young a Sub: to ever have a good Quarters. In consequence of which, I cannot enjoy reading or doing any thing else, whereas Marching passes away the time and varies the Scenes. Yet I look forward with hope and pleasure when I may have choice, and then perhaps some worthy Lady, who is as fond of Change, may take a liking to me, though you must know that I am so indifferent at present that I declare it to be my intention to refuse anyone who shall offer herself without an annual Income of £500, for, as I am not a Rich Man, I cannot supply her expences. Therefore, I authorize you, in case any one offers herself, to declare my intention. There would be a number of candidates if they saw me in my Marching Trim; an old ragged Coat which has more of the dirty Brown than Red about it, a Pair of Shoes that admit the water freely if I happen to walk on wet ground.

Castel Branco March 19th: Thus far have I travelled on my way to join. I left Sebugal on the 15th: in Company with some Commissaries who had charge of Sixty Carts loaded with Balls for Badajoz. I left them the 2^d days March, as they only travelled a league & a half or two Leagues a day, which I considered too slow. I arrived here yeasterday, about One o'Clock, with a complete wet Jacket, and found my Messmate Ill at this place. Whitley, one of the Gentleman Preachers, is here also but is considerably changed since Watson left the Reg[t]: He is not so great a Methodist as he was.

I mentioned in one of my former Letters to my Father I had drawn £10, the 26th Dec[r]: 1811, on C & B. The man lost his papers on his way to Lisbon. I gave him another Bill of the same tenor and date, therefore they must only pay one of the Bills. I am in hopes of receiving some Letters from you when I join the Reg[t]: as I understand Packets are arrived from England, and to have news from our D[r]: Betsy and Ferd[d]: I assure you I often think of all my Dear Freinds when going over some wild and Steep Mountains, many of which I have had to cross within the last Days. The weather is very wet at Present and has all the appearence of continuing so. I shall halt here to day for Certain. If I can get all ready, I shall make another start tomorrow morning for Nisa & Portaligre. I wish much to have a travelling companion as I find it rather dull to travel alone.

My Health and Spirits continues as good as ever. I walk, in general, from fifteen to Twenty Miles a day. All that I am affraid of is knocking up my valuable Baggage Animal, which would put me to considerable inconvenience as I have not the means at present of purchassing another, should that happen.

I am in a very good Billet in this Town, which is a thing I could not have had if the Reg[t]: had been here. The Town seems not to have suffered from the French. The Army have swallowed up every thing wherever it passed, so that what can be had is nearly double its former price. The People are more civil about this part of the Country than farther North, but they all seem tired of this War. Their Oxens are pressed and are left without the means of tilling their Grounds, and often looses their other Animals.

My Route from Sabugal to this place was Minao, Penamacor, Pedroga, Loja & Castel Branco. These are the principal places I passed through. I shall join in the course of Five days, if the Reg[t]: is not beyond Portalegre.

My best love to all &[c]:

Wellington invested Badajoz on 16 March. Though the French garrison of 5,000 was heavily outnumbered, Badajoz boasted some strong defences. 'All the arts of war then known were brought into play on both sides, for the attack and defence,' explained Bell, 'Many were our difficulties. Torrents of rain at night poured upon the working parties, shot and shell continually striking down the men, provisions scarce, our pontoon bridge carried away, artillery and engineer officers being killed and wounded every day, but no suspension of the fiery trial.'[3]

As he had done before, Wellington left his siege guns to batter down the walls. By 6 April two large breaches had been opened up and the troops were ready to attack. The 4th and Light Divisions would stage the main assault on the breaches, while Major-General Thomas Picton's 3rd Division stormed the castle at the north-east angle of Badajoz's defences using scaling ladders. The 5th Division would take the San Vicente bastion at the north-west corner of the town wall. The 1/9th was deployed to the south, opposite the Fort Pardaleras outwork, on a hill called the Cerro del Viento, from where they were to take pot shots at the enemy as a diversion.

D[r]: Julia   Camp near Badajoz April 8th: 1812

As I shall have an opportunity of sending this tomorrow morning, most probably by the same conveyance with the Dispatches announcing the fall of Badajoz, I thought you might be pleased at having a few lines as our Division, with the exception of the Royals and 9th:, were engaged and you might be anxious on my account.

On the Evening of the 6th: we marched from this Place, which is about Six miles from Badajoz, to a Hill fronting Pardeleira* Battery, about half a mile from the Town, from whence we had a most complete view of the whole Business.

About 9[o]: Clock the Assault began; the Description of the sight then, it is beyond my power to give you. C'etoit un beau terrible,[†] the light Balls, Shells, Guns, Musquettry, all at the same time playing on the Town, was most Beautiful, but the Idea of the Heroes that fell during the Time was dreadful. Our Reg[t]:, with the Royals, were kept as a kind of reserve, in case anything happened. Lord Wellington was close to us the whole night, so that we had early intelligence of all that passed. The pleasing intelligence that Gen[l]: Picton had got into the Castle with his Division was

* Pardaleras.
† 'That was a terrible spectacle'.

counterbalanced in some degree on hearing that the assault at the Breaches had failed. That part of the 5th Division that was engaged, Escaladed the Town near Perdeleira but met with rough usage. From what I can learn, about 500 Men of this Division alone were killed & wounded.

We remained under Arms all night and, about Four o'Clock yeasterday morning, the pleasing information reached us of the Town being in our hands, together with Philipon* and the whole Garrison, about 4500 men. Their loss I understand was trifling. They had cut Trenches behind the Breaches and had placed Chevaux de Frise† on the Ramparts. Genl: Leith was wounded slightly in the Arm.

The Division have received thanks, to which, unfortunately, we have no claim, from the Commander in Chief of the Forces. We have a little consolation left, that is (Earl Wellington informs us),‡ after giving an Order to have the Arms repaired immediately, that he expects we shall shortly have another opportunity of meeting the Enemy and of course the result is not doubtful.

Tell my father I am of his Opinion in regard to a Compy: I shall wait with patience for sometime longer. And as to the Cooking, tell him he gave me a receipt for a thing I should walk a league to get; that is, a prime piece of Salt Beef. No such delicate meat is too good for us Poor Subs in this country. Here, at this present time, we get Beef from which the Guernsey People would hardly allow their dogs to eat the prime parts, and we have nothing to eat with it of the vegetable kind. However, I manage to keep my health and Spirits unimpaired, and that is the chief thing. At present I am writing, Shaded under a hut, and my portfolio resting on a <u>Camp Table</u>. For want of a better, we have traced a square and made a small trench so that we can Sit comfortably & eat our Dinner, but

---

* General Armand Philippon (1761–1836), Governor of Badajoz.
† Literally, 'Frisian horses'; frames with projecting spikes used to stop cavalry, or in this case, infantry. They were 'composed of a strong beam of wood, with sharp-pointed sword blades fixed in every direction ... so closely set together that it was impossible either to leap over them or penetrate between them, and the whole so firmly fixed to the works at the top that it could not be moved' (Surtees 141).
‡ Wellington had been given an earldom that February.

it does not answer so well for writing, as I am obliged to stoop too much.

We are receiving Three days' provisions, from which it is probable we may move tomorrow. Albuera I belive will be the place where we are to gather our Laurels. I have said nothing of the doings in Badajoz after its fall. They were such that I shall be sorry to witness any thing more of the kind, for every enormity you can conceive were committed by our own Soldiers.

I shall write immediately, if possible, after any Brush we may have. The day after I joined the Reg[t]: I found the 24th: Reg[t]: in the same place, but was unable to find W.L.M., though he was with them. They marched early next morning. I have had but little rest and feel rather fagged. A good night's rest will put all to rights again. Remember me, &[c]: &[c]:

In the storming of Badajoz, Hay's brigade (2/38th, 3/1st and 1/9th) suffered minimal casualties. Forty-two men from the 38th Foot were killed, wounded or missing. The other two battalions survived without loss. Le Mesurier was fortunate to have been only a spectator. Those troops who mounted the breach encountered fire 'so heavy and so incessant that it appeared like one continued sheet of fire along the ramparts', and soon the 'bottoms of the breaches were nearly blocked up with the bodies of those who fell'.[4] 'Bags and barrels of gunpowder with short fuses were rolled down which, bursting at the bottom or along the face of the breaches, destroyed all who advanced,' recalled Captain Blakeney of the 36th Foot. 'Thousands of live shells, hand grenades, fireballs and ever species of destructive combustible were thrown down the breaches and over the walls into the ditches which, lighting and exploding at the same instant, rivalled the lightning and thunder of heaven.' At the castle walls Blakeney found the ladders of Picton's division 'warm and slippery with the blood and brains of many a gallant soldier.'[5]

The looting was even worse than at Ciudad Rodrigo. 'The truth must be told,' wrote Bell. 'The besieging army was promised the sacking of the town when taken, and, notwithstanding all the devotion and bravery of the British soldier, this promise of pillage adds to his courage and determination ... it became their reward.'[6] 'No house, church or convent was held sacred by the infuriated and now ungovernable soldiery ... priests or nuns and common people all shared alike,' recalled Surtees. 'Any who showed the least resistance were instantly sacrificed to their fury.'[7] Those officers who tried to stop the chaos were swept aside. 'Three times I narrowly escaped with my life for endeavouring to protect some women,' reported Blakeney. 'Lord Wellington found it absolutely necessary to order in a Portuguese brigade to force the stragglers out of the town at the point of a bayonet.'[8]

D[r]: Fath[r]:   Castel Branco April 20th: 1812

Yours of the 26th: Febr[y]: found me at Campo Mayor, on our return to the North, and gave me much pleasure, particularly at that time being rather in low spirits having lost one of my acquaintance at Badajoz, and a little annoyed at our Commd[r]: The day after our return from Badajoz he called the Off[rs]: together & told them their Conduct at that place was bad, for instead of paying any attention to their men they had gone about plundering. He did not want their favour or affection, but he would have the Duty done in a very different way for the future.

This would have been very right had that been the case, but, with the exception of One or Two, I can safely say none went to plunder.[*] They were so fatigued that they sought a shady place to sit in (the heat being excessive), and there remained till they got their Quarters. In consequence he has put three times the number of Off[rs]: on Duty than their used to be. Since his most Gentlemanlike speech none of the Off[rs]: have spoken to him, except on Duty. Thus we stand at present.

We expected to have remained in the Alentajo sometime longer but were suddenly ordered to the North, the French having pushed as far as this place. We are come at the rate of Four Leagues a day, except yeasterday; we came Six Leagues in a deluge of rain, the

---

[*] Blakeney records the 9th as imposers of order, as at Ciudad Rodrigo, though he may be conflating the two sieges: 'The 9th Regiment were marched regularly into town. A gallows was erected in the principal square and others in different parts of the town. A general order was proclaimed that the first man detected in plundering should be executed; but no execution took place. The soldiers well knew how far they might proceed, and no farther did they go. The butcheries and horrible scenes of plunder and debauchery ceased in Badajoz' (Blakeney 277).

whole day. We started at ¼ past Five yeasterday morning and were in Quarters at Five in the evening (Croté jusqu'au Genoux[*]).

Abr^m: says he attributes my preserving my health so well to living Regularly and Temperately. The latter, well and good, but as to the former, I do not agree with him; sometimes up at Three in the Morning & breakfasting at that time; sometimes at Eight, and my Dinner as uncertain, so that I cannot attribute presuming my health to regularity.

The day before yeasterday my Donkey knocked up. However, through great care and good feeding I have brought it as far as this place, part of my Baggage being carried by Dallas's animals. To day it is so lame that I am greatly affraid this will be its last Day's March. I am in hopes we shall halt tomorrow, in which case I must look out for a Mule. My Baggage, I suppose, weighs Sixty pounds, so that it could be only from excessive Marches she knocked up. I am not the only sufferer in this march. Several Off^rs: have lost Animals. What distresses me most will be my being obliged to draw on you, for how much, I cannot exactly tell.

I can assure you our Life at present is not a life of ease & Idleness, but of care and hard work which, however, we could go through with comfort with a pleasant *******[†]. I sometimes get a lift from my Freinds on the March which helps me a great deal. I have an enormous appetite when I come in, having accustomed myself to fast on the March, be it ever so long.

The Inhabitants of this Town were rejoicing for the Fall of Badajoz when an express arrived & informed them that the French were within three leagues of the Town. They immediately collected all they were unable to carry with them, such as Flouer and Rum, &c:, &c:, and Burnt it publickly in the Market place. We march tomorrow for Alcains and Ledrosa.[‡] I have a Poney in view which I shall be obliged to take for 80 Dollars.

Marmont had crossed the border into Portugal, leaving a division outside Ciudad Rodrigo to worry its garrison. The first allied fortress inside Portugal was at Almeida. Marmont sent General Bertrand Clausel with two divisions to reconnoitre,

---

[*] 'Muddy up to the knees'.
[†] Here the original transcriber has left a short line with six vertical strokes.
[‡] Lardosa.

but Clausel was 'deterred from pressing in upon the place by the defiant attitude of the governor', Lieutenant-Colonel Havilland Le Mesurier, another of Peter's cousins.[9]

Marmont instead turned south towards Castello Branco. In the face of this French offensive the allies abandoned the town on 12 April.

D^r: Abr^m: Leomil May 9th: 1812

Since my last from Castel Branco I have received Three Letters, two of which I suppose came with my Clothes by the Speculator, as there was no post mark on either, from which I am in hopes the things you sent are safely arrived at Lisbon. Though I have heard nothing from that Quarter, I have written and expect an Answer every day from Ens^g: Carver,* which I hope will arrive ere I send this.

You will see by the Map† that our marching has been (I may call it) severe, for since the 1st: March to this present time we have hardly had any rest; always up an hour before Daylight that we might have a cup of Coffé & a piece of Bread & butter, ere we marched. We are about half a League from Muimenta de Beira, which you will find on the Map about four Leagues to the southward of Lamego. I am Quartered in the Juiz de Fore's‡ house, which is rather decayed and very cold. The only advantage I have over better Quarters is from a nice little Garden behind the house where I study Spanish. When the weather is fine the Trees about it are filled with Nightingales that sing most delightfully.

How long we shall stay here is very uncertain. The Orders are for the Soldiers to be provided immediately with Shoes and the Public Mules to be inspected to see if they are fit for active service. Some imagine we shall make a Dash in Spain shortly. I wish something decisive was done one way or the other, that we might not be kept here much longer, for I think the people of this country begin to be very tired of the war. We are obliged to cut their Corn for forage, to press their Cattle to carry Stores, so that they almost starve. Their Labourers are obliged to serve the Army. With the exception of

---

* Ensign Charles Carver (9th Foot).
† No map appears in the letter book.
‡ A 'juiz de fora' is literally an 'external judge'.

those that live near the sea port Towns, I cannot imagine how it is possible for them to live.

My Messmate Dallas is gone to Oporto and will bring up a Stock for us. The only Luck I have had was in selling my Donkey, which was completely knocked up. It went for 20 Dollars, so that after carrying my Baggage Three months I have only lost 4 Dollars on it.

I bought a Poney at Castel Branco for 70 Dollars from an Off^r: of the 38th: Reg^t:, for which I am to pay him at the next issue. I shall get a Bill cashed for that purpose. We are only paid up to the 24th: February and are not likely to get money for sometime, so that the money I received for my Donkey has been of great value to me.

As all the Off^{rs}: are complaining for want of Cash, our Dinners now consist of Beef & soup and vice versa, which we eat with good appetite. Sometime, by way of great relish, we put a little Cabbage in. Our great comfort is a Pipe of Tobacco and a Glass of Egg wine,* for, tho we are close to the place where the Opporto wine is made, what we drink here is little better than Vinegar.†

Sunday May the 10th: We are just returned from hearing Divine Service at Muimenta del Beira. The Chaplain of the Division Preaches well and gives us very good Sermons.

Our supplies of Meat are very short at present, so much so that they now give us Mutton. Whilst that continues there is not the least chance of our moving from hence. I wish we could remain here untill the parcels you sent me come up. The Army is Divided in Three Corps at present; the North, Earl Wellington with the 3^d: 4th: 5th: and Light Divisions; the Centre, Genl: Graham, 1st: 6th & 7th Divi^{ns}; South, Genl: Hill‡ with the 2^d: Division and Portugeeses. It is reported we shall enter Spain in that manner.

The Portugeese Militia that fled from Guarda on the approach of the French, have acquired the Appelation of Tropa Fandango. I was told that General Baccellar§ fled with so much speed that he killed two Horses on the Road from Guarda to Viseu. All the staff have been ordered to Lisbon by the Regency to give an account of their

---

* I have been unable to establish what egg wine was, unless he means egg nog, or possibly Alderney milk punch which uses eggs.
† Even today, while the Oporto region produces superb ports, the local unfortified wine is often terrible.
‡ Major-General Rowland Hill (1772–1842).
§ General Manuel Pinto de Morais Bacelar (1741–1816).

conduct on that Occasion. Coll[s]: Trant and Wilson are among the Numbers. They were for making a Stand at Sabugal, but Baccellar told them he could place no dependence on his troops and refused to make a Stand.[*]

With sincere wishes for &[c]: &[c]:

My D[r]: Mother   Leomil May 23[d]: 1812

By the last packet which arrived from England I had the pleasure of receiving my D[r]: Father's & Abr[m's] Letters of the 20th: Ult[o]: and according to my Father's orders, will give you an account of myself every fortnight, though nothing very interesting is passing at present. I have received a Letter from En[gn]: Carver announcing the safe arrival of my Clothes at Lisbon, which he will send up by the first opportunity. My Father will have received, long before this, the Letter I wrote immediately after the fall of Badajoz, by which he will find that I came in for a share of the honour our Reg[t]: reaped at that place.

We are living very peaceably here. We have had two Balls lately in this Town: about a Dozen Couples, but the Ladies are not fond of Dancing. They are the Laziest set of Mortals on the face of the Earth, so that we are obliged to have Off[rs]: for Partners. The sideboard agrees with the state of our Purse; nothing but Sour Wine is to be found there, and that even scarse. However, that does not affect our Spirits, so that these Balls are pleasant enough. Next week our distress will be relieved by a Month's Pay which our Pay master is gone for.

Stores are forming in our front at present. An Immense number

---

[*] To meet the threat from Marmont, General Bacelar had Portuguese militia troops under the command of British officers, Captain Nicholas Trant and Colonel Robert Thomas Wilson. Marmont had divided his troops, sending some with Clausel to Castello Branco, but keeping his main force at Sabugal.

Trant wanted Wilson to help him surprise Marmont's troops at Sabugal, despite overwhelming French superiority. Bacelar thought the idea mad. Wellington agreed: in his opinion it would have resulted in the loss of both Trant's and Wilson's divisions. The plan was not adopted.

Then, on 13 April, Trant's force was surprised by Marmont at Guarda. Trant and Wilson retreated, pursued by French cavalry. When the militiamen tried to make a stand they found their muskets would not fire in the pouring rain, so they fled.

of Carts & Mules loaded with Biscuit, &ᶜ: pass through this place every Day, but I do not think that we shall move yet. We have not at present One Genˡ: Offʳ: with the Division. Genˡ: Leith is in Lisbon, Genˡ: Hay in England and the Portuguese Brigade gone to Abrantes for their Clothing. The Division is at Present Commanded by Lᵗ: Colˡ: Barnes* of the Royals, our Brigade by our Comᵍ: Offʳ:, and the Regᵗ: by Lᵗ: Colˡ: Crawfurd.

I am sorry everything is so dear in Guernsey. The good people ought to have a peep at this Country and thank God for the Blessings they enjoy – Bread One Shilling a pound, and that not always to be had.

Marshall Beresford has given a very severe reprimand to the Militia for their conduct at Guarda. He says they retreated very well as far as Guarda but when they came there they fled shamefully, because some of their arms, which had got wet, would not go off. In consequence of their shameful retreat he has taken the Colours from Five Regᵗˢ: and drafted Sixteen hundred men into the Line.†

Our Messmate, Dallas, arrived last night from Opporto. I had been on the look out for him for several days as he had a stock with him which we wanted much. From the Account he gives of the Place I should have no objection to take a trip there. He was treated with the greatest hospitality by the Inhabitants.

I had a peep at the Dispatches from Earl Wellington to the Portugeeses' Government & found the names of many of my Old acquaintance among the killed and wounded. By the last Packet we received the Thanks of His Royal Highness the Prince Regent for that affair. He says he is sorry to see the long list of Brave men who fell, but that the loss was unavoidable. I hope we shall have no more storming business. Our Men are ungovernable after. One of our Men lost his Leg there because he refused to give a few Dollars he had found to a Soldier of the 88ᵗʰ: Regt.‡

We have very little to do at present. Colˡ: Crawfurd seldom has a parade, which has suited me well these last days, as I have felt a little the effects of our long marches by stiffness and weakness in

---

* Lieutenant-Colonel Sir James Stevenson Barns.
† According to Oman these five colours were taken by the French at Guarda (Oman, V, 287).
‡ The 88th Foot, the Connaught Rangers, were 'regular bronze fellows, hard as nails, and as ready for a fight as for a ration of rum' (Bell, 52).

the Legs, which I hope will not last long. The extent of my walks are confined to my Garden, where I amuse myself all day long with a book in my hand. I manage my rations pretty well, of Biscuit and Beef. This is the worst place we have been in for a Market. We can buy nothing but Sugar, Rice and Sardinias – no vegetables of any kind and White Bread seldom.

There is no talk of a move at present. Every thing seems to be at a stand. I should suppose that something will be done when they begin in the North. We may perhaps make a push at that time in Spain, as the French will not be able to reinforce their Army whilst at war with Russia.

I am happy to hear that my Old freind W^m: Metivier is settled for his own account. I hope he may succeed in his business, as also his Brothers. Wishing you all &^c:

Marmont had heard that Badajoz had fallen and that Wellington was marching to meet him. Short of food, the French marshal decided to withdraw into Spain, past Ciudad Rodrigo towards Salamanca.

There were five French armies in Spain and while Napoleon could direct them from Paris, albeit with some time lag, it would be impossible from Moscow, so, while he prepared to invade Russia, the emperor appointed his brother King Joseph to supreme military command in Spain. Joseph 'had a fine command, a great and brilliant army, an obedient army, but that soul of armies, the mind of a great commander, was wanting'.[10] 'The King for two years had been allowed to have no direct relations with the generals-in-chief; he had no exact knowledge of the military situation in each of their spheres of command, nor was he better informed as to the strength, organisation, and distribution of the troops under their orders,' explained Marshal Jourdan, Joseph's chief-of-staff. [11]

Though the weather was like 'Vulcan's smithy',[12] Wellington pressed ahead to Salamanca to exploit the confusion in the French high command.

D^r: Ann.   Sarzedas June 6th: 1812

Yeasterday we left Leomil on our Route to Spain, and, in consequence of other troops marching at the same time for the same Destination, we were obliged to halt in this place to day, not to clash with another Division. Our Departure caused many Tears in Leomil. The Ladies declared they had never passed such an agreable Month as the time we were there, and the lower class praised the good conduct of our Soldiers, so that you cannot wounder that we felt something like regret at leaving the place. Latterley our Balls were well attended and the Ladies began to take some pleasure in Dancing. It was our intention to have had a Ball on the 4th: till the Order for Marching arrived, in consequence of which we had it on the First and took our farewell.

We have now other amusements and, if I can prognosticate from the looks of our Com Off:, we shall not find much pleasure in our march. I shall take good care and not come under his Clutches, for since our pleasant conversation at Castel Branco we have had no other confab save when duty obliges me to go to him, and then he is civil enough. I am more inclined to pity his temper than hate the Man, for when he is well and not on a March he sometimes tries to please the Offrs:

We have received another Packet since that which brought me your Letter and learnt poor Mr: Percival's Death.* We are now anxiously waiting for another mail to know his Successor. I am also in hopes it may bring me the agreable news of our Dear Napolitan's arrival in England, in good health.

It is reported that we are going to Madrid, which would please me much, and perhaps I may pick up some Dona with a little Fortune if the French do not secure them before. You must know that that my heart was almost stolen at Leomil by a Young Lady who, as I afterwards understood, was worth a great Deal of Money, having houses and lands in many villages round about, but it would have been necessary to become a Roman Catholic which did not answer my purpose at all. I am therefore in hopes that absence and new faces may eradicate her image from my poor heart for the arrow went very deep indeed.

We are at present in a little room about 9 feet square with a loop hole by way of a window, a chest for a Table, and a Sack of Corn

---

* Prime Minister Spencer Perceval (1762–1812) had been shot dead in the lobby of the House of Commons on 11 May. He was succeeded by the Earl of Liverpool.

for a chair, from which you may suppose it is not a very pleasant place for Three to use as a Sleeping and Dining room. Our Route extends as far as Espija, Three Leagues this side of Ciudad Rodrigo, when I understand we are to be reviewed by Earl Wellington. We are to Bevouac there. I understand it is a fine country in the environs. If we do not halt again we expect to be there on the 10th: as it is only four days' March from hence, part of it abominable roads. I have not time to finish this Letter to day as I am on duty and I just learn that, till our arrival at Espeja, no Letters will be forwarded to England. I shall therefore keep this open till there.

Camp near Rodrigo June 11th: We arrived yesterday at Espeja. We expected to have Bevouc'd for a short time, but last night about five o'Clock a fresh route arrived. We have Three days' march more, which will take us close to Salamanca where I suppose we shall have a little fun, as we understand the French are fortifying it now. We are about Three Miles from Rodrigo. I should wish much to see it now, but after a march in a hot Sun that is not my first thought.

We are up every Morning at half past Two, and March at Four, so that we are arrived at our destination early. We are at present encamped on the Banks of the Agueda, a bad situation as there is no shade whatsoever. I am affraid we shall be but badly off on our advance, as the Country between this and Salamanca is an immense plain, and I understand that for many Leagues a Tree is not to be met with. Yeasterday we were in a most delightful part of the Country; a large Forest and pasture for our Animals. This was between Poza Velha and Espeja.

We received a packet with papers to the 15th: and I must own I was a little disapointed at having no Letters from any of the Family, but I learnt this morning almost all the Letters had been lost by some accident.

Our Division has been reinforced by the 2d: Battn: of the 4th: Regt: and 58th:, and we shall soon have the 1st: Battn: of the 38th: so that if any thing is to be done, I think we shall have a finger in it. Our News by the last Packet informs us that we shall soon have a reinforcement of Ten Thousand men. If that is the case, I think we shall soon have a view of Madrid.

I belive by the time our Campaign is over we shall be pretty well reduced to Skelletons from the heat. The unfortunate Soldiers suffer much by it, with their Arms, accoutrements and Ammunitions, they have sufficiently to load a Donkey.

Gen¹: Leith joined us at Trancozo a few days ago and brought two Amateurs with him, Lord Manners and the Marquess of Worster.* If they wish to know what a Soldier's life is, I would advise them to enter as Ensign in his Majesty's 9ᵗʰ: Regᵗ: of Foot. There they would be much better able to form an oppinion on the subject.

We have a General Court Martial sitting for the trial of some Offʳˢ: for spreading a report tending to alarm the Portugeese Militia, when the French made their late incursions into Portugal. One of them, of the 42ⁿᵈ:, in his defense accused the Prosecutor, a Portugeese Col¹: of Militia, of cowardice. The Prosecutor, in his reply to the Defense, allowed that he had been twice affraid in his life; once one a Boy on hearing Thunder which, however, he afterwards conquered, and the other was of Marshal Beresford. He made, I understand, a most excellent Reply to the Defense.

I was in Badajoz with the Regᵗ: at the time we were accused of Plundering, and had under my protection about Twenty Ladies, in whose house I was Quartered, and prevented the Soldiers entering the House. I lost a pair of Shoes in their defence, in Shewing a Portugeese Soldier the most expeditious way of retreating with an Enemy pressing hard on him. I tore one completely from the sole.

I am on better terms with the Comᵍ: Offʳ: He has shewn more inclination to become freind than formerly. He is become more tractable and now uses the appellation of Le Mesurier. He commands a Brigade at present. We are Brigaded with the 2ⁿᵈ: Battⁿ: of the 4ᵗʰ: and 58ᵗʰ: Regᵗˢ: We were removed from the other Brigade that he might have the Command of the Brigade.

The 6ᵗʰ: Division is in Salamanca, the French being entirely confined to the Forts,† and amusing themselves firing at the Amateurs who go and look at them. They are Volonteers and will no doubt hold out to the last. We are encamped on the Torres about

---

* The Marquess of Worcester (1792–1853, Duke of Beaufort from 1835), a notorious womaniser and roué, had served with the 10th Hussars since 1810. He was in Spain as aide-de-camp to Wellington, as was Lord Charles Manners, lieutenant-colonel of the 3rd Dragoons and son of the 4th Duke of Rutland.

† Three convents in Salamanca had been fortified; 'one very strong and capable of containing about 500 or 600 men; the other two were smaller, to cover and act as supports to the principal one' (Surtees, 160). These Wellington besieged.

5 miles to the West of Salamanca. I intend going to town tomorrow if we do not march. Tout est bien cher ici, une livre de pain d'orge 18^d: & tout en proportion.*

Camp near Salamanca June 19th: We have been here two days. Marmont has left from Six to Eight hundred men in the two forts at Salamanca (and retired himself to Toro). They are so well fortified that the English are obliged to Batter them. We expect they will fall in our possession tonight.

Marmont left the Town on the 16th: at Midnight in great haste. His Army is not more than 12 to 15 Thousand men Strong. We expect to move forward every day, to follow the Enemy, and it is supposed that he will make a stand between Toro and Valadolid.

Camp Fuente Lapena June 30th: 1812

As I have no doubt of my Dear Sister's arrival ere this, I thought a few lines would not be unwelcome, with her joy on her return from her Travels. I have lately undergone a few hardships, which are almost rendered light by hearing that my D^r: Freinds in Guernsey are in good Health. I had the pleasure of receiving my Father and Abr$^{m's}$: Letter of the 6th: inst^t: yeasterday, in which they mention being in dayly expectation of your arrival at the Beaucamp. I have often expressed a wish to be present at that moment, but am moving on a contrary direction, therefore cannot be accomplished.

On the 19th: I wrote from the Camp near Salamanca, which did not fall into our hands till the 26th: when the Convent was burning & the Enemy were in danger of being blown up. You will no doubt see the account of this affair in the Newspapers. I shall therefore continue my Journal from the 20th: When we left the Camp we had so little time given us to prepare ourselves (the Baggage not being allowed to move with us) that we took nothing but our Blankets. We were completely drenched as it began to rain as soon as we began our March. We took our position near Aldea Seca and at daylight next morning move[d] to the heights over Vilares, from which we had a ful view of the French army, who were formed in Columns in a plain about Castillano Morisco and adjacent, not more than

---

* 'Everything here is very expensive, a pound of barley bread eighteen pence and everything else in proportion.'

Threequarters of a Mile from us. We were in expectation of having a General engagement every moment, but were dissapointed as the Gentlemen retreated.*

On the 25th: we had very little rest, being under Arms at Daylight, and changing our Positions according to the movements of the Enemy, perhaps twice or Three times a Day under a scorching Sun. During their stay we had Skirmishing every day between Cavalry and the Light Troops, in which we were generally successful.

I went to Castillano Morisco and saw two Bodies which had been strangled and were then Burning. On enquiry, I found they were two men of Don Julian's Corps who had fallen in the hands of those Barbarians. They completely destroyed the Villages they occupied by pulling down the Houses for firewood.†

On the 26th: we moved to our Right near Salamanca, the Tormes running in our Front. I rode to Salamanca, as I was enabled to Clean myself, the Baggage having joined us. I was agreably surprised on going in the Plaça Major to see a most regular and handsome square. It is not large but the houses are good and appear comfortable. In other parts of this Town I could trace the hands of the French. The Colleges are destroyed as well as their Libraries. They destroyed many buildings to fortify the Convent. We were received with open Arms. The Cathedral is a beautiful Building. The inside is ornamented with Paintings, &c: Its lenth is about 400 feet, breadth 200 feet. I paced it, therefore cannot be exactly correct.I had a sight of those Gentlemen that defended the Convent about an hour after their surrender. They appeared rather low spirited as they had just been plundered by our Soldiers.‡

Last Sunday a Te Deum was sung in the Cathedral for their Delivery from the French, and in the Evening a Grand Ball was given by the Inhabitants to the Offrs: of the Allied Army, which I did not attend as we were to March next morning at day light.

---

* On the 24th Marmont's troops had crossed the Tormes and pushed back troops of the King's German Legion. Wellington responded by sending Graham forward with the 1st and 7th Divisions. The 4th and 5th Divisions were also brought up, ready to attack, but Marmont pulled back (*see* Oman, V, 375).

† The 1/9th Foot had also pulled down houses for firewood on the retreat to Corunna (Hale, 29–30).

‡ The fortified convents actually surrendered on 27 June.

In our progress after the French we are welcomed in every Village we pass through by the Bells ringing and the 'Viva Inglezes' of the Inhabitants, who are very liberal indeed of their Water which is in great requisition among the Soldiers as Springs are very scarce in this part of the world.

Though every precaution has been taken by Earl Wellington, as far as lies in his power, to prevent Corn being destroyed by the Allied Army, yet I am sorry to say that many Thousand Acres have been destroyed for want of other Forage for the Animals, which cannot be procured in all parts of this Country. You cannot imagine the number of Mules requisite for the supply of an Army of about Forty or Fifty thousand men, besides Baggage and Riding animals. By a Proclamation I saw at Salamanca every thing is to be paid for which is destroyed by us.

We followed the French so closely as far as Fuente Lapena that our Commissariat found Five thousand Rations in that place which those gentlemen had ordered, and which they had not had time to receive when our Cavalry drove them from it.

We are now a little to the Right and in the Rear of Toro, about one league and a half from the Douro. We have received no orders to march to day and various reports are in circulation. (July ye 3^d) The most probable is that the French have crossed the Douro at Toro and destroyed the Bridge, in consequence of which our march may be retarded for a short time. At this moment we hear the report of Cannon in our Front, but cannot learn any thing about the Enemy. Since their retreat we have made but few Prisoners. A few Deserters have come over. We met four yeasterday that were on some advanced Post and deserted. They were so very Drunk that we could get no rational answers from them.

I have met with Hardy dayly since the Capture of Salamanca. He is in good health. He appears to understand his business well. As he knew we were short of Corn he has very kindly offered to supply me, but I thank him as we can get nothing to buy – a pound of Bread, when it can be had here, is sold Eighteen pence. Let the good People in England follow the example of these People: when they are told the Price is enormous, their answer is <u>Patience</u>. These are bad times. They appear willing to sacrifice everything for the good of their Country.

I shall thank you to inform my D^r: Father, I drew on him a few days ago for the payment of my Poney, £19"5ˢʰ", payable to my order, which I gave to our Pay Master's clerk, Mʳ Plymton, who cash'd the Bill for me at the rate of 5/6ᵈ per dollar. We are now paid to the 24ᵗʰ: of March, so that, including Bat & Forage Money,* we are Five months in Arrears, without the least prospect of of any Issue from the Pay Master Genˡ:

I have written this as I may have an opportunity of sending it by one of our Officers to England, who expects to obtain leave every hour & will Start immediately for Lisbon. 'Il dit qu'il prefere le joug de l'Hymen au joug Militaire'.†

I have lost much of the pleasure I took in Rising before the Sun. It has happened so constantly lately that I enjoy a Feather Bed, when I am allowed to Sleep in one, till Seven. The mornings are very Cold before Sun Rise and, during that time, we are almost always standing quietly by our Arms for an hour and a half or Two Houres, and, till the Winter comes on, I am afraid we shall have no more rest.

I went to Medina del Campo a few Days ago and was well paid for the trouble of going a league and a half by a peep at the Town, which is very ancient and most of the Houses are built like Castles such as you read of in old Spanish Romances. The Inhabitants have not returned to their houses which they left on the retreat of the French.

Adieu.

---

*   Bat money was an allowance paid for an officer's baggage. Hence batman.
†   'He says he prefers Hymen's yoke to the military yoke.'

Salamanca and the Occupation of Madrid

After the fall of the convents at Salamanca, Marmont retired north-east, beyond the Douro, towards Valladolid, to wait for reinforcements. Wellington sent three columns after him, including the 5th Division and the 1/9th, but rather than engage in a battle, Wellington instead directed Portuguese cavalry to clear the north bank of the river and confound Marmont's foraging parties.

Once reinforced, on 15 July Marmont again advanced south-west towards Salamanca. Wellington withdrew in the direction of Ciudad Rodrigo, closely pursued by the French. By the morning of 22 July, the British were south of Salamanca. Marmont thought Wellington was still retreating and moved to outflank him. Spotting the 7th Division in a wood, Marmont assumed it was the British rearguard covering that retreat, but concealed beyond the ridge was the rest of Wellington's army, ready to fight.

D[r]: F.   La Nava de S[t]: Raval July 24th: 1812

After undergoing great fatigue, we have at lenth gained a Brilliant Victory over the French near Salamanca. On the 22[d]: in the Morning, the French began their Maneouvres in front of our Army and shewed a disposition to attack us. After waiting for some hours under Arms, we received the welcome inteligence that our General intended to bring them to action, and about Two o'Clock we were ordered (the 5 Division) to support some Artillery towards our Right which oppened on the Enemy. This was not a very pleasant position as the Enemy's shot came thick about us and killed and wounded many of our Men.

At Four we were ordered to advance in Line. A Village lay between the two lines, in consequence of which we broke in Colum of Sections and advanced in double quick time, Shot & Shells pouring on us. When we had passed the Village we formed line and moved on in the same order as a Reg.^: would do on l'Hyvreuse,* that is to say, Admirably well. Here the 9th: pushed forward before the Brigade, the Enemy about Two hundred yards in our Front. When we came within a hundred yards they faced to the Right about and moved off in ordinary time, which, however, they quickened as we advanced on them till such a time that, finding us too close, They ran as fast as they could, put leg to ground, and we following them, cheering. We had lost the Division then, and, after advancing over Two Hills, we were ordered to halt, as our men could heardly draw breath and were almost choaked with Dust.

It is almost a miracle that we had not above one third more killed and wounded of any other Regiment in the Brigade, which must have been owing to our rapid advance. We lost no officers & only 42 Men killed and wounded, Eleven of whom belonged to Percival's company, to which I belong. Six of them were killed and wounded by the long cannon Shot of the Enemy.

You will have a more correct account of the whole in the Gazette than it is in my power to give you. We have followed them (the Enemy) as far as this, and I am so tired for want of rest that, had I not been fortunate enough to buy an old Animal for my Baggage & Ride myself, I should undoubtedly have been in the rear at present. Percival and two Ensigns left us this morning, Sick. I am in hopes of seeing my Cap^tn: in a few days. I attribute his Illness to want of rest and food fit for our work.

Genl: Le Marchant fell in front of our Reg^t: and his Body was delivered by one of our Serg^ts: to his Son. Col^l: Barlow† was killed also in the attack of the last position the French took before their

* A road in St Peter Port, Guernsey.
† Lieutenant-Colonel Frederick Barlow (61st Foot).

Retreat. I have not heard of any more of our acquaintance falling. Pottinger had left us before the action, I belive from fatigue.*

As the Letters may be called for at a moment's notice, I have scribbled, which I thought would be acceptable. If I have time I shall add more. I am in good spirits & health at present, which I pray God to continue, as also that you may all enjoy health and happiness is the sincere wish of your affectionate son – P.L.M.

25th: July. After a good night's rest and a good Breakfast I feel considerably refreshed. We halt at this place to day for the purpose of collecting the straglers. Report says that the French have taken a Position Eight Leagues from this. If this is true, you may expect to hear of another Victory.

Before we advanced on the 22^d:, General Leith road along the Ranks, telling us this was to be a proud and glorious day for England. He was very cool, but I am sorry to say he was wounded a short time after. Col^l: Crawfurd was near getting a wound in his hand; a Ball scratched his Thumb. One of our Lieut^{ts}: was scratch'd in the foot.

The fatigue we have undergone has Weakened our Army. Sick are continually going in the Rear; our Division sent this morning 140 away. However, our strenth is more than a match for the Enemys after such a drubbing as they have had.

We were tired of the maneouvering between the Armies and could not account for the advance and retreat of the Allies. We have now full proof that Marmont has been out-General'd. We expect to move forward tomorrow.

I have seen nothing of my Guernsey Freinds since the Battles. I saw Tuppur Carey on the 21st:, in good health. I have my clothes up with the Reg^t: My Cap is a little too small & the Cloth for the Great Coat rather light, but altogether I am highly pleased with the execution of my order to LM & Co: I have not been able to make use of any thing yet as we have had other employment for the Taylors. I wait anxiously for Letters from Guernsey announcing our Dear freinds from Naples arrivals.

Please to remember me to all &^c:

[SIX PAGES MISSING]

---

* Lieutenant Thomas Pottinger (8th Light Dragoons). Father of Eldred Pottinger who was to serve in the disastrous retreat from Kabul in 1842.

Salamanca was a great triumph for Wellington. The French lost 14,000 men, twenty guns and two imperial eagles. It was, declared the Liverpool Mercury on 21 August, 'A victory complete in every respect, and from which the best and greatest results may be safely prognosticated,' news to 'fill the bosom of every Englishman with exultation.'

After their defeat 'the enemy continued retreating, taking the nearest direction to Valladolid (which was about twenty-four leagues from Salamanca),' explained Hale, 'and our army continued advancing in like manner, forming our camp as convenient to wood and water as possible every night. But nothing in particular happened till we came to Valladolid, from which place a division of the enemy took a fresh route towards Madrid, and the main body formed a line about one league beyond Valladolid.'[1]

D[r]: J[a]:   Camp on the Cega River near Cuellar
                                                 August 3[d]: 1812

Since my last of the 24th: Ult[o]: we have been continually on the move. We have gone within two Leagues of Valadolid, where I understand we took Two thousand Sick and Wounded Frenchmen. From thence we have changed our direction and are now on our Road to Segovia, where the Spaniards tell us Joseph is with some Juramendos[*] and surrounded by the Guerrillas.

When we were near Valadolid, Earl Wellington thanked the Army in Orders for their Conduct on the 22[d]: and at the same time Observed that particular attention ought to be paid to the formation of the Troops in Action. This was a rub at the Reg[t]: who were charged by the French Cavalry and Cut to pieces. He afterwards desires particular attention be paid by Off[rs]: to prevent any Straggling on the March, as it has been reported to his Excellency that the French took above One hundred men on the 20th: Ult[o]: when we were retreating from Nava del Rey.

His Excellency seems much out of humour, occasioned, I believe, by the Sickness of the Army which is very great at present. Our Reg[t]: is not Four hundred Strong, which Two Months ago was near Seven hundred. But the fatigues of this Campaign have

---

[*] Spanish soldiers serving under King Joseph.

NAPOLEON EMPEROR OF FRANCE.

What ho! young Boney, ho! — 'Tis Johnny calls!
I hate thee, Boney, —— for thy savage cruelty!
Now if thou dost —— not hide thee from my cudgel,
Now while the —— Mighty Sir-loin turns upon the spit,
And Christmas —— cheer invites us all to feast,
Boney I say —— come forth, and singly face me!
Johnny is —— hoarse with daring thee to arms!!!

JOHNNY BULL'S DEFIANCE to BONAPARTE!
A Parody on Shakespeare's Richard 3.

Above left: 1. Napoleon Bonaparte.
Lithograph by N. Currier *c.* 1847.
(Courtesy of the Library of Congress)

Above right: 2. Johnny Bull's Defiance
to Bonaparte. (Courtesy of the Library
of Congress)

Right: 3. Ensign with colours of the
9th Foot. From *The History of the
Norfolk Regiment* by F. Loraine Petre.
(Author's collection)

4. Front of Les Beaucamps, Castel, Guernsey. (Courtesy of The Guernsey Society)

5. Landing troops. From *The Martial Achievements of Great Britain*. (Author's collection)

6. The 9th Foot after first landing in Portugal. From *The History of the Norfolk Regiment* by F. Loraine Petre. (Author's collection)

GENERAL JUNOT.

Above left: 7. Marshal Jean Andoche Junot. From *Battles of the 19th Century* by A. Forbes. (Author's collection)

Above right: 8. Sir John Moore. From *The Diary of Sir John Moore* edited by J. F. Maurice. (Author's collection)

Below: 9. Battle of Vimeiro. From *The Martial Achievements of Great Britain*. (Author's collection)

10. Lugo from *Letters from Portugal and Spain* by Adam Neale. (Author's collection)

Above left: 11. Marshal Soult. From *Napoleon's Marshals* by R. P. Dunn-Pattison. (Author's collection)

Above right: 12. Attack of the Black Watch at the Battle of Corunna. From *Glorious Battles of English History* by C. H. Wylly. (Author's collection)

13. The Battle of Corunna. From *The Martial Achievements of Great Britain.* (Author's collection)

14. The Death of Sir John Moore. From *The Martial Achievements of Great Britain.* (Author's collection)

15. The Burial of Sir John Moore at Corunna by the 9th Foot. From *The History of the Norfolk Regiment* by F. Loraine Petre. (Author's collection)

Above left: 16. Lieutenant Colonel John Cameron. From *The History of the Norfolk Regiment* by F. Loraine Petre. (Author's collection)

Above right: 17. André Masséna. From *Napoleon's Marshals* by R. P. Dunn Pattison. (Author's collection)

Below: 18. Gibraltar. From *England's Battles* by William Williams. (Author's collection)

19. The Battle of Barrosa. From *The Martial Achievements of Great Britain*. (Author's collection)

20. Taking a French Eagle at Barrosa. From *The Martial Achievements of Great Britain*. (Author's collection)

Above left: 21. Sir Thomas Graham. From *Life of Thomas Graham, Lord Lynedoch* by Alexander Delavoye. (Author's collection)

Above right: 22. Marshal Auguste de Marmont. From *Napoleon's Marshals* by R. P. Dunn-Pattison. (Author's collection)

Below: 23. The Storming of Ciudad Rodrigo. From *The Martial Achievements of Great Britain*. (Author's collection)

24. The Storming of Badajoz. From *England's Battles* by William Williams. (Author's collection).

25. The Battle of Salamanca. From *The Martial Achievements of Great Britain*. (Author's collection)

26. The Battle of Vitoria. From *The Martial Achievements of Great Britain*. (Author's collection)

27. The Battle of Vitoria. Bringing in the Prisoners. From *The Martial Achievements of Great Britain*. (Author's collection)

28. French escaping Vitoria.
From *Battles of the 19th Century* by A. Forbes.
(Author's collection)

29. Marshal Jourdan. From
Napoleon's Marshals by R.
P. Dunn-Pattison. (Author's
collection)

30. The Siege of San Sebastian. From *The Martial Achievements of Great Britain*. (Author's collection)

31. The Storming of San Sebastian. From *The Martial Achievements of Great Britain*. (Author's collection)

32. Irun. From *The Campaign in the Western Pyrenees* by Robert Batty. (Author's collection)

33. Bivouac in the Pyrenees. From *The Martial Achievements of Great Britain*. (Author's collection)

34. Sir Colin Campbell, ensign in the 9th Foot with Le Mesurier. From *The History of the Norfolk Regiment* by F. Loraine Petre. (Author's collection)

35. Street in Fuenterabia. From *The Campaign in the Western Pyrenees* by Robert Batty. (Author's collection)

36. The Duke of Wellington at the Crossing of the Bidassoa. From *The Martial Achievements of Great Britain.* (Author's collection)

37. The Passage of Bidassoa. From *The Martial Achievements of Great Britain.* (Author's collection)

38. The Quay at St. Jean-de-Luz. From *The Campaign in the Western Pyrenees* by Robert Batty. (Author's collection)

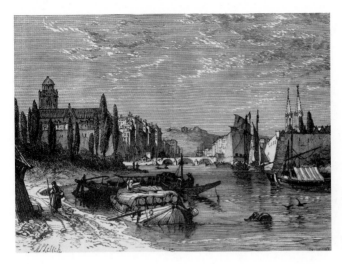

39. View of Bayonne. From *British Battles on Land and Sea* by James Grant. (Author's collection)

40. The Field of Battle. From *The Martial Achievements of Great Britain*. (Author's collection)

41. The Journey of a Modern Hero to Elba. Published by J. Phillips 1814. (Courtesy of the Library of Congress)

been very great. I have been better within the last two or three days than I had been for some time before. I am not near so jaded as I was then. Our Rations, on which we have lived for the last month, have not kept us in high condition. We are as lean as Whipping posts. We are to have an addition to our Rations dayly of Two Oz^s: of Rice, or flouer, or wheat, or Barley to put in our Soup.

We were agreably surprised yeasterday morning, before we commenced our March, by receiving Orders for a Month's pay, which we received yeasterday afternoon and which will make us a little more Comfortable. Since we left Valadolid we have marched for many leagues through a Pine Wood & Sandy ground which is very fagging to the Men. Last night many Spanish Ladies came to see the Camp &, after some persuation, we made them Dance on the Sand, but as we had no refreshment for them save Adam's ale, they did not keep it up long and went off well powdered from the Dust.

Lord Wellington has been forced to issue very severe orders with regard to Women plundering. I must do them the justice to say that they are ten times worse than the Men. A little wholesome discipline is now administered to them when they are found at it. A few days ago the Provost of the Division desired one of them to walk out of a Field where the Industrious Lady was very busy digging Patatoes, else he would punish her. With a tremendous Oath she replied 'You may Flog me every Day for a Meal of Praties', and went out well loaded.

Genl: Leith has thanked us in a very pleasant manner for our Conduct in the field on the 22^d: He says he was excessively sorry for being obliged to leave the field so soon after the Commencement of the Action, but he hopes to be able to join the Division shortly, and will be happy to lead them to any place or in any enterprize they may have to undertake.

The Portugeese of our Division behaved uncommonly well when the Cannon Shots were thinning their ranks; not a Man stirred. Their Col^l: shewed them a fine example.

Where the French were not hard pressed in their retreat, they recommenced their Barbarous system of Burning the Villages & plundering every Article they could possibly carry away.

I have not heard which road Marmont has taken since he

left Valadolid. Col^l: Cameron is gone to England on leave of Absence. Col^l: Crawfurd now commands the Reg^t: I am left in the Command of Percival's company, who is still unwell at Salamanca. Since our retreat from Naval del Rey we have gone smoothly and quietly; every indulgence given to the Off ^{rs}:, for which the Off ^{rs}: exert themselves to the utmost. We have been as comfortable as circumstances could admit of since the campaign began.

I saw D^r: Hardy a few Days ago, in good health. He eat Soup and Beef with us. Their Department have much to do, but they are well fed and can therefore undergo fatigues. The Commissary of our Division (the best we have been blest with for a long time) has been put in arrest for not having made his appearance with Liquor of some kind after the Battle of the 22^d, which I think would have saved many Men who were obliged to Drink Cold water after being heated to the utmost degree. I had charge of the water Party & I am Certain I took very near a Gallon to wash the Dust down.

I sometimes wish I could make my appearance, after a long day's March, before your free and easy Clubb. I very much doubt if you would know me immediately; a Meagre Face covered with Dust almost an Inch thick, a Sigar in his mouth, his ration of Rum in his hand, with the new Regulation Cap* & Great Coat on.

We have halted to day to get Stores up and rest the Men. About half past two this Morning I called my Servant, who told me that I might lay in my Blankets a little longer as the men were not to be disturbed, and I followed his advice willingly. I have had a Sumptuous Breakfast; Beef Stakes and Tea, which I constantly make a rule to get when I halt, which is once a week or ten days.

You have seen the handsome Provision Government have made for wounded Off^{rs}: I should not be surprised if, in the fullness of their hearts, they gave us an additional sixpence a day when they hear of our fine doings in this Country – defeating the Enemy with a loss on their part of Sixteen Thousand men. I certainly deserve a triffle.

Though close to Valadolid, I did not go to see it. I had a little touch of Rheumatism. The Town is very old, every thing to be procured there for Money.

Remember me &^c:

---

* A regulation forage cap had recently been introduced.

D^r: F.   Camp near Madrid August 14th: 1812

Yours of the 7th: Ult^o: reached me at Cuellar on the 4th: ins^t: and gave me but little pleasure on opening it and not finding any of my D^r: Elizabeth's writing. I felt something which seemed to say that some misfortune had befallen them. I sincerely hope that, by the time this reaches you, their sufferings will be ended and that in the Centre of their Family the past will be forgotten and the future have a brighter and happier prospect.

I have long thought of seeing Madrid, and my expectations have been most fully gratified. On the 11th: we marched within two leagues of the Escurial, which, being mentioned as a remarkable place, I was curious to see and in consequence rode Eight leagues. The view of the Escurial at the distance of a Mile did not please me much; it strikes as an immense heavy building. One of the few things that are worthy of notice is the Mausoleum, one of the most solemn appartments and finest I have ever seen. There are about Seventy cells for Kings. Only Seven are filled; Charles 5th: occupies one. The inside, which is about 20 feet long, the same breath and 15 or more high, is all beautiful marble.

The Library is a fine Appartment but as all the Books are taken by Joseph it looks rather naked. As to the appartments occupied by his Majesty, they are small and very shabby. Altogether, I think I paid pretty well for the sight of the famous Gridiron.[*]

We marched yeasterday to the Casa del Campo, a Mile from Madrid.[†] In passing near the Suburbs, immense crouds were gathered to Cheer us as we passed. I was on Baggage Guard, but was allowed to march with the Reg^t: 'Viva Inglezes' resounded from all parts. We were nearly dragged from our Horses by the Ladies, shaking hands a Dozen at a time. They were mad with joy, hurled their caps in the Air, and waved their handkerchiefs. After passing through this Gentry we hurried our Breakfast & rode to Madrid about Four o'Clock in the afternoon, where we were again greeted by the Inhabitants. To our infinite pleasure we saw a

---

* The floor plan of the Escorial resembles a gridiron.
† As Wellington advanced on Madrid, so King Joseph retreated with his troops, leaving only 2,000 soldiers to defend the Retiro arsenal.

Proclamation by the Corregidor* saying that the new Constitution would be proclaimed that night, and mentioning the Order of the Ceremony. First came the Guerilla Comp^y: of Don Juan D'Avril, Trumpets sounding. Then part of Don Carlos D'Espana's army; the Alguacils† & Guerillas.

The Constitution was read in Four different parts of the city, but such was the Buz that I could not hear a word. After the business was over there was a general Shout of applause. I got in conversation with some Spanish Ladies in the Balcony of the Town House and they pointed out the different people & their names as they passed.

The Ceremony lasted near four hours, after which I walked till near Eleven o'Clock to see the Illuminations which are to last Three nights. The Balconies of all the Houses are adorned with Silk hangings, some of them Beautifully decorated. The Post House was particularly fine last night. Crowds of People paraded the Streets and stopped us every moment to embrace us. At Eleven I retired to Bed, but I am sorry to add not to rest, for a host of Bugs anoyed me so terribly that they succeeded in expelling me from it at half past four this morning.

I strolled to Market which is well supplied with Vegetables, Poultry (algo caro‡), and fish. Bread is scares, tho not dear.

To night a Ball is given by the Inhabitants to the Allied Army. I am inclined to go if I can obtain leave. The French left a force in the Retiro (which they had fortified) to check the Inhabitants, who were very refractory during Joseph's stay in Madrid and on his retreat from it. There is a report at present that the Men in the Retiro have just surrendered, which I hope may be the case, and that we shall have a few days' rest in this place. I am greatly pleased with it. The Houses are fine, the streets good, though not very broad, and I should like to have time to see the place, which I am told is worth seeing, & any other fine sight that is to be seen.

Joseph, on leaving Madrid, was very civil, Bowing to all his good subjects. He has retired to Toledo where I suppose we shall follow him.

---

* In effect, the mayor.
† Royal official.
‡ 'somewhat expensive'.

If I had money and was going to England I should get some of the Ancient Spanish dresses here, which are very fine. One of the Nobility was dressed in one of those yeasterday and I seldom have seen anything so handsom. He had an immense sword on one Side and a Stilleto on the other.

D. Hardy is gone to the rear. I understand he has been unwell. I saw or heard nothing of him till I sent to repay him some Dollars he had lent me in time of need.

August 15th: Yeasterday, at Four in the afternoon, the French marched out of the Retiro and laid down their Arms on the Glacis.* A finer Body of Men, 1700 in number, were seldom ever seen. They appeared to be a Set of picked Men. The stores in the Retiro are, I am informed, beyond conception.

Last night Earl Wellington honoured the Theatre with his Presence. The representation was l'Enganador Enganado (Biter Bit) and Lo Sourdo de la Posada (Deaf in the public house). They are pretty good actors. After the Representation some Spaniards cried out 'Viva Lord Wellington', on which he came to the front of his Box and bowed. The number of Spaniards was small, not being aware of Ld Wellington's coming there.

After the play I walked home and had the pleasure of finding my purse flown on waking this morning. I suppose some of my Portugeese neighbours had the luck to put their hands on my Pantaloons, as they were found on the outside of the Tent, Ten Dollars minus.

Please remember me &c:

Dr: M-   Arevalo August the 28th: 1812

My Dr: Father's letter of the 23d: Ulto: announcing the arrival of Ferdinand & Elizabeth at the Mother Bank found me at Madrid the day before I left it, the 16th: The news gave me the greatest pleasure. I now hope my Dear Sister is entirely recovered from her dissagreable voyage and that she enjoys good health in her native

---

* A slope of earth, inclined towards the top of a defensive structure, allowing a garrison to keep assailants under fire from the parapet without adjusting the elevation of their artillery. It also shielded the walls from enemy cannon.

Island. I hope my D^r: Mother will welcome them in the Island by Proxy for her Absent Son.

I was inclined to be in very low spirits when we received the Order to leave Madrid for the Escurial.* This was on Sunday, about four in the afternoon. I resolved to take my last ride in the place and, after buying a few things our Mess wanted, I went to the Prado, the grand public walk of the Capital,† and enjoyed the sight for about one hour. Immense crowds of Spaniards that seemed delighted at having the English among them, were promanading in a Beautiful Piece of Ground with Two or Three Rows of Trees on each side, and Bands of some of the Reg^{ts}: Quartered in Madrid playing in different parts. I could have amused myself here much longer, but we were to March at day Break next morning and I was oblige[d] to quit it with regret. Madrid has brought to my recollection several views of Naples that are in the front Parlour, in which some of the Streets are seen with a row of Trees on each side.

A Proclamation was issued by the new Government for confiscating the Property of those People who went off with the French as well as Joseph's, and any Person conceiling any part of the said Property is liable to very severe punishment, or if they do not deliver within a period of Forty Eight hours.

On my return to Camp that night I found my D^r F's letter (laying on what answers to my Table, a pair of Paniers) which had the effect of raising my spirits considerably.

On the 18th: we marched to Escurial, a solitary place with very few Inhabitants, and on the following days were followed by the 1st: 4th: and 7th: Divisions. Both Men and Off^{rs} were crowded. I took my Quarters in a field about one Mile from town.

On the 22^d: we marched from the Escurial to this place, which I assure you is not at all to my liking. They are completely a Frenchified set in this Town and are as rude as they possibly can be without absolutely insulting us, so that I hope we shall not stay any lenth of time among them.

---

* After enjoying their reception in Madrid, the 1/9th were billeted at the Escorial. 'They have taken care for the present that Madrid shall not be our Capua,' explained Gomm, 'and have quartered four divisions of us in and about this very large house' (Gomm, 284).

† The boulevard, the Paseo del Prado, rather than the building now housing the Museo del Prado.

Our Prospect appears very promising at present and, if some very favourable Change does not take place for the French, they are in as bad circumstances as we could wish them. On retreating from Madrid, Joseph left a Garrison at Guadalascara* of 900 Men, who followed the laudable example of their Brethren in the Retiro and surrendered the moment our Dragoons made their appearance.

The remains of Marmont's Army, who retired to Burgos, seemed inclined to make a Diversion in favour of Joey and pushed some of their Troops to Medina del Campo on our advance to Madrid, in consequence of which we were ordered to this place, where the 6th: Division, who had been left with the Recruits at Cuellar and retreated when the Enemy advanced, has joined us.

The Divisions which we left at the Escurial have moved on the Road to Burgos, and the Enemy, afraid of having English troops in his rear, have wisely retired from Valadolid to Burgos. The last news we had of Joey was of his arrival at Cuenca. Genl: Hill, it is reported, had advanced as far as Talavera de la Reyna.

After the Battle of Salamanca the papers at Madrid said that Marmont had been recalled to France and that the French, in a Skirmish with the English, had taken some Prisoners. These news were publish'd before the retreat of the French from that place, and the People heard nothing of this Battle before the 9th: inst: when a report was Spread that the French had been defeated. On the 11th: French Offrs went out of Madrid to reconnoitre & soon brought the intelligence of the allied Army passing the pass of Guadarama. All was consternation and bustle among the French, and Joey took his departure bowing very respectfully to his good Subjects as he went along the Streets. The spies and police were very active and put a great number of Spaniards in Prison for expressing their joy with a little too much clamour at so unseasonable a time.

What does Elizabeth intend her Son for? From what I saw of the Rogue he would make a good Soldier & would often deceive his enemy by manoeuvering. However, I do not recommend it as a lucrative Life or even as one I shoud wish him to enter into. This last year I think I have fully earned my wages, all which I have not yet received. We are paid to April, besides allowances which are not paid, so that, any rate, if it is not considered a lucrative, it must at

---

* Guadalajara.

least be honorable, which together with one pound and a half of Bread, the ingredients of which are too numerous to mention but in which Straw, Bran, & Fetches* predominate, a Pound of Beef and two ounces of Wheat for Soup, and sometimes half allowance of Grog (or 1/6 of a Pint), keep us alive and in good spirits.

29th: Yeasterday a forage Party of the 44th: Regt: was terribly beaten by the Inhabitants of a neighbouring Village. The Alcalde† began the battle by knocking the Offr: off his Horse, & it is reported the Spaniards killed a man of that Regt: When this was reported to the Genl: he ordered an Armed party of 60 Men to go for the Alcalde, who, conscious of having done wrong, had fled, & in his place they brought back the Chief Inhabitants of the Village who have given security for the appearance of their Magistrate, who most probably will swing for it, if he can be found. I do not hear from any person that the party behaved any ways ill.

I expect by the next Packet to receive a few lines from my Dr: Elizth: Have the kindness to remember me to &c:

---

* Common vetch, normally fed to horses.
† Spanish magistrate.

8

The Siege of Burgos

D^r: Abr^m: Camp before Burgos Sept^r: 21st: 1812

I had the pleasure of receiving my Dear Elizabeth's announcing her safe arrival in Guernsey on the 3^d: ins^t: as we were marching out of Aravalo for Valadolid, which is the reason I have been rather longer than usual in acknowledging the receit of the Letter. I had been in dayly expectation of having another with the agreable news of my having a Nephew, and that E: was in good health, but have been disappointed. Though we have Newspapers to the 26th: August, the last news I have from Guernsey are no later than August 1st:

On the 6th: we crossed the Douro at a Ford about a League from Valadolid, in front of which the French had taken a position with a view, apparently, of making a Stand. Owing to some negligence of the Staff of our Division, our Artillery was delayed some hours, the necessary Orders not having been given, which were to follow the 6th: Division over a Ford where Carriages might pass, whereas at the place where we crossed, Horses could with difficulty pass, on account of the Steepness of the Banks on both sides. It was reported that the Marquis* gave these Gents a severe lecture for their negligence, as we were to have attacked immediately after crossing with another Division, and when the Artillery came up it was too late in the Evening, and next morning the Gent^n: retired

---

* Wellington had been made a marquess on 18 August.

from Valadolid, blowing up the Bridge which crosses the Pisuerga River.

We entered the Town on the 7th: which was in great confusion as the French had not been gone above two hours. The People did not say much on our entering; I understand they are greatly in the French interest. We halted here on the 8th: & 9th: The new Constitution was proclaimed and the Town was Illuminated, if putting a Candle in the front of a large House, or two or Three in a Street can be so called. As I am no great amateur of that kind of Illumination, I went to the theatre which was honoured by the Great Lord in his Uniform as Captn: General of the Spanish Armies; A Blue Coat with Three broad Stripes of Gold embroidery on the Cuffs & one of the same round the Colar.* He had the Star belonging to the Order of the Golden Fleece, which is very brilliant and cost, I am told, one Million of Dollars. He received it on his entry in Madrid from the Cortes.

The play was Christopher Collumbus, who on his return from America was disgraced by Ferdinand & Isabella, in consequence of the representation of Bobadilla. Collumbus, in a Dungeon at Seville, bewails his hard fate, that he should be treated thus, who has done so much for his Country and gained Kingdoms for his King. At this time some Spaniards Roared out 'Viva Duque de Ciudad Rodrigo!' and it was a long time before silence was restored, and not till after His Lordship had come forward and made some low bows.

On the 10th: we bent our course this way, but here fine weather forsook us and instead of Hot and Dry we had cold & wet nights. Such a change could not take place without affecting our Men considerably, and our Batt^n: paraded about One hundred and fifty men this morning, exclusive Servants & Batmen. We have sent above 80 Men Sick to the Rear in the course of a Week, and though we have had dry weather for the last two or three days, since yeasterday morning 31 have reported themselves sick.

On the 12th: Our Dragoons took 150 Prisoners, which they were obliged to abandon afterwards as the French sent 15 Squadrons to release the Prisoners and our force consisted of Two Squadrons only.

---

* Wellington had also been given supreme command of the Spanish forces.

On the 16th: and 17th: the Enemy seemed inclined to make a Stand, but retired after a little Skirmishing in which a few Men on both sides were killed and wounded.

On the 18th: they left this place and retired towards Vittoria, leaving a Garrison in an old Castle* which they have fortified and which commands the Town, and which is commanded by a Hill close to it, on which they had raised an Outwork which was escaladed by the Scotch Brigade of the 1st: Division.[†] The Villains in the Castle amuse themselves firing on the people in Town. They have killed seven or Eight of the People and only one Soldier.

Our loss in the Escalade is variously stated; some say Two, others Four hundred. It is supposed that one Week's work will put the place in our possession, when I hope all those Rascals will be put to the sword. The General that commands the Garrison (2000) commanded in Burgos before, and though he was there but a short time, put about 100 Spaniards to Death. I have not been able to learn his name.[‡]

We have been employed making Fascines & Gabions,[§] which I suppose will be the only share we shall have in this business as we are reserves for greater deeds than having our heads broken against a Stone Wall. We are in a fine piece of Ploughed Ground, something like the Ruette[¶] with regard to stones, which we have not taken the trouble of picking to afford us a smooth Bed, but we are pretty well accustomed to it now and sleep equally well.

Castanos and his Army are here. He rides in the Rear of one of his Divisions in this Order; Four men of the Walloon Guards in front; the General, with Staff on his Right and Left and in the Rear; and the Rear is brought up by two Troops of Dragoons. The men are Stout but have bad appointments and do not appear to be fed on Roast Beef. They shew but little mercy to the Kitchen Gardens

---

* By which Le Mesurier means the castle at Burgos.
† Including the 24th Foot (South Wales Borderers), the 26th Foot (The Cameronians), the 42nd Foot (The Black Watch) and 79th Foot (The Cameron Highlanders).
‡ General Jean-Louis Dubreton (1773–1855).
§ Fascines are bundles of brushwood used to fill in ditches or strengthen entrenchments. Gabions are large cylindrical wicker containers filled with earth to provide cover from enemy fire.
¶ Guernsey has several 'ruettes'. It is another name for a lane (from the French 'rue').

when they come across them, devouring Cabages, Peas or any thing they can lay hands on.

Our 2nd: Batt^n^: is still at Gib. They were detained till another Reg^t^: relieved them. I wish a few Subs more would join us. Our grand total of office^rs^: is now 19 instead of 43: We have 3 Capt^ns^: and 11 Subs doing Duty. The remainder are Sick and absent on leave, so that Duty sometimes is Short.

I saw D^r^: Hardy yesterday. He is attached to head Quarters and complains of having too much to do and being kept up till passed Midnight. He does not look ill from too much work, though I belive they work them pretty hard in his Department.

If ever I return I shall be thought a most accomplished Man in Guernsey having acquired the Habit of taking a Pipe of Bacco at Daylight of a Cold morning, and sometimes an Inch of the Raw (dram), accomplishments which I think have preserved my health lately, and which you would soon acquire if you ever came to this Country Campaigning.

The French, in their retreat from Valodolid, have destroyed many Houses and plundered every article they possibly could, which I think shows they have no Idea of ever returning to a country they have ruined.

The Castle at this place is strongly fortified, if we are to believe the Inhabitants who say that the French have been working at it constantly for upwards of two Years. The garrison consist chiefly of Dutchmen who keep up a continual fire of Shot and Shels, with what execution I cannot say, but apperently great, if we may judge of the direction of their Shells.

We have papers with the account of the Battle of Salamanca. In them I see some Gentlemen gave their Tenants Hogsheads of Beer to Drink our healths. Which would you prefer? Reading of these fine things, or getting a Pot of Beer yourself when laying on the Ground and the Sun Scorching you? I think if they sent us a few Tons it would be much better applied than giving it to a parcel of over fed Country men and then publishing their Liberalities in the Newspapers.*

---

* Free beer on victory was widespread. The officers of the Royal Military College distributed 'two hogsheads of strong beer ... amongst the delighted Populace' (*Morning Chronicle*, 21 August 1812), and at Launceston the people were

I am anxious to hear from the Beaucamps as the Letters I last received are almost Two months old. Rem^r: &tc.

P.S. Pack's* Brigade of Portugeese behaved well the other night. They made a false attack on the outwork whilst the Highlanders scaled on the other side and went close to the Fort.

The French resisted the allied siege fiercely. 'Begging me Lord Wellington's pardon, I think we have not respected the castle of Burgos sufficiently,' wrote Gomm on 9 October.[1] 'Several attacks were made to take the castle,' explained Hale, 'but it being so strongly fortified, they proved unsuccessful.'[2]

The 1/9th was not directly involved in the siege, other than sending Captain Kenny and Lieutenant Henry Dumaresq as assistant engineers.

D^r: Eth: Camp near Burgos Octo^r: 5th: 1812

On the 23^d: I had the pleasure of receiving Letters from all the family announcing the agreable intelligence of my D^r: Elizabeth having a Daughter. I received my Letters by some mistake, two days after the arrival of the post and therefore had given up all hope of news from the famyly, when this package was brought to me with all the kind wishes of my D^r: Friends, for which I am most grateful and wish them in return prosperity and happiness. I hope by this time my D^r: Sister is entirely recovered, and that my niece has a sweeter voice than when she made her appearance which, I am told, astonish'd all the family, from which I conjecture that she is a Stout Lass.

Our time here has been rather Idly spent. We moved from the place from which my last Letter was dated about Three Miles to the left of the road leading to Vittoria, and encamped near a wood where all the Off^{rs}: have taken refuge. We are about 6 Miles from Burgos, which place we can see by going half a mile from our Encampment. We made but little progress towards the reduction of that Fortress till last night when the 24th: Reg^t: carried the Outwork

'regaled with strong beer, by the munificence of the much-esteemed Mayor of that ancient borough' (*Royal Cornwall Gazette*, 29 August 1812).

* Brigadier-General Denis Pack (1772–1823).

in a most gallant manner, and I am in hopes the place cannot hold out much longer as their chief supply of water is cut off.

The Operations are carried on by Mining. Two mines have been blown up. The First blew up about Twenty French men in the Air and they were so panic struck that they left every place, we wished to obtain possession of, unprotected. Through some unnacountable reason or other, the Scaling ladders, under charge of an Off^r:, could not find the Breach, though a Serg^t: and three Men of that same party got on the Breach and remained there for about ten minutes when they were obliged to retire. A Court of Enquiry is Ordered on this Off^r: and, if sufficient reasons are not given, he most probably will be brought before a Court Martial.*

One of our Capt^{ns}: volunteered his services as acting Engineer at the beginning of the Siege, contrary to the wish of our Com^g: Off^r: who said he had no Off^{rs}: to spare and did not conceive that much credit could be obtained by an Off^r: in such a situation, and therefore did not wish them to volunteer. He was obstinate and went on the 28th: Ult^o: After releiving another acting engineer, he was amusing himself with firing at the French from a Riffle Gun above the Trenches when a Messenger was sent to seek if he had any Brains and executed his mission so roughly that the Off^r: followed his Corpse on the 2^d: to the grave. What renders his volunteering more ridiculous was that he had no idea of Engineering, besides which he was one of the Senior Capt^{ns}:, maried and a large family, his name K^y.†

All the family appear greatly displeased with me, particularly Sister A, for drinking Cold water after the Action of the 22^d: They must be aware that if wine or Spirits could have been procured I would not have run any risk by drinking Cold water, but of two evils I chose the least one, the risk of taking the beverage rather

---

* The first mine blown on the night of 29 September had been limited in its effect. Nearing the breach, 'the main body of the forlorn hope and its officer went a little farther along the wall, reached a section that was wholly impracticable for climbing, and ran back to the trenches to report that the defences were uninjured. The supports followed their example.' Fortunately the second mine, exploded at 5 p.m. on 4 October, 'was fired with excellent effect, throwing down nearly 100 feet of the rampart, and killing many of the French'. In the confusion, the 2/24th carried the breaches. (Oman, VI, 32–3).

† Captain Kenny's widow, Mary, was granted a pension of £60 p.a. in 1815.

than to choak, which I think I must have done had there been no water.*

I take pretty much exercise which I find agrees well with me. I have been out shooting and have had pretty good sport. There are plenty of Pigeons here about without any owners and when they are at some distance in the fields we have some sport. A few days ago I brought home five which made a Capital Stew.

I was very busy about my Paneers, setting every thing to rights a week ago, when I received a Slap on the Shoulder and, on looking round, found my Old play mate S. Dobree who had just arrived from Cadiz. He is appointed commissary to our Brigade. He Dined with us and partook of my game. He is just as Stout and as Rosy as ever.†

From the report in Circulation, I shall once more visit Madrid before I rest. Tis said that the 5th: and 7th: Divisions will proceed there the moment this place falls. Tis almost too good a place for Soldiers to Winter. I expect our rest will be very Short for, if we do not exert ourselves this winter and oblige the Enemy to cross the Ebro, we shall meet with more opposition in the Spring when they will be able to reinforce him from France.

Whilst I am well fed and not too much harrassed I have no doubt of doing well, but Starvation and hard work do not agree with me. At present we are well supplied by the Commissariat in every respect.

A General Order appeared yeasterday (Octr: 6th) censuring the inactivity of the working parties at Burgos. When the 24th: stormed the outwork a Covering Party of the 6th: Division was ordered to attend them, which, however, was not in time, in consequence of which a party of our Division, who have been employed in making Gabions & Fascines, were ordered on that Duty. Out of [blank] Offrs: belonging to that Party, four were Wounded, one of which has since Dead. The Offr: Comg: (Captn of the Royals) was wounded & received a visit next day from Lord Wellington who expressed himself highly pleased with the behaviour of this Party.

---

* Le Mesurier's fear of 'Cold Water' may have been due to the risk of disease from unboiled, fresh water. Spirits and wine were considered much safer.

† Dobree, as a commissary, was charged with supplying food among other things, so the fact that he was on the heavy side must have been amusing. Le Mesurier refers to it several times.

We are ordered to be in readiness to turn out at a Moment's notice, particularly at night and towards Day light in the Morning, from which we conjecture the French have moved as if with an intention of forcing us to raise the Siege, but I do not think they will be so uncivil as to disturb us from our miserable Beds in such Cold nights. The French made a Sortie from the Castle the night before last, and took some entrenching tools and killed about a Hundred men.* The weather was so bad yeasterday that we had not the Particulars correctly.

An immence number of our Men have died lately; out of 67 sent in the rear lately, 17 Died on the Road. Rain and cold winds rouses us pretty early from our Beds, for the sake of warming ourselves near a large Fire. I think it is just cold enough to go under a warmer cover than Canvass, and what comes hard upon us is that our Stock of Tabacco is nearly out and good is not to be procured here. A pound of common Tea is sold here for Four Dollars and a pound of corse brown Sugar 1/9ᵈ: and we are glad to procure it at that rate.

Octʳ: 10ᵗʰ: A few nights ago the French made a sortie – Killed & wounded all the Offʳˢ: employed that night. Dumaresq of ours was severely wounded in the Thigh by a grape Shot. However, his life is not considered in danger. Tis said Lord Wⁿ: goes to Madrid shortly. I hope he will take us with him for we are most miserable here, and no expectation of ameliorating our Condition by an issue of Money to pay for provisions, from which I suspect there is very little Coin. Remember me &ᶜ:

Further attempts by Wellington to assault the town failed. 'The inadequacy of the means with which we attacked the castle of Burgos allowed the French armies of the north time to assemble and reorganise a sufficient force to induce them to assume the offensive,' reported Gomm.[3]

On 20 October the British started pulling back their guns from Burgos. The next day Wellington began a full withdrawal towards Valladolid. 'We were obliged to retreat,' wrote Hale, 'for our army was then getting very weak by sickness, being obliged at that time of the year to encamp without tents.'[4]

---

* 'The French had carried off 200 picks and shovels which could not be replaced, the stock (as usual in Peninsular sieges) being very low' (Oman, VI, 37).

Retreat from Burgos. Battle at Villa Muriel, &c:

D^r: A. Camp near Tordesillas Nov^r: 2^d:1812

Our time has been most dissagreably occupied lately. About the middle of last Month the French moved down to relieve Burgos. On the 21st: Ult^o: the Seige was raised and we began our Retreat the same night at dark, and marched till Four o'Clock next morning over ploughed fields, ditches, &c:, &c:, the men to their knees in mud. After a few hours' rest we recommenced marching and halted about four in the afternoon.

On the 23^d: we marched from Six in the morning till midnight to Cordovilla. We left an immense number of Stragglers in the rear, having marched upwards of 8 Leagues in bad Roads.

On the 24th: we had a march of Seven leagues (the road was strewed on both sides with men completely knocked up) and we arrived about dark at Villa Muriel,* a village situated on the Carrion River between Duennas and Palencia. We were buoyed up with the hopes of a halt on the 25th:

On our arrival at this place I was ordered on Guard in the Town to protect the property of the Inhabitants and was comfortably lodged in a house that night with plenty of forage for my Poney, which he seemed to enjoy greatly, having fared hard since the commencement of the Retreat.

About Seven o'Clock on the morning of the 25th: the Adj^t: Genl: of the Division passed by the Guard and astonish'd me a little by an Order to go and support the Picquet on the Bridge, about 200 Yards from this Village. On my arrival there I found the Picquet lining the Bridge and preparations making for Blowing it up. We had not been there long when some Spanish Dragoons, who had gone out to Skirmish, returned, told us the French were coming on with about One Thousand Cavalry and 600 Infantry, but soon found our information was false. Artillery made their appearence, took a position and oppened a heavy fire of round and Grape on the Artillery that was supporting the Bridge. A short time after, a Gun moved to their right and took post in a situation which raked us completely. They then oppened on the Bridge with Grape and round, and wounded Three of our Men.

---

* Villamuriel de Cerrato.

The Spaniards were taking their positions on the heights in the rear of Villa Muriel and appeared to us to be in great confusion, every one trying who could reach the Top first, but formed on the Hill as soon as the whole had got up. Our Division was supporting the bridge. The 9th: were on the left of the Bridge when we were ordered to leave it as the Mine was ready. It blew up very shortly after we had left it, and the principal Arch was completely destroyed. We joined the 9th with the Picket and extended along the Banks of [the] River to the left of the Bridge in light Infantry order. In the course of a Quarter of an hour, four Offrs: were carried off the Field wounded.

Two Companies of Ours had been detached to the right of the Bridge, of which we received no intelligence. We continued along the River till Two in the afternoon. The French, having crossed a Ford half a mile below the Village, turned our Right and obliged us to retreat to the Hills.

At Four the Spanish Light Infantry advanced to Skirmish with the French who had crossed the River (about two thousand in number), but the Spaniards would, I belive, have made a bad hand of it if English troops had not been at hand. As we were an Independent Battn: we seized a favourable opportunity, Gave the Spaniards Three Cheers, and rushed down the Hill. This had a capital effect; the Spaniards pushed forward and took some Prisoners. Others (of the French) attempted to cross the Ford near the Bridge but, being closely pressed, leaped into the River and never reached the opposite Banks.

We then took our posts for the night on the left of the village and, on mustering our force, found Eighty Three Offrs:, N. C. Offrs: & Privates Killed, wounded & Missing. No: 8 Compy:, one of the Detached Companies, was completely cut up. Only four Men have returned that belonged to it. The Offr: Whiteley* and men that were not killed were taken. Only four of us escaped untouched. Poor Ford was severely wounded in the thigh and Leg, and had balls through his Coat.

We had a good supper after our <u>Halting day</u> and retired to Cabezon next morning, where I left the Regt: and went to the Baggage Guard, Completely lame from a tumble I had running

---

* Lieutenant James Whitley, the Methodist.

down the Hill, and sprained my knee, which is quite well at present. We joined the Reg^t: yeasterday with the Baggage.

Since we left Burgos, I have had only one <u>halt</u>. This will be, I hope, the first quiet Day, though we are within range of cannon shot from Tordesillas, but the French are I hope too Civil to disturb us in that manner.

I have given up all hopes of rest this winter. We hear that Madrid is left open and that Sir R^d: Hill is on the way to join us. Salamanca also is evacuated, so that affairs seem to have completely changed. Our loss has been very great in this retreat but we now and then looked back on the French and growled at them, which checked them.

All the Bridges over the Douro & Pisuerga Rivers are blown up. I think the Marques will trounce them soundly for this shortly, though we hear they will have Sixty Thousand men in the course of a few days when their reinforcements come up. We lost half of our Batt^n: on the 25th:, having only 168 rank and file in the Field.

I hear from D. Hardy that he has lost all his Clothes in the retreat. I have been fortunate in loosing nothing, though my old Animal's back is in a horrid state.

We are obliged to send two leagues for forage and have no wood, though the weather is far from being hot. I continue in as good health as ever. Cold or Wet seem to have no effect on me, except my hair which are turning grey, so that if we continue long at this work you may expect to see a grey headed Subaltern one of these days.

We have a great number of Sales* to day of the Dead and missing Off^rs: We are much reduced at present, not having an Off^r per Comp^y. I have, or am to have, the charge and payment of the remainder of N^o: 8, which will not be very troublesome at present; Two files only.

I expect news of the Family every day. Remember me affectionately &^c:

P. S. I drank no cold Water on the 25th: I had wine and Brandy given me, as much as I chose. (Mem Dr Sister)

---

* i.e. auctions of the chattels of dead officers. 'It was usual to sell their effects,' explained Bell, 'and remit the amount of sale to the agents at home. In this way, most of us got our supply of clothing' (Bell 31).

It is worth including Hale's account of the defence of the bridge near Villa Murial as a counterpoint: 'Our regiment was ordered to defend this bridge and soon after dark at night, a party of engineers was set to work, boring the bridge, in order to blow it up. We remained there very quiet till about nine o'clock on the following morning, the 25th of October, 1812, when we discovered a division of the enemy advancing at a very short distance from us, in consequence of which, about two hundred of our regiment were placed very convenient to the bridge, and the remaining part of the regiment was extended along the river.

The enemy seeing so small a party left to defend the bridge, they made a grand push for that place; but fortunately, before they could make their object, the bridge blew up, which put a stop to their pursuit, so then they extended themselves along the river, in about the same direction that we were, by which a sharp skirmish immediately took place, and continued about four hours. One company of our regiment was very convenient to a grist-mill that was on this river, and while they were busily skirmishing with the infantry that was on the opposite side of the river, a troop of the French cavalry rushed out from behind the mill, quite unawares to us, and swept away the whole company as prisoners of war before we could give them any assistance. The remaining part of our brigade was formed along the river on our right, which continued skirmishing in about the same manner; but at length, having kept up a continual fire for nearly four hours, it was thought necessary for us to fall back a little, and place a brigade of Spaniards in our places for a while, in order for us to have a little rest ... We had not been sitting more than half an hour when we beheld the enemy fording the river, and the Spaniards retreating in an unsoldier-like manner; in consequence of which our brigade was again ordered to stand to our arms and give them a charge, which we immediately did with great vigour and in a few minutes we captured about four hundred prisoners.'[5]

D^r: Ju –   Heights of St Christobal Nov^r: 15th:1812.

Since my last we have taken our old Position on these Heights, about a league in front of Salamanca. Genl: Hill is on the left Bank of the River near Alba de Tormes. We have been at work since our arrival here fortifying this Position, which I am inclined to belive Master Soult will not be inclined to Force. If reports prove true, we shall stay here about one Month or five weeks, and then push towards the Ebro.

Tis said that his Lordship is quite pleased with his retreat from Burgos as it has drawn all the Enemy's forces to this Quarter and left all the South clear. During the retreat most of our Off{rs}: suffered losses. Their Animals were Stolen or lost on leaving Tordesillas. I lost my Old Horse through the carelessness of my Servants. In consequence of his having a horrid back, I bought an Animal of Whitley's and the old gentleman travelled at ease tied to my Baggage Horse. When passing some narrow place it dissapeared and I have heard nothing of him since. The loss is not great as it cost me Thirty Dollars in June last and it had worked very hard since. The Animal I bought cost me Fifty four, which I mean to pay with my Walcheren Prize money.*

Our Position is not very pleasant. We have no good water within two Miles. We are obliged to use water from a large Pool which serves almost for meat and drink, and our Wood is brought from Villages where parties are sent to pull down houses, and of that we are obliged to be sparing. Forage for our Animals is not to be had within Two leagues, so that it has very little to recommend it, the Strength excepted which His Lordship says is equal to Twenty Thousand men.

Every article is sold at an exhorbitant price, so that I shall not grumble when we are moved from this. We have been reinforced since our arrival here by both Off{rs}: and Men. The former, having lived in houses for a long time, are too delicate to come to camp, and therefore will not leave Salamanca till we move from this. J'ai payé une Compagnie depuis l'affaire de Villa Muriel étant un des plus (?). Je fus appointé à commandement de N° 8 – depuis cela quelques uns de nos Messrs: qui ont joint ont demandé le commandement étant plus anciens que moi, mais ont été refusés le Col{ls}: croyant que ce ne seroit pas juste que j'ai crois pris le

---

* The British occupation of Walcheren had yielded some loot. Plundering was supposed to be left to official prize agents who distributed the proceeds across the army. Surgeon William Dent of the 9th Foot recorded his share as £12 (Dent, 31).

Commandement dans le temps ou ils y avoit du danger dy perdre beaucoup & que le moment que nous sortions de ce danger j'en perdrois le payments.*

We have a new Division Gen¹: & Brigade Gen¹: just come out from England and that anoy us greatly.† They wish to parade us continually. We have not one single day we can call our own. Immediately after a March, instead of rest we have a Parade. They are to be removed to the 6ᵗʰ: Division as soon as Genˡˢ: Leith & Hay arrive, so that we shall be comfortable again in a Short time.

Ituero Novʳ 25ᵗʰ: 1812.‡ I had proceeded thus far when the word 'Stand to Your Arms!' passed through the Camp, and in a moment the Tents were Struck. We encamped that night near the Zamora Gate, Salamanca, and on the 16ᵗʰ: passed the Tormes about Daylight and halted about 500 Yards from Salamanca. We expected every moment to be ordered to take our old position of the Arapiles§ but about Two in the afternoon we moved on the Road to Ciudad Rodrigo. The weather had been Cloudy all day and we were deluged with torrents of Rain. On our March we had to cross a rivulet near Traguas and there the Marques took his position. To see the Troops pass under heavy Rain, he appeared rather pale.

On the 17ᵗʰ: we continued our retreat without any thing extraordinary happening.

On the 18ᵗʰ: Our Baggage was Ordered to start two hours before the Troops. We had not moved far before the Enemy's Vedettes¶ made their appearance and we expected to have something to do. We moved off slowly (fast it was impossible) over ploughed ground, the Cavalry covering our retreat. About Four we halted near Salmonita where some Skirmishing took place between the

---

* The original text is almost impossible to translate but it runs something like 'I am being paid for a company, since the Villa Muriel business was one of the most (deadly?). I was appointed to the command of No. 8. Since then, several of the gentlemen who have joined, and are older than me, have requested this command but have been turned down by the Colonel, [and] believe it is not fair, that I would have taken command in time, or they were in danger of losing much, and that the moment we left this danger behind, I would lose my pay.'

† Major-General John Oswald (1771–1840) was appointed to command the 5th Division in Leith's absence.

‡ Presumably he means 15 November.

§ The site of the battle outside Salamanca the previous July.

¶ Mounted sentries or scouts.

Light Division and the Enemy. Sir Ed^d: Paget* was taken by the French that day, a circumstance of which they will, no doubt, boast greatly, he being Second in Command of the Army. We did not see our Baggage from that time till our arrival at Rodrigo, and were obliged to shift with our Boat Cloaks on the Damp Ground with nothing to Eat & no drink.

On the 19th: and 20th: we were quiet, but had to retreat through horrible roads. Baggage Animals were strewed on it by half Dozens. Even Greyhounds† could not stand it. Our loss, I am afraid, has been very great from the state of the roads and weather. I assure you, tis not at all agreable to sleep in the open Air in the month of November. I have not suffered from it, except a slight Cold which annoyed me for a couple of Days after my arrival in Quarters and which has left me entirely.

I hope we shall take our winter Quarters in Portugal where two or three months rest would be very acceptable. I have drawn on my Father for £10 in favour of Greenwood & Cox – Bill dated 5th: Nov^r: I had the good luck to find my old horse on the retreat from Salamanca. If my worthy Cousin W.L.M. has not left Guernsey before this reaches you, have the kindness to send me a few Strong Shirts, which will be very acceptable for mine are nearly worn out.

I had the satisfaction of receiving my Father's Letter dated Oct^r: 6th: two days ago. I am happy to find all the Family are in good health. I hope my niece, Miss Adela Blackley DeLisle, continues to keep her good health. I long greatly to see her Ladyship as well as Master Fardinand.

You will see by the Army List I am getting up. Col^l: Cameron a remoudi, qui quns des Oiseaux qui etount a ne rien faire en Angletere,‡ and rather than come out again some resign and some sell out, so that I expect, by the time the Business is over, I shall be left 18th: or 19th: Lieut^t: – a long list to work up.

A Detachment from the 2nd: Batt^n: is on its way to join us with 5 Off^rs: I am about effective in this Batt^n: at present. Tell Abr^m:,

---

* Lieutenant-General Sir Edward Paget (1775–1849).

† Since greyhounds are not notably hardier than many other dogs, Le Mesurier may mean Foreign Office messengers who carried silver greyhound badges.

‡ Again the original text is almost untranslatable, but the gist seems to be 'Colonel Cameron reminded me that some of the birds which return home find nothing to do in England.'

Greenwood and Cox have my Power of Attorney for the Walcheren Prize Money.

Our Brigadeir Gen[l]: has returned thanks to S. Dobree for his exertions in supplying us during the retreat and says he will report it to the Com[y]: Gen[l]:

I have not seen D. Hardy lately, his Division being in the rear. Tis reported Salamanca was given up to the French to plunder for Three days, and a Contribution raised on the unfortunate Inhabitants of 80,000 Dollars.

His Lordship says he will take the Field next spring with 70,000 British, and make the Gents pay severely for the loss we have suffered lately.

Tell Abram to get a couple Pairs of lacing Boots from his Shoemaker and send them as soon as possible to the care of Carver – Belem. Let them be very Strong. Rem[r]: me affectionately &[c]:, &[c]:

Wellington's losses on the retreat were due to the same mixture of circumstances which had beset Moore. 'It revived many of the recollections of the dreadful race to Corunna,' wrote Gomm. 'In some respects the hardships were greater for on that occasion the troops were generally under cover, such as it was, during the night; but here the only resting-place, after a day spent as I have just described, was a bleak, swampy plain.'[6]

As with Moore's retreat, indiscipline was the root of the problem. 'The Duke made a great fuss about all this insubordination,' complained Bell, 'but it is to be remembered that the line of march from Salamanca was through a flooded and flat clay country, that the troops, ankle-deep in mire, mid-leg in water, had lost their shoes, and with strained sinews had heavily made their way upon two rations only in five days, feeding on acorns, when Wellington supposed that the commissaries were supplying the army with their usual rations.'[7]

Fortunately the French did not hound Wellington as intently as they had hounded Moore, and the allied army reached Ciudad Rodrigo on the 19th without being closely pressed. 'His retreat has been masterly,' wrote Gomm. 'He has withdrawn the army upwards, I believe, of 200 miles, the greater part of the time before a superior force, which has never once found him in a situation to attempt anything serious, except upon Carrion, where they failed.'[8]

Napoleon's troops did not follow Wellington into Portugal and so the allies went into winter quarters, the 1/9th at Lamego. Le Mesurier was quartered 2–3 miles south at the village of Mós.

D[r]: F.   Mos. Dec[r]: 29th: 1812

I had the pleasure of receiving yours of the 4th: ins[t]: Christmass Eve, whilst drinking mulled Wine, for though we are in the Country where the real Port is made, tis but seldom we can get any that is good. We have passed our Holidays comfortably enough, considering the place we are in. S. Dobree Dined with us the day before yeasterday and was greatly pleased when I informed him of his Brother's promotion, for he had received no Letters from Guernsey since he joined the Division.

I am still keeping up the Holidays. I am engaged for this day and tomorrow to Dine out. His Lordship has issued us pay with which we have been able to keep up our spirits. I am sorry to see Guineas brought to this Country to pay the Troops, which I understand Govern[t]: have purchased at a very high rate.

We have papers to the 4th: Dec[r]: which have greatly increased our hopes of leaving this Country shortly, for it depends entirely on the Russians and, to all appearences, their affairs are going on at present so prosperously that the French will, we hope, shortly be obliged to leave this Country.[*]

Some time ago the Off[rs]: were called together to hear a Circular Letter from Lord Wellington to Gen[l]: Off[rs]: of Divisions, to be by them communicated to the Off[rs]: of the several Reg[ts]: under their command, the substance of which was to impress on the mind of Off[rs]: the exertions they ought to make on a Retreat to keep their Men in Order, and stating that in the Retreat from Burgos some Reg[ts]: were in the utmost state of insubordination, that Off[rs]: lost all command over their Men, in consequence of which a great number were taken by the Enemy, straggling, and recommended the greatest attention to Discipline & regularity during our Stay in Winter Quarters. The Brigadier, in transmitting the Letter to

---

[*] Le Mesurier's appreciation that British prospects relied on Napoleon's defeat in Russia is noteworthy. Many Peninsular War memoirs tend to suggest Britain beat Napoleon virtually single-handed.

Col^l: Crawford, said that he would leave it to himself to make the necessary remarks on the Letter, though he was convinced it did not at all apply to the 9th: We only lost one Man during the retreat straggling, and that Villain had leave from an Off^r: to fall out and put another pair of Shoes on.

Last Sunday, after Divine Service, Genl: Hay looked at the Reg^t: After going up and down the Line, he ordered the Off^{rs}: to the front. He told us he was very happy to see us all and that we looked like ourselves. The men appear healthy which shows that proper attention had been paid to them. This was intended as a compliment to the Off^{rs}: for we are a favourite Regim^t: of his, but the Person who enjoyed it most was our good Commandant, who was pleased before the Genl:, rubbing his hands and assenting to all the Genl: said.

Genl: Hay told Col^l: Crawfurd that Genl: Oswald's report of our Conduct at Villa Muriel had been sent in too late for any of His Lordship's observation in the Dispatch. Seven Men that had been severely wounded at the Hospital Station which was on the Top of a Hill in rear of the Village, and were left there by the Waggon train,* are returned missing instead of wounded and missing, but it would not have looked well in a dispatch to have said that our wounded were left on the Field.

I have receiv'd a Letter from D. Hardy dated Cea.† He was in good health and had plenty of work on hand. He is Quartered in a much finer Country than this and expects to go hunting the moment his accounts are made up.

The views about this Country are very fine but the Country is so hilly that I cannot go ten yards from my Door on a strait road. I have tried Shooting, but I am rather out of practise. I have had some fine Shots at woodcocks and Partridges but have not killed one. The only Bird that I have murdered was an unfortunate Thrush. The country around here is very promising for Sportsmen, but we have found but little game, most probably from want of Dogs.

We have many Freinds in the neighbourhood. They supply

---

* The Royal Waggon Train was the army's own dedicated transport corps, dwarfed in size by the number of carts and muleteers privately hired by the army during the Peninsular War.

† When Le Mesurier writes 'dated' he often means 'written from'.

us with fruit. I have now my Room ornamented with Grapes, Oranges, and Aples. At Christmass we had a Lamb given us. In the Village where the Reg^t: is Quartered they are very partial to us, but when we have to go for forage (the most dissagreable duty of a Sub) we do not escape without abuse. It certainly is very hard on the Inhabitants to have all their Forage taken away from them, but our Animals must be fed. When we advanced in Spain in June the people were satisfied at our cutting their Corn, and now these Gentry grumble at our taking their Straw.

My Stud, tho numerous, are certainly not of the best quality. I mean to sell two old Animals who were knocked up in the retreat & purchasse a good Mule.

W. L. Mesurier's Reg^t: is gone home as well as several other Reg^{ts}: The Men are left behind and formed into provisional Batt^{ns}: They are four in number and each consists of Men belonging to two Reg^{ts}: formed in Eight divisions or Companies, four from each Reg^t: and Off^{rs}: in proportion.

We are in expectation of seeing Col^l: Cameron every day. He left Lisbon a long time ago. I have no more the payment of a Company. Some of our Sick Off^{rs}:, having joined, have deprived me of the emolument.

As I think it probable that we shall have peace ere long, I intend, should I be placed on half-pay, to offer myself in Matrimony to any Lady with a decent fortune and retire to live quietly in some little cottage. My Sisters may be able to give me advice on the subject.

I am very happy to hear that Ferdinand has recovered the amount of his Cargo. I hope fortune will bestow her favor a little more freely for the future on them. Please do remember me most affectionately, do, &^{c}:, &^{c}:

Despite persistent disease, Wellington's army enjoyed their winter quarters. 'Every sort of innocent amusement, at least generally innocent, was had recourse to, both by officers and men,' reported Surtees, 'not only to pass the time of inactivity with pleasure but to keep up that readiness for action always so necessary in a state of warfare. We accordingly had races, balls, plays and every other description of pastime our situation admitted of.'[9] Hunting was popular and General Rowland Hill had a pack of hounds shipped over from England. Theatre also thrived: 'We had amongst so many regiments capital actors, scene-painters and really a first-rate company,' explained Bell. 'The delicate-looking, pale-faced, slim ensigns distinguished themselves in petticoats, and right well they played their parts. All we wanted was an audience!'[10]

D[r]: M.   Mos Jan[y]: 11th: 1813

I have to acknowledge the receit of two Letters, one from Ferdinand of the 22[d]: Oct[r]: and the other from Sister Anne, 19th: Dec[r]: Both gave me the greatest pleasure. It is great satisfaction to me to know that wherever I go the kind wishes of all the Family attend me. I am indebted to all the Family more than ever will be in my power to repay. Their great attention to all the little comforts I wanted here have enabled me to go through the last campaign with as much comfort as my situation could admit of.

From the favourable appearence of affairs in the North, I am inclined to think that our work this year will be triffling in comparison with last. If I can judge by our Reg[t]:, the sickness in the Army must be great. We have accounts of many Deaths in the Reg[t]: Our strenth is not above 400, and last year we had nearly double the number.

At present we think of nothing but amusements. Last week I had an invitation to sup with one of the Chief people in the Neighbourhood and I assure you I never saw any thing equal to it; every delicacy that could be procured made its appearence. As the Supper was on the Table at Eight (and we Dine past five), I was a Spectator, and the Ladies did ample justice to it. I have seen people with good appetites but I never saw any Persons eat so Voraciously. After Supper was removed, and they had washed it down with plenty of wine, we proposed a Dance. As the Band of the Reg[t]: was not to be had, we were obliged to be contented with a Fife & Drum, and kept it up till Three o'Clock in the morning. A Stout Damsell, who had made rather free with the juice of the Grape, made several attempts at a Country Dance, to our great amusement.

The Reg[t]: in General are very popular hereabout. The Inhabitants are highly satisfied with the conduct of the Soldiers. Col[l]: Cameron, who joined us the last day of the year, seems equally pleased with us. We have no parades except for Divine Service once a forthnight, and the only disagreable Duty we have is taking the Forage from the Inhabitants which, however, is unavoidable.

It gives me pleasure to hear Ferdinand is going to settle in London. It will be pleasant for Elizabeth to be so near home and in a place where they will not be subject to heavy contributions except, now and then, a freind calling in. I intend taking up my Quarters with them whenever I go to London. I should have no objection if my good Ferdinand's prayer was granted for a Short time. I should give him a hearty embrace for his good wishes for me. Should we be recalled from this Country, there is no doubt but we shall have a trip to the East Indias. I should dislike going there as a Sub, for promotion is very slow and I might be an old grey headed Sub all my life.

C. Percival has received Letters from his Brother from Martinique. He says they touched at Barbadoes on their way and the first thing he heard was the Dead March in Saul.[*] He seems in good spirits and likes Martinique well.[†]

I have had a Step lately. When Col^l: Cameron went to England he was at the Depot, where he found a Mr. D,[‡] a Gentleman who obtained leave after the taking of Badajoz to go to England to get maried, on Condition that he shoud return at the expiration of Three months. He pledged his word of honour for returning, instead of which he went to the Depot and filled the situation of Adj^t: and Quarter Master. When Col^l: Cameron found him, he was so displeased with him that he gave him choice of Resigning or coming to this Country to stand a Court Martial, and he very wisely preferred the former, and by that got a Step and rid of a bad subject at the same time.[§]

I am very glad to find that Shirts are coming out for me, for mine

---

[*] The West Indies had a reputation for high mortality among soldiers.

[†] Martinique was seized by the British in 1794, handed back to the French under the Treaty of Amiens in 1802, recaptured by the British in 1809, and finally handed back to the French for good in 1815. It remains a French colony today.

[‡] Quartermaster David Durs.

[§] Le Mesurier's references to officers being persuaded to resign, rather than suffer a court martial, are significant. As Bell wrote, 'Commanding officers had almost unlimited power in those days to dismiss officers without court martial for grave offences ... It saved a great deal of trouble and inconvenience, and kept young fellows and old ones *in terrorem*' (Bell, 44).

are not worth much; they are only fit for Tinder. My Set out at present is not in very good order, however, I hope ere long to refit in England.

I am excessively sorry to find by Anne's letter that, instead of raising in the estimation of the Ladies, we have fallen so much. This unfortunate war in the Peninsula has, I suppose, been the cause of this great falling off, for instead of a Blooming Fresh countenance that Off[rs]: have on leaving the Home Station for service, they return with a Tanny, Emaciated face,[*] some wanting legs, others Arms & Eyes, &[c]:, &[c]:, which, I suppose, is the cause of their dislike to Soldiers. If, at some future time, our Duty consisted only of Field Days in Guernsey for their amusement, perhaps we may become favourites again.

The Parson of the Division yesterday told us that Bony had published his Twenty ninth Bulletin from Paris, in which he admits the loss of his Army. I am in hopes that the first part of the Parson's report is not true, for I should be sorry to see Bony safe in his Capital.[†]

I received a Letter from D. Hardy a few days ago. He is in good health and spirits. I have not seen S. Dobree lately. He lives in an out of the way place beyond Lamego and, as my Poney has been very Ill, I have not gone that way. I had an invitation to dine with him but I do not like to leave my Fireside for a very cold country house. I intend going to him one of these days.

W. L. Mesurier will meet his Reg[t]:, or at least the few that are sent home about Lisbon, for they have left the Army to embark for England. L[d]: W[n]: has not returned from Cadiz.[‡] He went escorted by one of his Servants only.

A Corporal of ours that was taken at the Bridge of Muriel, having been wounded, has joined us. He made his escape from Palencia. He says that, after being there three or four days, the French retired in consequence of a Spanish force advancing, and left all their Sick & wounded behind. The Spaniards immediately

---

[*] The ideal complexion for a gentleman was white but ruddy-cheeked. Tans were for farm labourers.

[†] In his 29th Bulletin of the Grande Armée, Napoleon reported the appalling losses he had suffered in Russia. He was not in Paris at the time, but his bulletin was reported in Parisian newspapers. This is probably the root of Le Mesurier's confusion.

[‡] In early December Wellington headed to Cadiz to 'see how far I can venture to go, in putting the Spanish army in a state to do something' (Wellington, VI, 207).

collected as many Mules & Horses as could be found and sent the English away. We have heard nothing of Whitley who was missing; tis generally supposed he is Dead of his wounds.

Please to tell Abr^m: to direct to the care of L^t: Carver any parcel he sends, for that Gent is promoted & he might think it a mark of disrespect to direct Ens^g: as he is a very punctilious, though very useful man in his way.

On the 1st: Jan^y: Col^l: Crawfurd entertained Genl: Hay and his Staff and Col^l: Cameron. After taking a fair allowance, the Genl: retired to Bed, but left his rest in a Short time. On his Son proposing a bumper* to the 9th: he found the company perched on their chairs, preparatory to giving Three times Three. He (the G^l:) took his post under Co^l: Crawfurd and drank his Bumper. on which the Col^l: made him a long speech, beggin he would not go on leave again. He was shivering for the time the speech lasted with cold, his hands joined and making solemn promises not to leave us again. I understand it would have been an excellent subject for a Painter.

Tomorrow we are to have a grand review for the amusement of the Ladies of Lamego. You see, My D^r: M^r:, by the journal I have given you, that the new year has begun well with me. I hope you have had a happy begining also. If the Family enjoy as much happenings as I wish them, they will not be the most miserable in the world. If Fortune favours them a little more than she has hither to done, so much the better, however, as it is, May God grant you health and happiness is the sincere wish of [letter ends abruptly here].

D^r: A^m: Mos Jan^y: 28th: 1813

I had the pleasure of receiving your Letters of various dates, brought by W and H. Le Mesurier three days ago at the same time. I felt hurt at you not receiving any of mine, which you might attribute to neglect. Did I not assure you that I have written often? I wrote from Ituero & since our arrival have written every forthnight. However, long ere this, you may have received my Letters which will convince you fully. Julia hints in her Letter Nov^r: 6th: that it would be better if I sent my Letters via Corrunna. The choice is not with us; our Letters are given in to the Adj^t: General's

---

* A glass filled to the brim, raised in toast.

Office of the Division, by him sent to the Head Quarters where the Mail is made up and sent to Lisbon.

If reports are to be belived our stay here will not be much longer. I am pretty well off, Linnen excepted. My Shirts are fit for Tinder only. I have bought Soldiers Shirts from our Quarter Master which will prevent my going without entirely. I would have written for some, long ago, but mine appeared so good that I expected they would last another Campaign when, to my astonishment, I found them all rotten.

I was obliged on the retreat from Burgos to purchase an old Animal to bring my Baggage here. I was well aware that I had paid through the nose for it, as I could make no further use of it the next Campaign. I was on the alert and found a Mule for Sale. I went to the Man and offered to change, on my paying a difference, and, on my giving him 35 Dollars, the Bargain was Struck. He had seen the Horse and said it would require much Corn to bring him about.

The day after the Bargain, the Gentleman went to Lamego and on his return I happened to meet him when he informed me that, on the road, in the first half League, the Horse had fallen with him Six or Seven times. He offered to annul the Bargain which I of course refused as the Gentleman is a complete Jockey.* The Mule has turned out very well and will most probably be the last Animal I shall purchass in this Country. I have been obliged to draw on my Father £10, as they do not issue sufficient pay to refit and live. We are now above four Months and a half in Arrears, besides allowances.

We pass our time agreeably together here. Every body contributes as much as lies in his power to the comfort of the others. We have Balls and sometime Dinners. I should have amused myself shooting if I had a Gun, as their is abundance of Game in this part of the Country. When I am not on Duty I generally take a long walk or ride.

There is a Typhus fever among the other Reg^ts: of the Division which has carried off a great number of Men. The Parson of the Division, after reading the Funeral Service, was taken home and has been confined to his Bed since, with but faint hopes of his recovery. We have lost Three or four men in our Hospital since our arrival, but almost every post brings an account of the departure of Three

---

* Jockey can mean horse dealer and by extrapolation a cheat.

or four. Two months ago the strenth of the Batt[r]: in the Country was 827 – at present 773, and I belive we have not suffered more than other Reg[ts]:

On the 25th: of October we had only one Capt[n]: in the Field. Percival was with the Baggage Guard. Dallas I have not seen since the 21st: Octo[r]: when he went sick in the rear. He writes word that that I may expect him shortly. I suppose he will come with a Detachment from the 2[d]: Batt[n]:, among whom is Seaward & Robertson. If my calculations are correct, we shall see them next week. You will perceive by the Army list I am creeping up; I am now 22[d] Lieu[r]: so that, should I escape next Campaign, I may probably look out for a Company in the course of Four or Five years more.

Curzon has purchassed his company in the 69th: and is here on a visit, quite recovered from his wounds.[*] He most probably will exchange back to the Reg[t]: Dumaresq will get his Company shortly and be put on the Quart[r]: Master Gen[l]: Staff, should he recover sufficiently from his wounds. From all accounts it will be a long time first. Il etoit au Grand Bal a Lisbone qu'and le grand L[d]: etoit la & a fait une Caricature du principal R[t]: qui est un homme <u>Gros & Gras</u> par le desir du suidit L[d]:[†]

If we are to give Credit to the french papers, we are likely to have more work to do than was expected, as they say a reinforcement of Twenty Thous[d]: Men are on their way to this Country. Six Eighteen pounders are moving towards Spain, which looks as if there were walls to demolish. It is expected that the ensuing Campaign will close our opperations in this part of the world. I shoud have no objection, after a few months rest in Guernsey, to go to America by way of novelty.[‡] Portugal has very few charms for us at present. A Soldier's life at this season is not certainly a very busy one but we make up for it in the Summer. Even at this time I am 3 or 4 days of the Week on some duty or other.

By the time I return to Guernsey I shall be surrounded by a

---

[*] The Hon. William Curzon, son of Lord Scarsdale, went on to be a staff officer. He was killed at Waterloo.

[†] 'There was a grand ball in Lisbon, attended by the grand Lord [Wellington] and at which was done a caricature of the principal R[egent?], who is a big, fat man, by the wish of the said Lord.'

[‡] Britain had been at war with the United States since June 1812, so Le Mesurier may have been considering exchanging into a regiment stationed in Canada.

swarm of little relations unknown to me, my cousin Hounson too!!! Tis well, for we require a number of recruits for our Army, to replace the brave fellows who have fallen this Campaign. Tis natural for Man to return kindness when he meets with it. You may therefore suppose that I am not indiferent to my nephew, Master Ferdinand's. The little Anecdotes related by my D^r: Sisters have (if it was possible) strenthened my affection for him, for which reason I sincerely hope he may never be a Soldier but chuse some other profession where he may acquire a decent fortune without exposing himself to the hardships inseperable from a Soldier's life.

The Portuguese are recruiting at present. It might be called Conscription with more propriety, as all young men of a certain height, who are not married, are obliged to serve.

I should have been very happy could I have joined in the round games at my Uncles during the Holidays. I have only had Cards twice in my hand since I have been in this Country.

Remember me affectionately to &^{c}:

That winter Wellington's troops recovered quickly. 'We got good provisions and very regular,' recorded Hale. 'Also, some other articles that were needful, in particular shoes and shirts; for at that time we were got very bare of both these articles; and in a few days after we were supplied with every thing that was necessary, we received the balance of six months' arrears of pay that were due to us ... So we remained in our cantonments very comfortable till May, and in the course of this time several regiments joined the army from England or from some foreign stations; and most regiments in the army were joined by detachments from the depots in England, and small parties also frequently joined from the different hospitals, so that our army was daily increasing.'[11]

It was decided, rather than bring the 2nd battalion, still on Gibraltar, back up to strength, detachments from it should be used to fill the gaps in the 1st battalion wrought by the retreat from Burgos. Four hundred men were transferred to the 1/9th. The rest of the 2/9th returned home to England where they remained until the remnants of the battalion were disbanded on Christmas Eve 1815.

9

Vitoria and San Sebastian

Encouraged by the news that Napoleon had retreated from Russia with crippling losses, Wellington prepared for yet another summer campaign in Spain. The French empire seemed fatally wounded, so the British, Portuguese and Spanish concentrated resources for one great advance to force the French back to the Pyrenees.

D^r: Anne   Mos March 5th: 1813

I have not had the pleasure of receiving any Letters from my Dear Freinds at home since Abr^{m's}: postscript dated Jan^y: ye 2^d:, a longer period than I ever was without news from you, which, however, I am fully convinced is not your fault. This most probably will be the last Letter you will receive from me dated from Mos, as we expect to be on the move in a short time, though the Army will not take the Field in so effective a state as last year. Our Reg^t: is one of the most effective; from a good reinforcement from the 2^d: Battⁿ: we can bring 500 in the Field. The fine weather seems to have had the desired effect on the health of the Soldiers, as the sickness is abating considerably.

Orders have been given out for the issue of Tents for the Men, which Tents are to be carried on Mules formerly appropriated for the carriage of Camp Kettles but now done away with, a Thin camp Kettle substituted, which the men are to carry and which I think will be highly beneficial to the health of the Men. Formerly they were exposed to the Broiling heat of the sun by

Day and to heavy dews by night, which certainly caused great sickness.[*]

Some of the other Divisions have already moved. I hope we may be left till the latter end of this month in our Quarters to get my Animals in working Order, for they have suffered considerably from last Campaign and are now under the Doctor's hand and getting much better.

A Capt[n]: of the 2[d]: Batt[n]: was married a short time before the Detachment sailed for this Country. Some of the Off[rs]: called on him as he was dressing for the wedding. To shew his Zeal for the Service (though he was rather later than the appointed hour), he stopped and wrote to our worthy Col[l]: saying that, though he was on the point of mariage, his Zeal for the Service was not in the least abated and begged he would order him to join the 1st: Batt[n]: forthwith. This has caused much laughter in the Reg[t]: as other motives are ascribed than those he mentioned, and [he] found out too late that he had been completely taken in by the Pay master of the 2[d]: Batt[n]:, whose Daughter he married – a mighty fine prospect of Domestick happiness.

A grand Fair is held at Lamego at present which lasts from the 1st: to the 10th: of March, when a great quantity of Silver articles are brought. As I am satisfied with a Steel fork and Iron spoon, I very seldom honor the place with my presence.

I saw S. Dobree a few days ago, as Stout as ever. We seldom visit each other, though on the best terms, for if an Off[r]: is seen often in the Company of a Commissary he is suspected of having some interested motive in keeping him Company. When on the March, and quartered a little nearer one another, we shall visit oftener for he has always been remarkably attentive to me, especially on the retreat when he carried a Tent for me all the way from Burgos to this place.

We were review'd by Gen[l]: Hay Three days ago when he took an opportunity of thanking the Off[rs]: who brought up the Detachment from Gib[r]: Out of Two hundred men, Two only were left sick on

---

[*] Wellington was careful that the new tents should not draw the attention of the enemy. 'Strict orders were given always to encamp out of sight of the enemy, if practicable, that they might not be able to calculate our numbers,' explained Surtees. 'How very different from the ancient mode of encamping, each of which being more like a town laid out with regular streets, &c' (Surtees, 189).

the road between Lisbon and this place. Tis rather remarkable that those Men are much leaner than those with the Reg^t: and do not look half so healthy.

We have given up our Balls, and our own parties have decreased considerably for a very powerful reason – that money ran rather short. Last year, at this time, we were Two Months in arrear. We are now five, or nearly, so that I expect by the end of this summer we shall be 8 or 9. If I escape this Campaign I may have some chance of seeing you again, for I do not conceive it possible to carry on this business two years longer. When Guineas are issued for paying the Troops & salt fish for rations, it shews a want of resources not very favourable to us, added to the immense loss of Men we have sustained.

I think, my Dear Anne, that you will have the mortification of seeing your Grey headed Brother a half-pay Lieut^t: if something very fortunate does not befall him. I have had no news of the Parcel you sent to Lisbon by the swift, or of the articles inclosed in the Box of D. Hardy, though they would be very welcome at present. Whilst I enjoy my health it signifies but little if I have a ragged or Whole Shirt on. Whilst I am decent outside, I care little about what is hid.

I hope you will write often for you cannot guess the pleasure I receive whenever a Letter is handed to me from Guernsey. There is a report of a Packet being taken by the Americans, which may be the cause of my not receiving Letters from you.

Remb^r: me &^{c}:, &^{c}:

D^r: Ju   Mos March 20th: 1813

I had the pleasure of receiving two Letters from home by the last Packet, one of the 1st:, the other of the 18th: Ult^o: A few days Previous I received the parcel containing Shirts, Nightcaps, &^{c}:, which was brought up from Lisbon by an Off^r: of the 38th: Reg^t:

The last Bill drawn by me, which my Father mentions in his letter of the 18th:, was drawn since that paid by C & B on the 14th: Dec^r:, in consequence of being obliged to change an old horse of mine. I have been very unfortunate in horse dealing for one of my present Stud has been Sick ever since we came into these Quarters and has cost me above Twenty Dollars in purchass^d: delicacies to bring him round, which, coupled with other necessary expences, has made me exceed more than I otherwise should have done. The letter I wrote after drawing the last Bill mentions my having done so and the date.

Dumaresq got his Comp^y: through L^d:Wgⁿ in consequence of his being wounded at Burgos where he behaved well in some of their Storming parties.* He is now on the Staff of this Division, but I understand he will get on the Qu^r: M^r: General Staff shortly as he has some Idea of Drawing, so that he is likely to get on rapidly.

A Captⁿ: of the 38th: Reg^t: commanded the Picquet on the Bridge at Muriel and honorable mention was made of his name by Col^l: Crawfurd in his report of the Business, as the Picquet was attached to our Reg^t: during the whole of the day.

On the 17th: Ins^t: we were awoke about 4 o'Clock in the morning by the Band who were parading the Streets playing <u>Patrick's Day in the Morning</u>. After going round the Town they took post under our windows and continued playing there for half an hour, though not one of our Mess is an Irishman. We knew that, as it was intended as a compliment, we should have to pay for being disturbed at that hour if we were not beforehand with them, therefore the moment Dallas saw the Master of the Band he told him that he deserved severe punishment for presuming to disturb the whole Village in compliment of a few of the greatest Blackg^{ds}: we have with us, but that in consequence of his former good behaviour he would overlook it for this time, which maneouvre saved us Two or Three Dollars.

I had the pleasure of taking charge of the Forage Party that Day and was on foot from 7 o'Clock in the morning till near Six at night. We were obliged to go Three leagues from this place for it. We shall not be able to get much more in this part of the Country. I assure you the People are very anxious to get rid of such good Company, who take every morsel of forage they can lay their hands on. We cannot persuade them that, though they have the trouble of Mowing and making the Hay, they have no right to keep it for their own use, in consequence of which they take every opportunity of insulting our nice feelings by the gross appelations of Theives,

---

* For Wellington to promote subalterns on merit was rare and usually only for leading a forlorn hope.

and calling us Serg^ts^: though fully aware of our Rank. We bear all this like Christians.

I suppose, ere this reaches you, Elizabeth will have gone to England with her Family. I assure you I feel unde great Obligations to my worthy little Freind Ferd^d^: for his hearty wishes on my Account. I do not see much prospect of their being realized at the present; no great chance of Peace whilst that Monster lives.

I Dined with Dobree last Sunday. We were Three only and well entertained. I must return my thanks to my Dear Sisters for the parcel, which, I assure you, was highly acceptable. The Angola* night caps will come in play during the Summer Campaign. I have now Three good Shirts fit to see Company in, and three fit for Campaigning, that is to say Soldiers shirts. The others are gone as Pensioners.

I shall now exclude Elizabeth & Ferdinand from the family Roster. A seperate Roster shall be opened for them. Remember me most affectionately to &^c^:, &^c^:

No talk at present of moving for some time.

D^r^: F.   Mos. April 2^d^: 1813

Since my last to Julia, I have received no letters from Guernsey, owing to the honesty of some Soldiers who robbed the mail the night before last between this place and Lamego, bringing letters and Papers to the 10th: Ult^o^:, which I assure you caused great dissapointment to all of us, for, besides the pleasure of hearing from our friends, the papers were a great source of amusement in this very stupid place. The Royals have the credit of having committed this Robery as they were quartered in the Neighbourhood and some of their men were absent. We may yet by some fortunate accident recover the Mail.

Our Division is greatly scattered at present. The Royals crossed the Douro yeasterday in consequence of the sickly State they were in. The 38th: are also the other side and likewise very sick. Our Gents are not only healthy but getting stout, so that we have no chance of being removed, though Wood and forage are getting very

---

* A corruption of 'Angora'.

scarse. We are now obliged to send our Animals out for two days; go out one, and return the next with Rye straw.

The general oppinion is that we shall not Stir for a month or Six weeks to come, as we may expect a forthnight's Rain about this time, and the Roads will hardly be passable for a few Weeks after. We have had hopes at times that, if we moved at all, it would be for the purpose of Embarking for England, as the Report of a Peace having been signed were pretty Strong in this part of the world about ten days ago, which, I assure you, would have been very agreable to the greatest part of the Off[rs]: at present in the Peninsula, who, tho they are able and willing to carry on the War, would have no objection to a little rest among their freinds.

I understand that an Order has been issued from Head Quarters saying that, as the End has been gained for which British Off[rs]: were allowed to enter the Portuguese Service, none will be allowed to go in that service for the future, and any Off[r]: at present in that service not particularly wanted is to join his Reg[t]: This is in consequence of the high State of Discipline they have been reported to be in by General Off[rs]: Commanding Divisions.

We had a Field Day last Monday, the Caçadores[*] as French attacking a Bridge, and our light companies, supported by the Royals and 9th: British, 3[d]: & 15th: Portuguese, defending. I am happy to say we did not suffer quite so much as last time we had any thing to do, though, had it been in earnest, our Light Comp[ys]: would have been cruelly mauled by about 50 of their opponents, placed in ambush on their flank.

We shall be stronger in Off[rs]: this Year than we ever were before. Comme je suis mieux connu a present, j'ai le commandement d'une compagnie jusque ce que mon Capt[n]: qui est a Lisbonne arrive c'est un grand objet a cause des Rations d'Orge que je recois chaque jour 15[ll] au lieu de 5[ll].[†] I was a little astonished at the appointment as I thought the companies would have remained under their respective Officers till my Capt[n]: came up, but on the 25th: Percival

---

[*] Portuguese light infantry.

[†] 'As I am better known now, I have the command of a company until my Captain, who is in Lisbon, arrives. It is a big thing because of the rations of barley I get each day – fifteen pounds instead of five pounds.'

was ordered to take charge of Nº: 7 and I to take Nº: 6 till further orders.

I received a Letter from D. Hʸ: some days ago. He appears to have great hopes of getting his promotion shortly. He was at Cea in good health. He says he is trying to get his Clothes from Lisbon, so that I have some hopes of getting the articles that are in his Box when we come near one another. I have heard nothing of W. L. M. since his arrival in this Country.

My Animals are now fit for Duty. My Poney is very nearly recovered from his long illness and my Mule is getting Stout. I have borne many jokes on the subject of my Stud but, by perseverance, have them now very decent, with the exception [of] a little Sulphurous smell which they retain having been anointed for a certain complaint very prevalent in this country.

Notre C[olone]ˡ: nous fait l'honnneur de diner avec nous Dimanche la premiere fois qu'il a dine avec des C-ˡ comme nous. Il a donne Deux ou trios fois a Diner depuis son arrive, je ne crois pas qu'il y ait jamais eu une instance d'un si grand changement dans une personne en aussi peu de temps. Nous sommes en Paradis en comparaison du temps passé.*

Please do remember me to &ᶜ:

4 o'Clock. The mail has been recovered but I have no Letters or Papers up to the 8ᵗʰ: Ultº:

Dʳ: Mʳ: Mos April 16ᵗʰ: 1813

I have just returned from witnessing a most ridiculous procession at the Convent; the Internment of Christ which can compare to nothing, but raree Shows excepted.† A Centurion opened the Procession, followed by Cimon bearing the Cross, then a great number of the People, some with Dice, nails, hammers, ladders, &ᶜ:, all dressed in a most gaudy stile, the Body bourne on Four Monk's Shoulders.

---

* 'Our Colonel, we had the honour to dine with us Sunday, the first time we dined with the Colonel present. He has given two or three dinners since he arrived, but I don't believe he has ever done so when there has been such a great change of personnel in such a short time. We are in Paradise compared with previous such occasions.'
† 16 April was Good Friday.

The Monks have been very busy all this week and told us we might expect something very grand, in which I must own I have been dissapointed, perhaps owing to a little bad humour which I rose up with this morning and which has not entirely left me. The cause was this; Last Night, the Man who has charge of my Mule (publickly) was ordered to go and cut Barley and take the Mule with him, and about Nine o'Clock last night returned with the pleasing intelligence that, whilst employed in cutting forage, the Mule broke his halter and strayed away. I immediately dispatched a Party to look out. At Midnight they returned, without success. At Day light we started again and found the Gentleman in a Stable, after a walk of Three or four hours and paying the party who discovered the Animal 3 dollars, so that all together I have not passed a very pleasant day.

We were surprised a few days ago by the arrival of Two hundred more men from the 2^d^: Batt^n^: and 6 Off^rs^: If we have any more fighting, the chances are that Promotion will be more rapid than hitherto. We have about Seven hundred Men in Quarters and, by the time the others arrive, I think we shall muster near Nine hundred in the Field. The 2^d^: Batt^n^: are, by this time, on their way to England. On their arrival, the Depot will be broken up and the effective men sent out to this country.

I find that a Captn: of ours, who I mentioned in one of my last letters, whose Zeal for the Service induced him to apply to join this Reg^t^: when on the point of Mariage, has succeeded in tearing himself from the Dear Object of his affections by exchanging with another whose Zeal, on the contrary, bent his inclinations to go home. This is considered a very curious business, and where it will end, I know not, but from many circumstances I am inclined to belive it will go hard with the Gentleman who has been in the Habit of falling sick previous to a General Engagement.

We were dissapointed in our expectations of seeing our worthy Com^t^: for Dinner, in consequence of a rainy day. Since his arrival every thing has been carried on in a most pleasant way. Two Days ago we had a Field day, when he made us a long speech full of Compliments and expressing his approbation at the conduct of the Men and their appearence and Steadyness in the Field.

The Weather has been very favourable for the grass in this country and we begin to feel the effects of it on account of our Studs. The

People would not be sorry to see us start, for an Hundred Animals of different descriptions make great havock in a Meadow or a Field of Barley. This Country is so completely drained, and such miserable objects continually before our Eyes, that a change would be delightful. I should have no objection to a trip to N America for some time. Many of our Subs expect to get their companies shortly (all Seniors). If their hopes are realized, and that Peace follows, I shall still remain in the Reg.ᵗ: as I shall become effective on the Peace establishment.

Our Paper intelligence leads us to hope that the French are in a very awkward situation at present, and that the whole Continent will rise and scourge the Monster who has caused such Misery wherever he has been, notwithstanding he boasts of having an Army Sufficient to chastise the Russians for his Sufferings. I think he would not be averse to making peace and give up his Titles of King of Italy & Protector of the Confederation of the Rhine, &ᶜ:

As the address of Ferdinand and Elizabeth has not been made known to me, I must defer writing for some time.

I expect we shall move shortly to ease this part of the Country. Tis reported we shall advance by Miranda or Zamora when we do advance. We are very crowded here.

A Third application for change of Quarters has been made by Col.ˡ: Cameron, on account of the reinforcements being on its way to join, which I hope will prove successful as we are already so crowded that Three or four officers are put in one house, which is not very agreable. I am &ᶜ:

D.ʳ: Ab.ᵐ: Mos May 1ˢᵗ: 1813

On the Road from this place to Lamego yeasterday I had the pleasure of receiving my D.ʳ: Father's letter of the 9ᵗʰ: Ult.º: I must desire you not to be uneasy from Hardy's letters because I am sometimes a Month or more without writing.

Several Detachments are on the Road from Lisbon to join the Army, as also the 59ᵗʰ: Reg.ᵗ: Tis expected that as soon as they make their appearence we shall move, the 3.ᵈ: and 5ᵗʰ: Divisions on the Right Bank of the Douro by Mirandela, Miranda and Zamora. Our Sick leave us to Day for Viseu, about Thirty in Number. If the draft from the 2.ᵈ: Batt.ⁿ: join before we move, we shall start with 900 Rank and File.

I was a little surprised to hear of my Dear Mother's trip to England, though I think it will do her good and I hope aford her plenty of amusement. Should your wish, with respect to my return, be accomplished, I shall take a trip to London too, but our exertions must be great indeed if we succeed in driving those Vagabonds from Spain this Campaign. We must do something wonderful, else we shall not be thought of, and I am sure our Chief would not like to play a Second Fiddle at such an important Crisis. If we do not gain our object this year, I do not think we ever shall. Taking into consideration the Mighty deeds we have to perform, I shall not conceive myself very unfortunate if I lose a Wing or a Leg, though I shall not at all object to coming off with a scratch or a 'slightly wounded' as tis generally called.

Our Reg^r: has been inspected T[h]rice within the last forthnight by Gen^{ls}: Hay and Robinson* in Light Infantry Maneouvres, for which we are getting famous. The latter is just come out from England and expressed his astonishment at the rapidity and correctness with which we moved. We have learnt to move without waiting for the word of Command in certain Manoeuvres, which might prove of the greatest consequence in Action when the Commanding Off^r: cannot be heard. As you are only a <u>Private in the Militia</u>, your Capacity is not equal to understand those Maneouvres without seeing them put into execution & explained, therefore I shall reserve them till we meet.

I am sorry to hear of H. D.'s death. If a Man wishes to lead an unsettled life, let him enter the Army. He will not want variety and at the same time do some good, and gain credit for fighting for his Country. Who would not brave any Danger to have such Compliments paid him as Major Genl: Sir James Leith has, in one of the last Gazettes, for his Bravery at Badajoz and the ever memorable Action of Salamanca when he led the Fifth Division to Victory. This sounds so very beautiful that I am inclined to belive that, had I an opportunity I would not leave the Army, in hopes of having praises bestowed on me at some future time.

We begin to lay in a Stock of Tea and Sugar for the Campaign as we buy every thing much cheaper here than in Spain. The great comfort of a Soldier's life is not to be had now in Portugal

* Major-General Frederick Robinson (1763–1852).

(Tobacco), owing to the War with America, the Brazil Tobacco excepted, which is Villainous stuff to smoke. If you could find some good opportunity to send me some Sigars, I wish you would send me a few hundred. One of my Messmates, Dallas, is gone on Detachment and, as he is obliged to go to several Depot, I hope he may meet with some.

The Exchange is at present enormous between this and England, at the rate of 6/6^d a Dollar, so that I would sooner be in want than Draw. We are not very flush of Coin but if we can muster sufficient for a Stock we shall want little else. I have Strong Russia Duck Trowsers* which, though not very comfortable in cold weather, must do for this Summer's Campaign. I have had my Grey great Coat turned which has not improved its appeerence much as it is particularly coarse inside but must be worn out too.

Some of the Men whose period of service was nearly out have enlisted again for life for a Bounty of £16"16s, and as the wine is sold for 4½^d a Pint, you may suppose they have not kept very sober. We have had two accidents only by Drunkenness; an Arm and a Jaw broken, besides Black Eyes and blody noses without number. I am astonished the broken limbs have not been more numerous from the bad state the Streets are in here.

I am glad to find they begin to employ the Garrison Battalions[†] away from home for I think it is shameful to see People who are fit for Service, and who have no claims whatever, Skulking in those Reg^{ts}: That Parson you mention in your Postscript is one of that class, One of His Majesty's bad bargains. It will cause many to resign and make room for fit objects for promotion.

The allowance known to the Military under the name of Bat & Forage Money is discontinued in the Mediterenean and Reg^{ts}: on service only receive it. When you write to Newington, remember me affectionately to my good freinds there. You must not expect letters very regularly when we begin to move. I shall write as often as I can. May God grant you all health and happiness for many Years to come is the sincere prayer of &^{c}:

---

* White linen, lighter than canvas.
† The garrison battalions were formed in 1803 from the 'Battalions of Reserve'. The intention was to free up infantry battalions on garrison duty in England and the colonies so they could be used in the peninsula instead.

D^r: An.   Camp at Mirandela May 21st: 1813

This day a week [ago] we commenced our Campaign for this year and crossed the Douro below Lamego in boats. The Day was wet and it was near Six o'Clock before we could get under cover. Our Baggage was left on the Lamego side as well as our riding Animals, and on the 15th: we started without either for Villa Real through a most beautiful Country; for an immense tract nothing but Vineyardes can be seen, to the very tops of the Mountains. The Country Houses appear comfortable and decent, but to counterbalance this the Roads are most abominable and we had to ascend two very high hills before we were blessed with the sight of Villa Real, which is a very pretty Town and the largest in Trasos Montes. Our Baggage joined us here late at night, which I assure you was very agreeable for we were in a miserable plight (Crotté jusqu'aux Genoux*), and without meat or drink. We then proceeded on the road to Mourza.† We arrived on the 17th: We encamped on the 16th: and have done so since.‡

Tis much more pleasant to encamp in fine weather, when we are obliged to get up so early, than turn into a Miserable little Hovel full of Vermin for the Night. We halted one Day at Mourza, and arrived at this place yeasterday. I had been at these two last places before but recollected but little of them for we generally came in about dark and strarted at Daylight in the morning. This is a small place but some decent houses in it.

We marched from our Cantonements about Seven hundred and Fifty Men Strong. Some of the Gentry appeared verry sorry to loose such good company for we spared them as much as lay in our power in not cutting their corn, &^c: However, those who had suffered in the least, prayed for being freed from such great Thieves – the appellation they honor us with.

We have found ourselves short of forage on the March, from a wish of the Heads of Detachments that Off^{rs}: would reduce their Animals and walk, which can never be the case in this Country where we are doomed to Slave for years together. At least when the

---

* 'Muddy up to the knees.'
† Murça.
‡ This is the impossible chronology as it appears in the letter book.

Campaign opens our life is not much better, and it is impossible to be constantly on foot. After a long days march we require Rest, whereas we are obliged to look after the Men, agreably to General Orders, to see they commit no depradations. Returns of Animals in possession have been required but nothing further done as yet. Notre Col^l: fait tout ce qu'il peut pour nous & soutient qu'un officier ne peut faire sans deux animaux s'il veut conserver sa santé.*

We are encamped on a beautiful spot of ground, the River Tua in our front abounding in fine Trout and our Tents shaded by Olive trees. The Town is about a Quarter of a mile on our Right, the country round well cultivated; abundance of Rye and Barley, the former nearly ripe. The only disagreeable prospect before me is Two Animals who, having fared sumptuously on five pounds of Hay, are so gluttonous as to be eating the Bark of trees and what little weeds they can pick up round the Tent.

The First and Third Divisions follow us this side [of] the Douro. Tomorrow we proceed on our journey. I am not certain which route we take, by Miranda or Outeiro; the latter lays between Braganza & Miranda. As I am not certain when the Post will leave us for England, I shall leave this open and add a few lines after each day's March.

We are to reach the frontier Town of Portugal in two days after leaving this, so that we shall have pretty hard work at the rate of about Five leagues a day and bad roads till we get into Spain. I see S. Dobree every day. He looks in high health and spirits. We are, I belive, one of the best supplied Divisions in the Army in consequence of the exertions of the commissaries.

I have not heard from D. H. lately. I expect to fall in with him about Valadolid when the Army unites. I expect Burgos will be the first object of conquest. All our Detachments have (with the exception of 100 Men) joined us and, as we are to halt on the frontiers, I expect to see them somewhere thereabouts.

I am very impatient to hear from my D^r: Mother, for I hope she will have been well amused in London and seen all the fine Sights that have taken place there lately; the Processions, Cossacks,† &^c:

---

* ′ 'Our colonel does everything he can for us and supports the view that an officer cannot do without two animals if he wants to maintain their health.'

† A small Russian state delegation had arrived in London on 9 April with two Cossack guards, whose appearance was sufficiently unusual to merit considerable press interest (e.g. *Morning Chronicle*, 10 April 1813). Other

I hope my next will be dated from Spain, for we have but little comfort on a March in Portugal. We are just now made acquainted with the Departure of the British Post this Evening. I have therefore filled my Letter as well as I could.

Our worthy Coll¹: seems very sanguine about Peace, which I hope may be the case for I begin to think that we have had War enough for a spell.

May God grant you all health and Happiness is the sincere wish of &ᶜ:

Wellington's troops were fit and well-provisioned. 'The Army at present is in admirable condition,' wrote Surgeon Dent. 'It does not consist of less than seventy thousand Infantry, the Cavalry are likewise very strong: the Hussars have made them quite jealous of one another. General Graham with the 1st and 5th Divisions forms the left, General Picton with the 3rd and 6th forms the Centre, General Cole* with the 4th and 7th forms the right, the whole under the Eye of his Lordship.'[1] After nearly five years in the peninsula, Wellington had improved his ordnance and supplies to such a degree that when he marched into Spain in early 1813 his columns progressed at an incredible speed. The French obligingly retreated in front of him. Having had the heart ripped out of his military machine in Russia, Napoleon had no more men to send to help his brother defend Spain. This time it looked like Wellington had a strong chance of liberating the Iberian peninsula.

The weather was excellent, rations plentiful and the welcome warm. On 5 June Le Mesurier's column reached Medina de Rioseco. The French had evacuated the town at 3 a.m. the previous morning. Gomm, now a lieutenant-colonel in the 9th, found the place especially agreeable; 'The people of this town have received us most graciously. For want of something else to do, we have been laying ourselves out a good deal for

events in London that spring included the funeral procession of the Duchess of Brunswick (31 March) and a huge cavalcade, led by the Lord Mayor and Aldermen, from the City of London to Kensington Palace on 13 April to congratulate the Princess of Wales on her vindication by the Privy Council, following the second investigation into her private life demanded by the Prince Regent (*see* Plowden, 151).

* Lieutenant-General Sir Galbraith Lowry Cole (1772–1842).

receiving the compliments of the season, and we find it such a favoured spot by nature that it almost tempts one seriously to think the Spanish women grow handsomer every year.'[2]

D^r: Ju   Camp near Palencia June 7th: 1813

Since I wrote last from Mirandela, we have moved on pretty rapidly by Outeiro, Alcanizas* & Medina de Rio Seco to this neighbourhood. On the 30th: Ult^o: we moved from our Encampment at Los Sillos about 7 o'Clock in the evening, to cross a Ford at the River Esla, we supposed, in face of the enemy. On our arrival, within a couple of Miles, it was found the River was too Deep as some English and Portugeese Dragoons had been drowned crossing (or attempting).† We passed the night near the River without our Baggage and returned next morning to our old Encampment.

On the 1st: a Pontoon Bridge‡ was erected across and we passed quietly, the Enemy having retreated without troubling us. We have not seen their faces though we are getting close to them. Joseph passed through Palencia yeasterday, on his road to Burgos, as well as the Infantry. The Cavalry left the place between Five and Eight this morning.

Our Cavalry have been fortunate, as the Gazette will inform you. I should think the Enemy will not venture to show their faces this side [of] the Ebro. They are said to have immense Stores at Burgos which I hope they will not have time to destroy before our arrival.

The 1st: and 5th:, with Bocks§ & Ponsonby's¶ Dragoons, form the left wing of the Army under L^t: Genl: Sir Thos: Graham.

---

* Cañizo.

† Several men of the 51st Foot were also swept downstream and drowned (Green, 149). The cavalry tried riding across with infantry men clinging to their stirrups. 'In one minute were seen Hussars scrambling, their Horses now on a Rock – next minute, plunging over head, the Infantry dragged hanging at the Stirrup, and Horses Tails; some by a jerk, or kick lost their hold, and were struggling with the Torrent – others borne by the rapid Current of the Water, sunk, never to rise more' (Newcome, n. 201).

‡ Wellington had brought a purpose-made pontoon bridge all the way from Portugal. See *Royal Engineer Journal*, January 1871, p. 14.

§ Major-General Baron George von Bock, in command of the dragoons of the King's German Legion (Hanoverian troops fighting for Britain).

¶ Major-General William Ponsonby (1772–1815), in command of the Heavy Cavalry Brigade.

A Packet has arrived at Head Quarters and we are informed by report that the news from Germany are such as we wish them, from which we expect to see the Pyrenees before the end of the Campaign, and England before the end of the Year.* No part of the Army having been in that part of Leon we passed through since Sir John Moore's time, we have been received with much cheering, at Medina de Rio Seco particularly, where a great number of very pretty Signoras came in spite of wet weather and Waltzed on the camp ground with the Off^{rs}: of the Brunswick Oels Corps.† I am afraid we shall not be favoured to night by the Ladies from Palencia as we are about Two Miles from the Town and the weather is not very tempting being windy and wet.

A few days ago, when on Baggage Guard, I was a little astonished by seeing four or five troops of Portugeese Ladies in the rear with the Baggage. Formerly they scattered over the Country & plundered Right and Left without mercy. It was therefore expedient to find a remedy for the evil and none was found to answer as well as keeping them in Flocks and placing a Guard over them, for the Cat even could not deter them from Plundering on the March; it has been tried and found not to answer so well.

We are near the Scene, the closing Scene of last Campaign. Genl: Hay and Col^l: Crawford went to have a view of the Bridge at Muriel. I have some hopes we shall not close this Campaign in the like manner. We have not been much harrassed, yet we move regularly at Four and March about Three and a half to Four leagues every day. We have done so since we left Los Sillos on the 1st: ins^t: The roads are good so that our day's work is over about Eleven or Twelve o'Clock.

Sabagudo June 12th: I had the pleasure of receiving my D^r: Father's letter on the 8th: ins^t: The Papers arrived at the same time to the 17th: and only brought us the account of the 1st: Battle (or the Battle of Lutzen).‡ We are in anxious expectation of further news.

---

* To exploit Napoleon's losses in Russia in 1812, Prussia had declared war upon France and was soon followed by other continental powers.

† Troops of the exiled Duke of Brunswick fighting with the British.

‡ At the Battle of Lützen (2 May) Napoleon had forced the Russians and Prussians to retreat but at great cost in men. At Bautzen (20–21 May) the emperor won a second victory, but the casualties he incurred weakened him still further.

Several Bags of Letters and Papers are on the road to join the Army on Donkeys, I suppose from the great scarcity of Mules, so that we shall not see them for some time.

We have gone Four leagues since we left Palencia and the weather has been very unfavourable for us; the roads of course very deep, added to which it is not fashionable to serve out Bread as usual, but, as we had a little hard marching, they tried to accustom the Troops to do without that article. The Commissary Department not being able to keep up, and money so scarce, that they cannot pay ready money and the Spaniards do not like paper, in consequence of which they hide their Bread and Flour and we do as well as we can. For the last three days we have been short, yet our marches have not been reduced in proportion, which of course causes a little grumbling and makes the Duty a little heavier on Off^{rs}: who are obliged to growl to get the men to their Journey's end.

We are moving for the Ebro and are at present 6 or 7 Leagues from the River. Where we are to cross, I cannot tell, but from the direction we move in at present I think it will be at Miranda de Ebro, as it appears by my Map that we are nearly opposite. We are Eight Leagues from Burgos to the Right of it.

I hope the great scarcity of Red coated Beaux with you will operate in favour of my Country men and that they will make the best use of our absence, else I warn them that the moment we return they will be considerably in the back ground, unless they have been very fortunate in Privateering and have much money. We have only our Sun Burnt Countenances to recommend us, unless the Ladies, imitating Desdemona, Love us for the Dangers we have past; that may be tried at some future Period!

I shall thank you to tell my Father that I have been obliged to avail myself of his kind permission and drawn on C & B a Bill for £10. Il y a un raport que nous allons couper le passage d'un convoy de charrette charge de tout sorte de bonnes choses j'aimerez asser d'en prendre une avec un petit d'argent.*

Joseph passed through Palencia the day before our arrival there. I should suppose by this time he is at Pampeluna where I hope he may soon have the pleasure of seeing us. Our Army is about Eighty

---

* 'There is a rumour that we will cut the route of a wagon convoy, full of all sorts of good stuff. I like to think we'll take one with a bit of silver.'

Thousand men strong, English & Portugeese. The Spaniards are pretty strong also and, from what I have seen, in very fair condition. The Allied English and Portugeese Army were concentrated near Palencia, the whole within the space of Six or Seven miles. I heard the life Guards were in a most miserable state.*

A report is Current that our Dragoons have taken possession of a Bridge over the Ebro & that the French have left Burgos after destroying the Castle. I have not seen the 6ᵗʰ: Division nor heard any thing of D. H. lately. I expect we shall meet soon.

I shall write to Elizabeth in a short time. Remember me to all her family affectionately. I can readily conceive that Master Ferdinand is not fond of school discipline. Remember me most affectionately to &ᶜ:

June 13ᵗʰ: We halt here today. The commissaries are ordered to provide 4 days rations immediately. Tomorrow we move towards Miranda de Ebro. We are in expectation of a Skirmish after crossing the River.

The 1/9th finally met the French at Osma on 18 June. 'A sharp contest took place which continued more than two hours; but at length the enemy began to retreat so rapidly that our division was halted and the light companies dispatched in pursuit of them,' explained Hale, 'so we continued advancing, driving them before us like a flock of sheep for nearly two leagues, giving them a few shots when most convenient.'[3]

It was only a detachment of French troops under General Antoine Maucune and not King Joseph's main army. Two days later Wellington ran Joseph to ground at Vitoria. It was to be the decisive battle of the campaign. Vitoria was ringed by hills and Wellington wanted to advance on all sides to surround the French, so, on the night of 20 June, Graham's 5th Division (including the 1/9th) were sent on a detour, to attack Vitoria from the north and stop the French retreating eastwards. The 1/9th camped a couple of leagues outside town, in a 'sort of wild wilderness place, among brambles, thorns, &c.' 'We laid ourselves down two or three in a place, where it was most convenient,' wrote Hale, 'but hearing such music with the

---

* There seems no obvious reason why they should have been in a miserable state. The official regimental history describes their advance to Vitoria as generally without incident (*see* Arthur, 570–3).

vermin crawling and running about among the leaves, and sometimes running over us, caused our rest to be but middling that night.'[4]

Next morning they rose early, breakfasted and began to move south. 'Between nine and ten o'clock we arrived on a hill about one mile from Vitoria, where we had a fine view of the greater part of the French army; for they had formed all ready for combat along the river for three or four miles each way,' reported Hale. 'They thought to drive us down the country again, in about the same manner as they did from Burgos.'[5]

Dr: F.   Camp 1½ leagues in front of Vitoria
                                                    June 22d: 1813

Yeasterday we had a Brush with the Enemy in front of Vitoria, where, as usual, we had our good fortune of loosing few Men, though the Action was very sharp and we advanced under a Cannonade equal to that of the Arropiles.[*]

Joe commanded in Person and had the fortune to escape. Their Artillery and Baggage has been taken. The number of Prisoners, we know not. We fought about Lorango (Gamara Maior), or some such name, North of Vitoria about two or three miles. We advanced on this Village in double quick time, first in Line then in open Column of companies. We have lost one Offr: and about fifteen or Sixteen men.

Close to the Village ran a River over which their was a Bridge which the Enemy defended bravely, and the Second Brigade lost many Offrs: and men. We were under Shelter of the houses, having been ordered to keep possession of the Village which the Enemy wished to dispute. They were Spaniards under Casa Palaccios.[†] They had seven guns, Admirably served, which played on us for a considerable time and did execution on the other Regts: that advanced in close Column.

An officer of the Caçadores of Avila, taken by our Dragoons, breakfasted with us this morning, and says they had about Seventy thousand men, and he does not think we shall have more trouble

---

[*] The Battle of Salamanca is also known as the Battle of the Arapiles.
[†] General the Marques de Casapalacios, in command of those Spanish troops fighting for the French.

with the Enemy, but drive them quietly over the Pyrenees. God grant that may be the case. We pass uncomfortable nights after an Action. The Right of our Line carried every thing before them. A heavy fire was kept up for several hours by the Second Division. However, the Gazette will give you more correct details than is possible for me to do. Sanders is the unfortunate young Man who was wounded as we advanced in Open Column. A Cannon Shot hit him on the hip and shattered it. I suppose by this time he is Dead.

We followed the Enemy about two Leagues last night after their Defeat, and are about moving at present. I shall therefore keep this open in case I should collect any more news. As a Packet is expected to be dispatched with the welcome, I took pen in hand, tho rather tired having marched Five leagues yeasterday, Three before we had the pleasure of being Shot at. Our Baggage came up about an hour ago, and we enjoyed our Breakfast much. The Battles of Salamanca & Vitoria will be remembered by the French for a long time.

Given the importance of the Battle of Vitoria, and the role played by the 1/9th, Le Mesurier is coy about the details. As Surgeon Dent notes, 'Officers of Regiments know very little about an action except what is going on in their own immediate front',[6] so it is worth recounting what happened in broad terms. On all flanks the allies had pressed forward, but Graham's troops to the north of the town had found stiff resistance at the villages of Gamarra Major, Gamarra Menor and Abechuco. All three needed to be taken before Graham could cross the Zadorra River and cut off the enemy's retreat.

At Gamarra Major the French had possession of the bridge over the Zadorra. Marshal Jourdan had 'posted about fifteen thousand Men in rear of it, with Cannon on both flanks. It was evident that if he was pushed at this point he must lose everything'.[7] The 1/9th was one of the battalions ordered forward to take the crossing. For several hours the French held on tenaciously and beat back every allied charge. The bridge finally yielded to the British, in the main because allied cavalry cut in behind the French, forcing them to withdraw. 'Our regiment got off rather favourably in this engagement,' noted Hale, 'for I believe not more than one hundred were killed and wounded.'[8]

Though Joseph's army was routed, few of his troops were captured. 'Strange to tell, I believe we have not made 1,000 prisoners,' wrote Gomm.[9] The British were too busy looting. The booty found at Vitoria was immense. The French had dropped everything and fled. 'Unless I had actually seen it, I could not have believed that such destruction could have taken place,' reported Dent. 'Hundreds of fine French Carriages, Cannon, Ammunition, Waggons, Carts and Mules were laying in the Roads, Ditches and Fields for Miles round the Town.'[10] 'Joseph Bonaparte rode off towards Pamplona,' explained Gomm. 'The whole of his baggage, private papers, cyphers, in fact whatever he possessed, is in our hands; and his servants say that all his possessions are upon his shoulders.'[11] 'Camp followers were dressed up in the state uniforms of the King Joseph's court; the rough class of women-kind, drunk with champagne and Burgundy, and attired in silks and Paris dresses – once envied, perhaps, in a palace. The pride of France was, indeed, levelled with the dust after this signal defeat,' wrote Bell.[12]

In front of Salvatiera June 23d:

We have not been able to learn our loss on the 21st: and the reports are so various and contradictory that I can form no correct idea of it. However, I think if we had not Baggage, Guns and about Two Millions of Dollars to shew as a Trophy and a sure sign of Victory, one might imagine it was an uncertain Business.

It appears our Division had more real hard fighting than the others. We kept a Force of Fifteen Thousand men in Check whilst the Business on the Right was going on. When Joey, who commanded the Centre about Vitoria, saw that things went against him, he left his Carriage and mounted one of his best horses, of which I suppose he made the best use. Our Cavalry observed some bustle at the time but were not aware that his Majesty was taking to his Scrapers.*

We have been on short allowances since I wrote (June 15th). The Men, however, found plenty of Flour on the 21st: and treated themselves to such a degree that they were unable to march yeasterday and were Obliged to stop often to discharge their overloaded Stomachs – something like the Emigrant in Guernsey,

---

* King Joseph's carriage was caught up in the traffic jam on the road east of Vitoria. He had to transfer to a horse to escape.

who enjoyed la Preparation, la Fete & la Purification. I am in hopes we shall be better supplied as Santander and Bilbao are now open, and Mules may be dispatched there in a short time.

I had almost forgot that on the 18th: we had a skirmish with the Enemy near Osma. They were commanded by Mauqune.* We lost Ten Men killed and wounded, but drove them back.

Mules sold very cheap yesterday, for three and four Guineas. Mules were purchased worth from One to Two hundred Dollars. Some of the Soldiers who had come across Joe's treasure bought Guineas at the rate of 5 Dollars each.†

The Weather is uncommonly Cold, to such a degree that we are obliged to wear our warmest winter Clothes.

I understand there are many Strong positions about Pampeluna which the French can defend but, if they are so completely without Cannon as we are given to understand, I suppose they will retire quietly to the Pyrenees without giving us any more trouble.

A Packet has just arrived, but I have no letters from Guernsey or London. I have not yet written to London for want of time and, as we had been pretty sharply engaged, I thought you might be uneasy if you received no letters from me.

One of our Capt^ns: has taken his Departure for the other world; he had been sick in England a long time.

June 25th: A Division under Clausel are rather in an awkward situation. They were yeasterday about Bernado S^t: Cruz and another Village on our Right and Rear. They know not what has become of their Army and seem at a loss how to act. They are about Four or Five thousand strong. The Sixth Division are left to give an account of them.

Genl: Hay's Son and Aid de Camp, who was wounded on the 21st:, died yesterday, regretted by all who knew him. He was a most promising young man.

We are about 10 leagues from Pampeluna. The Weather has been much against us lately. The roads are very deep so that the Men are almost all barefoot.‡

Please to remember me most affectionately to &^c:

---

* General Antoine Maucune (1772–1824).
† They wanted to exchange bulky silver for more portable gold.
‡ i.e. they had lost their boots in the deep mud.

After he had taken Vitoria, Wellington sent the 5th Division after Clausel whose troops had been marching to reinforce King Joseph. Clausel outran them and Wellington soon gave up the chase. Napoleon's armies in Spain were pushed back towards the Pyrenees, but the fortified towns of San Sebastian and Pampeluna offered two chances to delay the allies' advance.

D^r: Elizabeth   Camp near Salvatiera June 25th: 1813
London

We have had so much work since we left our Winter Quarters that it has been out of my powers to write to you. I received a letter from Guernsey about a forthnight ago, giving me your address, and I take the first opportunity of a halt to scribble a few lines.

We have had some warm work with the Enemy lately. On the 18th: we first commenced Skirmishing near Osma in Biscay. We lost Ten men killed and wounded. On the 21st: we had something more than a Skirmish before Vitoria. We were under the Enemy's Cannon about Three hours, but fortunately we got in a small Village which sheltered us completely so we lost but few men in comparison with the other Regiments, and owing chiefly to our advancing in line and in open Column of Companies and they in close Column. Our loss; one Off^r: killed and fourteen or fifteen Men killed and wounded. The loss on the side of the Allied Army is supposed to be between Three and Four thousand Men killed and wounded. That of the enemy is not exactly known as to Men, but we have taken all their Cannon, Military Chest with Money (tis said) sufficient for Three months' pay for our Army, and Baggage, Joseph's amongst the whole with his Court Dresses and Crown, which I understand is very Rich. The Coaches of all the great People of Vitoria, the seat of Government of this Province, were all ready for a Start, but we came too suddenly and the good People were forced to leave them outside of Vitoria. The number is hardly credible.

Some of the Private Soldiers of other Divisions found immense quantities of Money. I saw one of the 40th: Reg^t: exchange Dollars for Guineas at the rate of Five Dollars for one Guinea and, when he had done, I suppose had about Four hundred Guineas. We got in for no share of the Loaves and Fishes. Our Division received more Iron and Lead than Gold or Silver.

The 2ᵈ: Brigade were ordered to advance and take possession of a Village and we were ordered to support the Attack. The General Orders, in thanking the Army, say that Major Genˡ: Robinson, with the 2ᵈ: Brigade of the 5ᵗʰ: Division, attracted the admiration of the whole Army, and were ably supported by Major Genˡ: Hay with the First Brigade. The 59ᵗʰ: and 47ᵗʰ: Regiment lost many men from the Canonading.

We are now about 10 leagues from Pampeluna where it is said the French will make a stand. We have not followed them so closely as they did us last year. The weather has been very unfavourable for us. We have had much rain which has made the roads so deep that the Troops are almost without Shoes.

The Commissariat have not supplied us with rations regularly so that the Men have sometimes received No bread for two or Three days, which they have borne with great patience and undergone the fatigue without much grumbling. I am in hopes that our Campaigning in this Country will shortly be over though the French have still many Strong positions.

The People in these parts are completely in the French interest and it is with much difficulty we can buy any thing from them. We have not been near many large Towns on our way up as we have moved on the left of the whole Army, with the 1ˢᵗ: Division under Lᵗ: Genˡ: Sʳ: Thˢ: Graham's command. The 1ˢᵗ: Division are gone, a report says to hunt after a Convoy of Provisions which the French had coming up. We have not seen them the last two days.

Wellington's next task was to overcome the French garrisons at Pampeluna and San Sebastian. The 1/9th were sent to join the troops besieging the port of San Sebastian. It was a challenging town to take, located on a spit of land extending into the Atlantic, with a tall rocky outcrop and castle at the far end; the 'strongest Fortification I ever saw, Gibraltar excepted', as Dent put it.[13] Any attack by land would have to be over the walls of the town, and to the east and west these were only accessible at low tide. The southern front was protected by a huge hornwork.

Dᵣ: Mᵣ: Camp near Sᵗ Sebastien July 10ᵗʰ: 1813

Nous allons commencer le Siege de cette place ce Soir. En deux heures de temps nous marchons a joindre les Espagnols qui sont en avance presentement.*

The Enemy have a Garrison of about Three Thousand men. When this is ended we shall have seen almost all kind of Service. We have every requisite for the undertaking. His Lordship will be with us tomorrow.

We have been in a delightful country since I wrote to my Father. We are most plentifully supplied with everything and only want fine weather to make us very happy.

We had a view of the Artillery at Vitoria on our Road from Penna Cerrada (wither we had been in pursuit of Claussel) to this place. A more pleasing sight I seldom witnessed. There were One hundred and eighty seven pieces of Cannon drawn up in three Lines, with Waggons, &ᶜ: without number.

We cannot understand the language of the People of this Province, Guipuscoa. They speak Basque which is entirely different from the Castillian. The Towns are very good and the Country thickly inhabited; Farm houses every Two or Three hundred yards.

We passed through Tolosa where the 1ˢᵗ: Division had a severe Skirmish.

I am affraid you will have been anxious at not receiving news from me sooner after the Action, but the dispatches were sent off without our knowing any thing about it. We have come at such a rate this campaign that very few or no mails have been made up. I am in hopes this rapid advance will opperate as a powerful diversion in favour of our Russian Freinds. The French people on the Frontiers are in a great State of Alarm. The Levée en Masse† has been raised to defend the country.

I should not be surprised if you saw shortly a Dispatch from Bayonne. The Army, considering the long Marches we have had, is in very fine order, with the exception of Shoes which begin to be very scarce. J'en ai une paire qui me serviroit a aller a la peque si je

---

* 'We will start the siege of this place this evening. In two hours we march to join the Spanish, who are presently advancing.'
† General conscription.

tois en Guernsey – il y a beaucoup de soldats qui n'en ont pas un Brin a mettre sur leurs pieds.*

We are about four leagues from Andaye,† the First Town in France where I suppose the Army will proceed. We have had disgusting reports of the Alicant Army which I sincerely hope may not prove true. If they are, I should conceive their Commandant will cut but a sorry figure.‡

On getting a View of the Sea the day before yesterday I felt a shivering fit. The Surveillante§ is here with Six Transports laden with amunition.

Gen¹: Caffrarelli¶ took several men of Bradford's Brigade** near Tolosa. On enquiring from the Off^rs: what nation they belonged to, and being answered Portugeese, he Spat in their Faces, made use of his Foot, cut their Accoutrements, broke their Arms, and told them to go about their business as they were not worth their Rations. This I assure you may be of great service, as it has irritated these good People amazingly. The British Off^rs: in the Portugeese service say it is a Fabrication of some malicious Rogue, but it is evidently True as I have heard it from the People about Tolosa.

There are several Mails in the Country but we have not received our Letters. We expect a little promotion by some of our Seniors getting it in other Reg^ts: I have not seen Hardy, though I was one day with the Sixth Division, but it was after they had had a Ten leagues' March and I suppose he was resting. I was rather tired

---

* 'I have a pair which would be all right for a peasant, if I were in Guernsey. There are many soldiers who have not so much as a rag to put on their feet.'
† Hendaye.
‡ An Anglo-Sicilian expeditionary force had landed at Alicante in July 1812. In April 1813 it defeated Marshal Suchet's troops at the Battle of Castalla, though its commander, Lieutenant-General Sir John Murray (1768–1827), failed to pursue the retreating French. He then exaggerated the number of French casualties (*See* Oman, VI, 297). Wellington ordered Murray to retake Tarragona. Instead, on 12 June, he embarked his troops, leaving several guns behind. For this he was court-martialled in January 1815 and sentenced to be 'admonished'. The punishment was waived by the Prince Regent.
§ HMS *Surveillante*, a French frigate taken by the Royal Navy in 1803, sent to patrol the harbour at San Sebastian.
¶ General Marie Francois August, Count Caffarelli du Falga (1766–1840), commander of the Army of the North, had in fact been replaced by Clausel in January, so this was probably hearsay.
** Major-General Thomas Bradford (1777–1853) who had commanded a Portuguese brigade at Vitoria.

myself, having trampled Five, and did not go to look after him, expecting we should have remained with them, but next day, as we were on the march to Logronno, we were halted and posted pretty fast towards this place. Tis not yet two months since we left winter Quarters; we have seen a good deal of the Country.

A post goes for England this evening. I have therefore scratched a few lines to let you know that I am still alive and in good Spirits. Please to remember me most affectionately to &ᶜ:

Where the spit of land leading to San Sebastian met the mainland, there stood a convent, fortified and manned by the French as an outwork. 'This convent was the first thing that took our attention, for nothing could be done till we could get possession of that place,' explained Hale.[14] Portuguese troops, supported by the 1/9th and three companies of the Royals, would assault it in two columns. Major-General Hay led the right column and Major-General Bradford the left.

Dʳ: An.   Camp near Sᵗ: Sebastian July 28ᵗʰ: 1813

I had the pleasure of receiving My Dʳ: Father's letter of the 28ᵗʰ: yesterday whilst in the Trenches.* Since I wrote to my Mother on the 10ᵗʰ: we have been constantly at work. On the 14ᵗʰ: Four twenty four pounders opened on the Convent in front of the Town and on the 15ᵗʰ: an attempt was made by the Caçadores of Bradford's Brigade to set the Convent on Fire.† They were unsupported and failed. On the 17ᵗʰ: the same Brigade were ordered to take the the Convent and a Redoubt the French had built close to it, supported by our Regᵗ: About Ten o'Clock we moved down in the following order: The Three left Compʸˢ: under Colˡ: Crawfurd to support the attack on the Redoubt, the Four Right companies under Colˡ: Cameron to the Convent, and the remainder in reserve, close to the four Right.

The attack was begun by the Portugeese on the Redoubt in very

---

* As well as bombarding San Sebastian, the allies dug a series of parallels from which to mount an assault.

† Both Dent and Campbell wrote that this was actually an attempt to gauge the enemy's strength, 'what Military People call Feeling the enemy' (Dent, 38; Shadwell, I, 20; *see also Jones*, II, 21).

good Style. However, they went no further than a hedge under the Redoubt, when our People were obliged to show them the way and C. Campbell* led in fine Style through the hedge, over the Ditch into the Redoubt which the French abandoned without making much resistance. They retreated into the Town, as well as the People in the Convent. A few were taken Prisoners.

From the secure position of the Enemy, our loss was rather heavy. Col¹: Cameron was struck by a spent ball in the Leg, which lamed him a little. Captⁿ: Woodham was killed, Thornhill ditto & Ruse wounded in the Eye by a Musket shot. Robertson was hit by a Shell in the Battery two days before, which broke his Leg and received such a contusion in the side that he expired the same night.

On the 20ᵗʰ: our Batteries oppened a Fire, from about Thirty pieces of Artillery, on the town. On the 22ᵈ: the Breach was thought practicable. On the 22ᵈ: I had the pleasure of being on Covering Party (French Guard), wither I went at Five in the afternoon and passed a comfortable night under heavy Rain. They did not think fit to releave us at Five the Evening following, as it was determined to Storm the Town at Daylight on the 24ᵗʰ: so I had the pleasure of keeping watch the second night, and when the Troops came, joined the Regiment. However, some houses being on fire near the Breach, Genˡ: Graham thought it best to differ the attack till next morning.

We moved down on the 25ᵗʰ: and the Attack was made by the Royals, but alas! something or other did not go right. Some of their men got in the Town and were taken for want of support. It was impossible for our Regᵗ: to advance, the French was blocked up. The Royals lost 16 Offʳˢ: Killed and wounded and Prisoners, and 329 Men. The 38ᵗʰ:, who were next, had 3 Offʳˢ killed. Il paroit que l'aile gauche des Res. n'ont pas supporte la droite & on na pu faire le 38ᵉ. bouger.†

We retired. I know not which was heaviest, our Loss or Disgrace. The 4ᵗʰ: Caçadores behaved like heroes. They went over the French

---

* Lieutenant Colin Campbell, later Field Marshal Lord Clyde, in command of the light company.
† 'It seems the left wing of the Res[erve] did not support the right, and we could not make the 38th advance.'

& leaped into the Ditch and, if ladders had been at hand, I doubt not but the Town had been ours.

It has been determined to turn the Siege into a Blockade and Redoubts are making for that purpose. Yesterday morning the French made their First Sortie (the Covering Party consisted of 600 Portugeese and 100 British). They sallied about Six o'Clock in the Morning, fortunately the time when the working Party was going down, for you'll scarse believe that Two hundred French were sufficient to make the above party fly. I was going down, being on the Working Party, and we had not moved far when the firing commenced, and an Order was passed from Genl: Hay for the working Party to move down in double Quick. We found the Portugeese and English near the Convent in the greatest confusion. As I passed I made use of my Sword which, however, flew in twenty pieces.* I then laid hold of a club which I found had much persuation in it. The Trenches were ours in a short time.

Percival was on the covering Party (with Syret† who was taken Prisoner). He says that the Portugeese carried our British off in the Crowd. He tried hard to make them stand and had a narrow escape. Two Frenchmen cut him off but seemed not to like closing, as he had picked up a Firelock and Bayonet. He made a rush past and in passing left the Bayonet pretty deep in one of them. He hoped therefore to move off quietly but found another Gentleman in his way, who leaped over the Bank and charged him at the same time. Percival had a Stick with which he paried the Blow and closed. After scuffling both fell and, a Portugeese coming up then, between both they beat the unfortunate fellow's brains out. Our loss in this business, I suppose, will amount to One hundred and fifty Men, so that you see instead of gaining laurels we Sink deeper and deeper into disgrace every day.

I was in the reserve the day the Convent was taken, as I belong to N^o: 6. The only good we did was repulsing the French who made a Flank movement to the left. Colin Campbell was mentioned in very high terms by Genl: Hay to Genl: Graham. He had the misfortune

---

* Standard issue infantry officer's swords were notoriously ineffectual. Lieutenant Campbell, for example, carried a light cavalry sabre instead.
† Ensign J. Syret (9th Foot).

to be wounded the night of the unsuccessful assault, not very severely.*

Our Subs are considerably reduced since we left winter Quarters. We have Nine only doing duty. I am about living by myself as one of my messmates has got Promotion and the Father of the Second has also promotion in his way, in consequence of which they live at a more expensive rate than I wish or am willing to do, particularly now when we are so far in arrear and no prospect of pay. We are paid up to January the 24th: though I see it asserted by one of the Paymasters Genl: that we are paid to the 24th: of March, and asserted in Parliament too!!!

I received a few days ago my D^r: Mother and Eliz$^{th's}$: Letters dated the 7th: and 8th: of April. I cannot conceive where it has been travelling since.

It is generally belived that a Genl: Engagement will take place shortly. Weither or not we shall have an active part, I know not. I do not like French duty, but I think we ought to take the Town.

My wardrobe is in most pitiful order. For wearing out Clothes, give me wet weather in Trenches. I wish you would tell A. to send me Strong high Shoes and one or two pairs of Trowsers by the First opportunity.

Remember me affectionately to &c^c:, &c^c:

From Le Mesurier's description one would think the 1/9th were barely engaged on the 25th, but they were at the heart of the attack. Lieutenant Colin Campbell led twenty men from the 9th Foot's light company in the forlorn hope. Many more soldiers from the battalion advanced in support.

Explanations for the failure of the assault were varied. 'The breach was small and so steep that we found great difficulty in getting up,' wrote Hale, 'and the enemy continued pouring down their small shot and hand-grenades from all quarters.'[15] Gomm blamed the engineers and artillery; 'Provided they can make a hole in the wall by which we can claw up, they care not about destroying its defences, or facilitating in any degree what is, under the most favourable auspices, the most desperate of all military enterprises.'[16]

---

* Campbell was shot twice and hospitalised. The *London Gazette* described his wounds as severe.

'After this, it was thought most proper to batter down the town walls by a heavy cannonading,' explained Hale, 'therefore an express was immediately dispatched off for the battering train to make all speed to this place.'[17] Unfortunately, the same day as the assault, Marshal Soult launched a major offensive at the allied lines in the Pyrenees, 'in consequence of which an order came from our division to hold themselves in readiness to leave this town at the shortest notice,' recalled Hale. 'Therefore our entrenching tools, &c. were immediately packed up, in readiness to march, and some of our heavy guns were put on board our shipping.'[18] Happily for the battalion, Wellington mounted a powerful counter-attack in the Pyrenees and stopped Soult's advance.*

Dr: Jua: Camp before St: Sebastien 11th: August 1814 [sic]

Since my last of the 28th: Ulto: we have been looking on this place and getting fresh Batteries ready for its destruction, I sincerly hope. They have also been at work inside the Town, barricading the Streets, cutting Trenches, &c:, so that by the time we have every thing ready to make fresh Breaches the Town may be ready to receive our attack in any point.

It is reported that a Battery of 20 Twenty four pounds will Breach from the sand hills the other side of the River. This side we are to have 7 Twenty fours, 5 Eighteens and two Nines to destroy the defences and scour the works. Some days ago, when we heard of the achievements of the Field Marshal[†] in front, a Salute was fired from our Batteries. A freindly one I shall not call it, for the Cannon were loaded with shot. We displayed English and Portugeese flags. The good Folks in the Town, not relishing the Joke, opened a tremendous fire of grape and shells on the Trenches and Batteries but fortunately did little or no injury.

They now amuse themselves firing at the Relief going to the Trenches at Five in the afternoon and generally succeed in wounding two or three men. They have given over making sorties

---

* Following Jourdan and Joseph's defeat at Vitoria, Napoleon had sent Marshal Soult to buck up the French war effort in the peninsula.
† After Vitoria, Wellington had been promoted to field marshal.

as our Men are more alert. They sometimes send two or three men to reconnoitre, but have attempted nothing more lately.

I am now living alone which I think, for the present, will suit me well, for living Three together, we had our rest broken often by one or the other being out and coming home from the Trenches in the middle of the night. Yesterday, about Two o'Clock in the morning, I was roused out of Bed to take down a Party of Men who had absented themselves from the works without leave. I was relieved at Seven, for which duty I shall be exempted from going on Trench duty to night.

We have the benefit of Sea Bathing here which I indulge in every day and which I think does me an infinite deal of good. I used to feel a constant lassitude which rest increased rather than diminished, but, since I have indulged in Bathing, has nearly left me.

I am in hopes this Year will finish our Toils on the Peninsula and that we may enjoy ourselves next year at home, at least those whose troubles are not put an end to before this place. The Army has had hard work this year and our losses have been heavy, particularly the last business where it is reported our loss amounted to near Six Thousand. But I belive Marsh^l: Soult had a sound drubbing. His Levies do not appear to be actuated by the same spirits as Bony's at Bootzen.* The Invalids fight well. I suspect they are something like my D^r: Father's brave band, for it is said that they were knocked up by Bivouacking and fatigue, in consequence of which a great number were lost.

Our Papers and letters are arrived to the 5th July only, though I understand there are some to the 29th: Ult^o: I therefore hope I shall soon have news from the Family. The last I have are June the 28th: which I look upon as very old. Considering we are so near a seaport (Passage†) we shall have a plentiful supply of every thing shortly as Vessels are expected with all kind of delicacies from England, and several Cargoes for our particular amusement at this place. Some cannon has been landed for the purpose of fortifying some pass his Lordship has possession of.

---

* The Battle of Bautzen (20–21 May 1813) had been a victory for Napoleon over the Prussians and Russians, but it was not the decisive battle the emperor needed.

† Pasaia (Basque) or Pasajes (Spanish).

I heard a few days ago the death of Col^l: Le Mesurier* from our Col^l:, who expressed great sorrow for the Death of so good an Off^r: I did not know him. My worthy cousin WLM was at Vitoria the last time I heard from him. When the Division passed that way he made some inquiries after me, but, as I did not know of his being there, I did not see him.

I understand a great number of the Off^rs: who were wounded at the Battle of Vitoria have Died. One of our Capt^ns: who went there on Detatchment says that Parties paraded every day for the Funeral of some Off^r:

We have a very good market here but the People who are something comme les Guernesias nous écorche d'importance des petits reste de sols que nous avons, nous reçumes notre solde jusqu'en mars l'autre jour & les miserables ont encheris tout du double ils pillent du cidre un jour & le vendent le lendemain après l'avoir bien Baptizé.† However, they have a much better right to squeeze the Coin from us than you have, for they supply our Animals with Straw, and a great deal of their corn was destroyed when we first came here, and the Soldiers have treated themselves freely with Aples.

If peace does not recall us home this Autumn, I suppose our Winter Quarters will be somewhere in this part of the world, for I have not the least Idea that Soult will force us to recross the Ebro. Pampeluna and this place will secure us if we can once lay our clutches on them, and I am in hopes the former will fall shortly for want of provisions, which we are told are beginning to get scarce. I think the Tyrant has as much on his hands at present as we could wish sufficient. I hope to send him to his proper place and give us a lasting peace.

August 12th: The packet has not yet arrived. As I shall not be inclined to take up my pen to morrow, after being at work the whole of the Night, I shall close my letter now. The good men in the

---

* Lieutenant-Colonel Havilland Le Mesurier (1783–1813) was shot through the back of the head while leading the 12th Portugese Infantry in the Battle of Sorauren on 28 July. He died three days later.
† 'like the Guernesiase; we understand the importance of what little land we have. We received our pay up until March the other day & the wretches have been doubly enriched. They plunder cider one day & sell it the next, having been well baptized.'

Castle are amusing themselves throwing Shells in our new Batteries pretty sharply.

Remember me most affectionately &c:

Dr: Abrm: Camp before St: Sebastien August 23d: 1813

I had the pleasure of receiving my Dr: Father's Letter of the 29th: Ulto: a few days ago and your P. S. to it. It would have given me more satisfaction to have caught Joe than any sum of money I could have picked up at Vitoria, but such good fortune is not likely to fall to the share of a Sub of a Marching Regt: That kind of Folk are generally too well mounted, and as I am not very swift and my wind is not improved since I entered the Army, I had but little chance of coming up with him, whereas with a Cart drawn by Oxens and well loaded with Treasure I had a little more chance, but even that I did not get.*

Since I wrote last on the 11th: Inst: we have completed the Batteries against this place and last night the Battering Train was put in, ready to commence afresh. I understand that the number of Cannon, Mortars, &c:, that are to open on this Place amounts to about Sixty. They are to be ready to commence the <u>First Act</u> on the 26th:

We read of your great Dinners and Vitoria fetes at Vauxhall† but, belive me, this will be by far more interesting than all your fine doings in England.

On the 14th:, in the evening, we were amused by a Salvo from the Garrison and on the 15th: at Day break, Noon and Sunset, by Three Salvos, each time from the Cannon in the Place, for Nap's Birthday.

---

* Officers like Le Mesurier were due proceeds from the prize agents' spoils at Vitoria. In the event each officer received less than £20 (Bell, 71).

† A 'grand military fete' had been held in Vauxhall Gardens on 7 July to celebrate the victory. In addition, London was bedecked with illuminations; shops, warehouses, gentlemen's clubs, insurance offices, theatres, consulates, even Carlton House, home of the Prince Regent, were all decorated. 'The Spanish Ambassador's, Grafton Street, was superbly illuminated, all the windows of the three fronts of the house were hung round with variegated lamps. Over the door was a beautiful transparency of the Marquis of Wellington, with three flags; over his head that of England, on his right hand that of Spain, on his left that of Portugal, with the words The Spanish Nation in variegated lamps' (*Morning Chronicle*, 6 July 1813).

On the Castle was, in letters about Six or Eight feet high 'VIVE NAPOLEON, LE GRAND'. They had the Impudence to illuminate that on the Castle at Night and to have Fireworks. They, following our example in firing the Salute, loaded with Shot and Shells, but did no Mischief.

Some days ago some of my Freinds came and wished me joy on my Promotion to nothing less than a Company. Fortunately I was not very credulous at the time and answered that I should conceive myself to be fortunate, if it turned out as they reported, but till I had seen it they must give me leave to doubt. They tried hard to persuade me but no symptoms of pleasure appeared, and it turned out that it was my Ens^y: that had been sold, vice Le Mesurier promoted, instead of my Lieut^cy: so that I escaped a great number of Jokes.

At this Morning's Parade we were cautioned to follow the Leader when we have the next assault. 'You have played at that when a School Boy, and punishment was always bestowed on the Boy that broke off. Well, such will be the case here. Disgrace is the mildest that can be inflicted'. Our Worthy Com^r: added that he was sure nothing of the kind would take place. 'Shew the front of a section and the Villains will Run. As to Plundering, let us secure the Prisoners first and then wait for Orders to help ourselves. Strict Order is what I require whilst we are pushing the Enemy. Obey the Orders of your Off^rs: promptly and I will answer for success'.

Il y a deux Cours Martiale assemblée presentement ; l'une Angloise sur le Major du 4e: et l'autre Portugaise sur le L^t: Col^l: du 15e & un meme Cap^n: du meme Reg^t: pour avoir été Ivre le jour de l'assaut & en consequence incapable de faire leurs devoir. Il y a deux punitions pour ce crime ; l'une la corde & l'autre les Galeres le reste de leurs vie.* We are not so severe on that score. If an Off^r: is guilty of that, in a case of that kind, he is told very civilly that he may walk off as soon as he pleases.

Poor people. They lacked for an ordinary share of courage, and,

---

* 'There are two Courts Martial sitting at present; an English one on the Major of the 4th, the other Portuguese on the lieutenant-colonel and a captain of the same regiment for being drunk on the day of the assault, and in consequence being incapable of doing their duty. There are two punishments for this crime; one the rope, the other the galleys for the rest of their life.'

trying to infuse a little, overdid it and are now exposed to ten times the Danger they would have been in the Trenches.

I am in hopes S^t: Sebastien may be our winter Quarters if we remain, for it appears to be a snug place and, when we have once taken it, we could make ourselves very comfortable with a little trouble, for some of the houses have been a little damaged by Shot and Shells and will be further damaged when we begin.

August the 24th: The effects of Syrett, who was taken when the French made the sortie on the 27th: Ult°:, were Sold this day, as it appears they have sent British Off^{rs}: to France. The Sale was very dull in consequence of our present situation, as Off^{rs}: do not care laying out their Money when they may not have an opportunity of enjoying what they purchass.

As you may not have seen a description of the Castle and Town of S^t: Sebastien, I shall try to give you an Idea of it. The Town is a square. Our Trenches go to about Twenty Yards of their defences. When we get possession of the Town there still remains the Castle for the Enemy to retreat to, where I belive we cannot disturb them, unless with Shells. The Breach is made from the other side [of] the River, and we must wait till the Tide answers to give the assault. The Hill on which the Castle stands is so steep that Men cannot climb up; at least it appears impossible. From this I am in hopes we shall give them such a dose in Town as to frighten the Castle into a Surrender.

You shall hear from me shortly and trust it may convey the pleasing Account of our success, and then I think I may venture to have Clothes sent out for I shall nearly be Naked. My Reg^t: Coat is the only decent concern I have. Every thing else wants replacing. I expect we shall see many Guernsey vessels here shortly. Everything would sell well in the Clothing way.

Remember me most affectionately to &^c:

D^r: F^r: Camp before S^t: Sebastien Septr 5th: 1813

Once more I have to thank Providence for getting clear out of the reach of the Enemy's Cannon. On the 31st:, about Noon, the Breach was stormed by the Second Brigade. The Breach was well defended by the Enemy and the remainder of the Division was brought into play. Our Reg^t: pushed on to Cut the Communication from the

Town to the Castle and succeeded in taking a good number of Prisoners. Before we had reached the Breach the rascals sprung a Mine which, however, hurt them more than us by blowing up a great number of their Men.* The Scene was horrible. Our Artillery was admirably served and did great execution at the Breach.

When once we got into Town, as is usual on these occasions, the Men plundered and all kind of irregularities went on. I was very happy to hear the report of a Staff Off^r: to Genl: Oswald (the Right Wing was detached from the left): on the Genl: inquiring how the troops behaved, he answered 'with the exception of the 9th: and 38th: who are formed and in good order, the remainder are in dreadful State'.

The Town has been burnt to the ground with the exception of a few houses. We remained on duty till yeasterday when we were relieved by Germans.† How the Fire commenced, tis impossible for me to say. A finer place I never saw. We were at one time completely cut off by the Fire, with the Enemy close to us in front. We were on our legs from the time we entered till relieved. We might now and then get an hour sleep, but I assure you I have never felt so completely tired.

I met Dobree yesterday, coming out of Town, who offered me a horse to ride to Camp, which offer was not refused.

We have suffered severely. The Gazette will give you more particulars than I can do at present. The Castle remains to be taken, with a Garrison of a Thousand or Twelve hundred men, and it is expected we shall have to storm it. The Villians seem determined to stand to the last and our fellows are determined to sacrifice the whole if they do. I shall give you a more particular account in my next. At present I can hardly keep my Eyes open.

Please do remember me affectionately to &^{c}:, &^{c}:

The second assault was by no means as quick an affair as Le Mesurier suggests. The allies found themselves pinned down at the breach for hours by heavy French fire, while allied artillery fired over their heads into the town beyond. The breakthrough came with the explosion noted by Le Mesurier.

---

* According to Fortescue (IX, 356) it was a French magazine.
† The King's German Legion.

It unsettled the defenders long enough for the allies to seize the initiative.

Behind the walls the men of the 9th Foot discovered further obstacles. 'The enemy had so blockaded the streets that we found great difficulty in making our way through,' wrote Hale. 'They had formed a sort of breast-work with barrels of sand across the streets in several places, which was a great disadvantage to us.'

The enemy eventually fell back to the castle, 'not, however, till after he had made some obstinate stands in the town, which was barricaded with great attention,' explained Gomm. 'The day closed as it always has done since the first town was taken; in riot and tumult.' Fire took hold and lasted several days. 'With the exception of ten or twelve fortunate buildings there is nothing left of San Sebastian but the walls of its houses, and these are falling every instant with a tremendous crash,' wrote Gomm. 'Never surely was there a more complete picture of devastation than this place presents.'[19]

Though the French still held the castle it 'did not command the town, for it being situated on so steep a hill, they could not bring one gun to bear on the town, therefore we could keep possession without much fear.'[20] A few days' bombardment persuaded the garrison to surrender, and so, as Dent wrote, 'after two Months fatigue and hardships we are now quite Masters of St. Sebastian'.[21]

D^r: M   Casa de Misericordia ½ mile from S^t: Sebastian Sept^r:
                                                                    14th: 1813

The place I date my letter from must not alarm you, for though it is an Hospital, or was one formerly, it is now converted into a Barrack where Four Regiments are crowded in, and Off^{rs}: at the rate of three in each very small room, so that we are very <u>comfortable</u>.

The day before the Batteries opened on the Castle I was detached to the Island of St^a: Clara with Thirty Men to releive another Party.* I had a fine view of the Castle and was much amused during my stay there. We had some Sailors from the Ships of War who,

---

* At 3 a.m. on 27 August a detachment of 100 men had rowed out to Santa Clara Island, west of San Sebastian. This small force defeated and captured the French garrison, allowing the allies to mount guns on the island, the better to bombard San Sebastian before the second assault.

I assure you, made some beautiful Shots. The unfortunate people in the Castle seemed to be excessively uncomfortable during a Cannonade of two hours and a half, at the end of which we had the pleasure of seeing a white flag hoisted, and the terms were settled in the afternoon. I was not present when the Garrison marched out but I saw them afterwards and was greatly astonished when I heard their numbers, and saw a parcel of Stout Young fellows, that they had not attempted to retake the Town the Night after the assault. As there was not covering sufficient for them at the Castle, they had made holes between the Rocks at the Castle and must have passed a most miserable time, as we had some very bad weather.

I called yesterday on some French Ladies; Wife and Daughter of the Commissary Genl: who were in the Castle at the time the Cannonade commenced and who did not appear to relish the salutations we had given them, though they are accustomed to that kind of work having been Five years in this Country. They dislike the Spaniards amazingly and, from their account, have passed their time dissagreably enough during the whole of the Time. They have plenty of talk and are very pleasant, so that I may be induced to call again. I have no occasion to talk much and I must own that I feel considerably at a loss for words to express myself, particularly before Ladies, for I have still a little of that Bashfulness which on one occasion made me run away from Mademoi^{le}: Josephine in the Gravel walk before the Beaucamp. I hope [by] my cultivating good company it may wear off in time.

I received yours and Elizabeth's kind letters whilst on the Island, dated Newington, August ye 3^d: I feel grateful for your affectionate wishes on my account, and hope ere long they may be accomplished. However, I shall try new dishes. I have often said I am fond of novelty and I intend treating you to some excellent Spanish Dishes, and drop the Macaroni Soup as I succeeded so badly last time.

We have still some work to do before that time arrives. In the course of a few days we expect to be encamped on the Heights of Irun,* in front of worthy opponent, Marshal Soult, though I am inclined to think he will not do much this Year as the weather will

---

* With San Sebastian destroyed, Wellington prepared to invade France at the western end of her frontier, where the River Bidassoa meets the Atlantic Ocean.

be very cold and wet in the course of a Month. I hope we then move into Winter Quarters.

If our good neighbours at the Presbytere* send anything to their Son, if you could send me Clothes by the same opportunity it would be the safest and best way as the Commissaries have always means of Transport which we have not. I have been set up in a very decent way in boots by presents from some of my Freinds, who had more than they could carry in consequence of the Deaths that have happened in the Regiment lately. I have a stock of Books for the Winter; some of Molière's plays and part of Florian's Works, but neither complete, though I work hard to get them. Florian's was a present.

I intended going to visit an old Messmate of mine this morning, but a stop was put to it by Lieut^t: le Mesurier, Reg^l: Court Martial. Shelton was the Person I was going to visit. He had his right arm taken out at the Socket at the Storm. Ford, whose name you may recollect to have heard, was wounded three days after the assault. The poor fellow was not very sensible at the time and went close to the French. We have so many sick and wounded that I am now doing duty as the 2^d: Lieut^t: with the Regiment. Fatigue has knocked up many Off^{rs}: I still continue in good health, thank God. J'navons pas asses de liberté. Les hommes sont comme des Diables – ayant vendu leurs Butin & bu tant qu'ils ont pu.[†]

May God bless you and grant you all health and happiness is the sincere prayer of etc.

The allies would attack across the estuary near the towns of Fuenterabia and Irun.

* There is a Rue Presbytere in the parish of Castel on Guernsey, possibly named after a house which stood in Le Mesurier's day.

† 'I haven't enough freedom. The men are like Devils – they sold their booty & drank as much as they could.'

10

The Bidassoa, Nivelle and
the Nive

D^r: Ab^m: Camp in front of Oyerzun Sept^r: 25th: 1813

The last letter I received from Guernsey announced my D^r: Mother's return to the Island from her trip to London, which I am happy to find she has enjoyed.

We are now encamped on the road to Bayonne, between Emory and Irun, surrounded by Mountains. We have a view of part of the Castle of S^t: Sebastian, which I must own I regret, on account of the Bathing which we cannot enjoy here as we are at least four miles from Passage, the nearest place where we could go, which is at present impossible as we do not know the moment we may be ordered to move. To make up for it, we are likely to have refreshing shower Baths if we may judge from the appeerence of the Weather.

I have not had the opportunity of thanking S. D. for the early communication you had of the attack on S^t: Sebastian, as I have not seen him since, as duty kept me pretty constantly employed in Barracks and when I had a little time of my own I called on our Sick and wounded Off^{rs}: However, he is in good health.

I understand a Post office has been established at Passage so that for the future I hope my Letters will reach you in a very short time. You cannot labour at present under the same anxiety as formerly, when we were subject to have our heads knocked off every day, till such a time as we make a <u>Dash</u> at Bayonne, which I should enjoy much. Though we could not survey the country far from the

Regiment, we should be in France. Wher^r the French are in Spain
we should be obliged to keep close to the Reg^t: Though the French
are a very polished People, on an occassion of this kind they would
be very apt to forget themselves and treat us in a very ungentlemen
like manner.

We left S^t: Sebastian yesterday morning. The Spaniards had
Garrisoned the Town with about Three or four thousand men. The
Trenches have been filled up and part of the Breaches cleared. The
remainder must, of course, be left to the Spaniards, who are not
remarkable for hard work.

I do not think there is the least likelyhood of the French ever
seeing the Place this winter. They have too much business on hand
in the North. We have heard of a great Battle having been fought
in which Genl Moreau* was killed, but that the French had suffered
a dreadful Beating. If that is the case, it would tend considerably to
give us good Quarters in England this winter instead of Skylarking
over the Pyrenees. As I have not much hope of the former, I must
beg you will send me to Passage, directed to S. Dobree, a Great
Coat. Let the fly be somewhat larger than that you sent me last
year (dark grey); Two pair of strong Webb overalls, strapped
and Leathered at the bottom, buttons at the bottoms only; Two
waistcoats, Kerseymere† (colour your own choice, white excepted),
a couple of Shirts and a few pair of socks. My Jacket must last me
another year, though I got it soiled the day of the Storm by getting
it wet and rolling in it at night, but on such a great Day as that I
could not forbear appearing dressed decently and I put on all my
best, just as if I had been going to a Ball. You may add a Pair of
Boots that lap over and buckle. I think those are by far the best and
most comfortable under overalls. If you could send these things at
the time Dobree's Freinds send his, it would do better as he has
always communication with Passage and he can send a Mule when
they arrive. He told me some time back to get my things sent in that
way and he would get them up for me.

* General Jean Moreau (1763–1813) had fallen out with Napoleon and fled to
the United States. After Bonaparte's defeat in Russia, Moreau returned to advise
the allies in central and northern Europe. He had been mortally wounded at
the Battle of Dresden on 27 August, which, contrary to Le Mesurier's version
of events, had been a French victory over the Prussians and Russians.
† A heavily fulled, twill-weave woollen cloth finished with a fine nap.

I wrote to Seaward a few days ago to enquire where Signor Acha lived at Bilbao. When I get an answer I shall inform Dobree who, I understand, has a Box come out by the same opportunity. Je remplis la place de mon vieux Messmate Shelton dans le commandement de la premiére Compagnie pour les derniers Dix jours. J'etois le plus ancien Lieut^t: qui faisois devoir les autres étant maladies ou blessés.*

We have some Off^{rs}: who have just joined us and who begin their Campaign at this time, which I conceive far from favourable to young beginners.† Some of our Sick Off^{rs}: who moved with us yesterday, I am inclined to think will not be able to keep up with us. The weather is too damp for Convalescents. Three out of four of our Medical Department are left behind sick.

La seule chose qui me donne de la peine est la grande quantité de puces qui me devorent. Quelque fois j'ai le Bonheur d'en attraper 3 ou 4 a la fois dans les plias de mon linceul & j'ai un grand <u>crac</u> – autrement je suis dans las plus parfaite santé Dieu merci.‡

Cap^{tn}: W [rest crossed out]§ has taken his departure having exchanged with Dumaresq. He was candid enough to own that he was not at all in his Element before the Enemy. We were on very distant terms. We used to pass like perfect strangers, as well as most of the Off^{rs}: Nous avons trois jeunes Garçons dans le Reg^t: de la même partie des Royaumes Unis, qui sont plus brave, mais qui ne font pas pour le Reg^t:¶

I do not pity you when you complain of hard work. It is a sign your business goes on gaily. Your work is different from ours, for ours makes us poorer in the Pocket but richer in Honor. I shall not say that yours is just the reverse. I shall decide that point here after. It will therefore be your interest to treat me like un gallant homme doit faire.**

---

* 'For the past ten days I have taken the place of my old Messmate Shelton, in command of No. 1 Company. I was the oldest lieutenant not sick or injured.'
† The 9th Foot took on seven new ensigns between 23 August and 23 September.
‡ 'The only thing that gives me trouble is the large number of fleas which devour me. Sometimes I have the good fortune to catch 3 or 4 in the pleats of my sheet and I give them a good whack – otherwise I am in the best of health, thank God.'
§ Captain Walter Snow.
¶ 'We have three young boys in the Regiment, all from the same part of the United Kingdom, who are very brave, but do not perform for the Regiment.'
** '[A] gallant man who does his duty.'

Remember me affectionately to all and believe me your affectionate brother.

Wellington's attack across the Bidassoa was made at the estuary, where Soult least expected it. The 5th Division advanced from Fuenterabia, leaving their tents standing to fool the enemy that they were still asleep in Oyarzun.

After wading across the estuary and subduing all resistance, they swung right to threaten the flank of the French troops opposing those British soldiers fording the Bidassoa at Irun. Once the infantry had secured the ground opposite Irun, a pontoon bridge was laid across the river to allow the artillery to cross.

Dʳ: An   Camp near Irun Department
                                 of the lower Pyrenees Octoʳ 8ᵗʰ: 1813

We crossed the Bidassoa River yesterday about half past Seven in the Morning, with Mud and Water to our midle, near Andaye, and shortly after came in contact with the Enemy who gave us a very warm reception, but were driven from Hill to Hill, beyond the village of Irun where the business ended for the day, which I humbly conceive would have been a most glorious one for England if our Cavalry and Artillery could have been up, but for want of it we were unable to do more than drive them without taking Prisoners.

We suffered considerably in Offʳˢ: Eight were severely wounded and Two slightly. Amonst the latter is my fortunate self. I was going on the Right of the high Road leading to Irun with some of our Men and Germans popping away at the Enemy, but were obliged to stop a Short time to give the Enemy time to get away, as they were much too Strong to think of cutting them off, when a Musket ball hit me in the Right shoulder, but so civilly and gently that it only cut the Skin without lodging. The thing that vexed me most was my Epaulet and Coat suffering; it cut two or three Bullion* off and made a hole in the Coat and Shirt.

I went as far as Irun with the Party. After being reinforced, we were then ordered to retire and join our Regiment and I had the

---

* A gold strand of the fringe of an epaulette.

pleasure of walking back a League and, I assure you, I never was so completely knocked up as I was last night, and this morning I feel very stiff. My Shoulder is not painful but swelled and perfectly able to handle a sword, which I suppose it must do again very shortly as we expect to have some more fighting, but let the Villians remember we shall be more on an equallity and I think they will get a dreadful beating.

We saw a tremendous fire of Musketry last night. Tis said to have been the Light Division and Spaniards. We have no particulars.

I understand the Great Lord expressed his approbation of the conduct of the Division. Tis rather extraordinary that we were the only Regiment that suffered in Officers. With the exception of a Surgeon of the 4th:, who was wounded by a Stray Shot, I understand no Off^{rs}: were touched.

As I was returning from Irun I met S Dobree going there, but he changed his mind when he found we had left the place and returned to Camp.

We are going to fortify our Position by Redoubts, though I do not think we shall stay here long but move on a little further to the front and take up our Quarters in France for the Winter. Comme nous retournions un de mes Galliards pris une grasse Oie dans un village & vint me l'offrir, comme je cragnois de l'offencer je suis obligé de la prendre & de l'apporter au Camp. J'enferai un bon Dinner dessus aujourd'hui avec mes compagnons, les Poules & les Brebis, & les Cochons, ont beaucoup souffert le Gen¹: qui commande la 2e: Brigade nous dit hier au soir que presque tous ses gens avoient chacun leurs Brebis & les notres avoient du Lard. Nous fumes appellés de nos lits a minuit la nuit du 6 au 7e: et nous arrivames sur les bords de la Riviere un peu avant le jour. Je crois que l'enemi ne s'attendoit pas a une pareille visite & que ce fut une surprise, parce que le Passage de la Riviere ne fut pas defendu, qu'oi que trés difficile, a cause de la Vase dans laquelle nous enfoncions jusqu'ance Genoux.[*]

---

* 'As we returned one of my gallants snatched a fat goose in a village & offered it to me. As I did not want to offend him, I was obliged to take it & bring it into the Camp. I enjoyed a good Dinner today with my friends. The Hens & the Sheep & Pigs have suffered. The General who controls the 2nd Brigade told us last night that almost all the people had a sheep each & ours had bacon. We were roused from our beds at midnight on the night of the 6th to the 7th and

If we have much more of this kind of Fun we shall soon be reduced in Officers. Our loss in Men is, I belive between fifty and sixty.

Health and happiness attend you all &ᶜ:, &ᶜ:

P. S. I should wish Abrᵐ: to let me know the direction of his correspondence at Bilbao as Seward has been enquiring at Signor Acha and, as there are many of that name, cannot find my things, which would be of use to me now. I live with Dallas who has joined me since Shelton was wounded. Give my thanks to My Dʳ: Father for his kind offer. When I am in want I shall avail myself of His kindness.

Half past 2 o'Clock: Heavy firing is heard at present on our Right.

After crossing the Bidassoa, the 9th Foot found the King's German Legion under heavy fire at the Croix des Bouquets ridge. As Blakeney explained: 'At this critical moment Colonel Cameron with the 9th Regiment, having arrived just as the Germans were checked, put them aside and, making a desperate charge, gained the summit.' French artillery 'poured a destructive fire both in front and flank into the regiment. Yet this did not retard their quick advance for a moment; while the enemy seemed no way moved by the vehement advance of Cameron until the regiment approached within a few yards, when a loud cheer and rapid charge so astonished them that they scarcely knew what they were about until they found themselves borne off the hill. Thus the 9th Regiment gallantly carried the key of the position.'[1]

'The enemy were pursued about two leagues when orders were received to fall back,' recalled Dent, 'and the position we are in at present was taken up; the left resting on the Sea and extending along a range of Hills across the Bayonne Road into the Pyrenees, as far as the Eye can reach. The heights have been crowned with Redoubts and our position is altogether very strong.'[2]

we arrived on the banks of the River a little before daylight. I think the enemy was not expecting a visit and it was a surprise, because the river crossing was not defended, although it was very difficult because of the mud into which we sank up to our knees.'

London Octr 26th: 1813

My Dear Papa, here is a Letter from Peter that will give you much pleasure after having seen his name in the Gazette.*

The Children are well. My little Adela grows more intelligent every day. She begins to say a few words.

With love to all. Believe me, your E. D. L. [Elizabeth de Lisle]

Dear Ferdinand   Camp in front of Irun Octr 9th: 1813
London

By a letter I received from my Father yesterday, I find I shall meet on my return to England Nephews and Nieces unknown to me pretty numerous, as I understand a newcomer is expected shortly. It would give me great pleasure to take a peep in the Nursery this winter, but I suspect we shall have other kind of work.

We crossed the Bidassoa on the 7th: in the Morning at a Ford near Andaye. We were up to our Knees in Mud. It was hard work to get through. Fortunately the Enemy made no resistance at the ford.

After crossing we advanced pretty rapidly for nearly two Miles without much opposition. We then came up with a body of the Enemy on a Hill with Four or Six pieces of Artillery, when we were Obliged to halt within about 150 yards of them as all the Men had not come up and were in some confusion. After keeping up a Sharp fire of Musketry for a few Minutes, we cheered and advanced, when they thought fit to take Leg bail.

Our Cavalry and Artillery were obliged to go to some other part of the River to cross, which retarded their coming up, or I think we should have given a good account of the Enemy, but our Men were so tired that it was impossible to do more than they did. Some of them went on a road to the Right and running parallel to the Main road, by which the Enemy were retiring. I was with these fellows. We pushed on towards Irun, but were obliged to halt about a Mile from the Town as we found the Enemy on our Right and Left in close Columns. We tried to hurry them as much as we could, and the German Riflemen did a little execution among them. They

---

* In the *London Gazette* of 18 October a Lieutenant 'Lemesurier' was recorded as 'slightly wounded'.

returned our Fire and I got a thump in the Right Shoulder which, however, is not severe. The worst part of the business was that they spoilt my Epaulet by cutting two or three Bullions off, and made a hole through Coat and Shirt. It drew a little Blood without lodging, and I do not feel it at present.

We then pushed on to the Town, having been reinforced by the Guards and Germans, but were ordered to retire immediately and join our Regiment, and I had the pleasure of walking back almost a League. To my great astonishment, I found the Division taking up a Position where we have been since.

I belive I never was so tired in my life, but I got a fine Goose and a little refreshment in the Town. I beg to recommend the Inn to you, should you go that way, for I luckily found the Adress or I should not have been able to give you the Gentleman's name as he fled on our approach -

Au Lion d'Or, No.93 à Irun, Roger, Traiteur, Restaurateur, loge à pied et a Cheval, à de trés belles Ecuries pour le roulage, et sert avec toute properté possible; offre ses services pour se render utile aux Voyageurs.*

If he treats all his Customers in as freindly a manner as he did us, I am sure he must give up business shortly for a bad Job.

Our loss was considerable; we had Eight Off^{rs}: Severely, and Two slightly wounded, and about fifty Men. The Four last Adjutants we have had have all been killed, with the exception of the last who is not expected to recover. He had a Musket Ball through the Body.

On the Right, the Light Division have had tough work. Report says they have taken several hundred Prisoners.

We expect to have more work shortly to do with the Enemy, and I make no doubt but we shall give them a surfeit of fighting.

Sir John Hope has succeeded in the command of the left Column. He was present on the 7th: On the 8th: Sir Thomas Graham took leave of the troops by an order in which he takes an opportunity of thanking them for their behaviour the preceeding Day.

---

* 'At the Golden Lion, No. 93 Irun. Roger – Caterer, Restauranteur, lodgings for those on foot and with Horses, fine stables for those passing through, and with every possible accountrement – offers his services for the benefit of Travellers.'

I hope all this bloody work may lead to a Peace. We have had fighting enough and a little rest would not be disagreeable, besides, it would give our Merchants an Opportunity of making up their losses and people of our Cloth of getting paid, for, you must know, Honour is all we fight for at present as they very seldom think of troubling us with our pay.

I sincerely hope, D^r: Ferd^d:, that as your Family increasses, your fortune may keep pace with it and on my return I may find you and my dear Sister surrounded by a number of little smiling faces.

Remember me affectionately to my D^r: Elizabeth and all the Family, young Ferd^d: particularly, and that you may enjoy Health and Happiness for many years to come is the sincere prayer of, D^r: Ferd^d:, your affth: Brother, P. Le Mesurier.

D^r: Ju.   Camp before S^t: Jean de Luz Octo^r: 23^d: 1813

Yesterday I received Abr^{m's}: letter of the 24th: Ult^o: It did not give me the pleasure I generally feel on receiving letters from home; it says that my D^r: Julia is not so well as we could wish. This, of course, is quite sufficient to put me out of spirits, for I take a lively interest in the health of a kind Family whose constant endeavours are to make me comfortable and happy. It cannot be, when I know that one Individual of that Family does not enjoy perfect health, therefore take care of yourself and recover speedily. This I trust you will do when you are so requested by your affectionate Brother.

Abr^m: mentions Anne's going to London to pass the winter with our Dear Sister. I should have no objection to take her place at the supper table, not that I should fill it half so well, but I would do my best and be rather more snug than we are at present. We remain in the same position as when I wrote before, though I date my Letter differently, but as the Division Orders are dated in the same manner, I have followed the example.

We have had very bad weather lately; Strong gales and Rain, which is not very agreable in Camp, as the Tents are apt to give way and admit the Rain freely, but we are accustomed to it so that our healths do not suffer from it. We are up betimes in the Morning – an hour before daylight is the appointed Hour – and Stay under Arms till Broad daylight. Though our Beds are not quite as tempting as some I have seen in England, I cannot leave mine without turning once or Twice and stretching myself, which I own is a very lazy habit.

Our Acting Pay master was wounded on the 7th: and I have had that Office given me, by virtue of which I had a trip to Tolosa since I wrote, to get a month's pay. The journey would have been pleasant had the weather been fine and my Poney able to carry me, but the weather was bad and I was obliged to ride a Mule as my Animal is quite lame. The emoluments of the situation are considerable, but I touch nothing except Five pounds of Barley a day for my Horse. The real Acting Paymaster is in England doing nothing, and his Deputy is wounded and shares the emoluments between them. I am not likely to keep the situation long as the wounded Man is coming up almost immediately and will resume his functions whenever he comes. Our wounded, with the exception of one, are doing well.[*] They have been removed to Renteria which is too far from us to go to, but we hear from them now and then. My shoulder is quite well now and I feel no inconvenience from it.

We have a little more amusement in front as a <u>bonne bouche</u>[†] before we get to our Winter Quarters. My French will not come into play if the Inhabitants do not chuse to take better care of their houses than they have hitherto done. I belive most of them have fled beyond the Adour River.[‡] It is not very pleasant to live so close to Hostile Armies. The poor Inhabitants generally suffer from both parties; their little Stock is destroyed and they may think themselves happy if they escape with their lives and their houses not burnt, for in the heat of action it is difficult to restrain a Soldier enraged by great resistance.

I understand the French have fortified Irun by Trenches and

---

[*] This suggests army medical care in the Peninsula was good. Hale's recollection was very different. Having been wounded at San Sebastian, he was placed in a ward infested with lice, with beds made of biscuit sacks filled with bracken. He was then moved to a hospital in Bilbao, a cavernous hall housing 1,200 men. 'There we lay for nearly two months without any beds or bedding, except our blankets that we always carried about with us,' he wrote. 'Our wounds were dressed several days with brown paper and oil, in consequence of which, many of the wounds got in a very bad state' (Hale, 115–17). The only facilities were kettles for boiling the meat ration, and slop buckets. Nursing staff were provided in the ratio of one wardmaster and six orderlies per 100 patients.

[†] Appetiser.

[‡] The Adour flows through Bayonne.

Barricading the Streets. We are more to the left and will have little or few fortresses on the Sea Coast.

It is the custom now to give the Senior Capt^{ns}: engaged Brevet Majorities but unfortunately Subs get nothing except thanks, which do not stay our hunger or Thirst.

S. Dobree is in good health. He is quartered in a large house which looks well outside but a complete Barn inside, however, stored with many good things of which I partook before I went to Tolosa; some of Bell & Brock's Port, mais chuna coute trop pour un miserable comme moi. Un verre d'eau & de Rum fait mon breuvage, J'achette le Rum pour Deux chelins la Pinte & une pinte du vin du pays qui ne vaut pas grande chose se vend un chelin – & on est obligé d'etre un tant soi peu ivrogne dans ce pays autrement gare les Fievres tremblante, &^c:.* However, I shall willingly give up the way of preserving health when I get by the Fire side at the Beaucamps.

Our Coll^l: has met with serious losses, since we commenced the Campaign, in his Stud. Yesterday he was obliged to shoot Two horses and two mules that were Glandered.† He, of course, gets an allowance for them, though very inadequate. To their Prime Cost he says his loss will come to about one hundred pounds. He bears it much better than I should do in the same circumstances.

When you write to London do not fail to remember me most affectionately to my Sister, Ferd^d: and Family. With sincere prayers for your health and &^c:

Pampeluna fell to Wellington on 30 October after a siege which had lasted since June. 'The garrison had eaten up all the prog [provisions] in the city, as well as every horse, dog, donkey, cat, rat and mouse they could catch,' wrote Bell. 'They held out bravely until starvation compelled a surrender, and no fortress now in our rear, Wellington prepared to enter and visit our old friends in la belle France.'[3] With this last major French stronghold in Spain now in allied hands, Wellington felt confident to advance on Bayonne.

---

* '[B]ut costing too much for a wretch like me. A glass of water & Rum is my tipple. I buy Rum at Two shillings a Pint, & a pint of country wine, which is not worth a great deal, sells for a shilling, & one is obliged to be a little drunk in this country otherwise you get shivering fevers, etc.'

† Glanders is a respiratory infection affecting horses and mules.

D^r: F^r   Camp near S^t: Jean de Luz No^r: 7th: 1813

Last Packet brought me your letters of the 22^d: Sept^r: & 16th: Octo^r: which gave me the greatest pleasure. I feel grateful for the kind interest you all take in my welfare and it will always be a great incitement to me to deserve such marks of affection from my D^r: Family in any situations I may find myself placed in.

You enquire what my Thoughts are about a Company. In the present situation of affairs it is difficult to decide. Promotion is, of course, a most desirable thing to a Soldier. Now that Bony seems hemmed in on every side, and that the most probable consequence may be a Peace, it would be better to remain as a Lieutenant than get a Comp^y: and be placed on half-pay. On the other side, if a Company could be purchased, or had in a single Battⁿ:, and that war continued a little longer, the chances are that before any reduction took place I should be effective in that Battⁿ: which would give me a lift of five or six years in the Army.* Under every circumstance, I do not think it would be acting prudently to purchass at present, but if a Comp^y could be had by interest in a Single Battⁿ: I, of course, would accept it most willingly.† If not, why, I shall stay in the Reg^t: with as much good will, for I do not think I could get in a better, even if my choice was given me.

We have had a few days' fine weather and, had it lasted, we expected to have been in S^t: Jean de Luz in the course of a very few days, but the Rain has set in again and the Roads are so deep that I am afraid we shall not start again for some time. Pampeluna has fallen and the Garrison are by this time embarked. I understand they are fine Men but greatly reduced. I have not heard the particulars of the Capitulation. That you will learn from the Gazette.

We have received a Reinforcement from England of Five Off^{rs}: and 126 Men, which has added considerably to the appearence of the Reg^t: We muster 650 Rank and File, which is a very respectable number at the end of a Campaign.

---

*   Le Mesurier was expecting reductions when peace came. It would be the most junior officers who were placed on half-pay first. If he got a captaincy soon, and war continued long enough for him to move up the list of captains within the 9th Foot, he might avoid forced retirement.
†   Regiments with second or third battalions would lose those first, so finding a captaincy in a regiment with only a single battalion was the safer option.

I have to thank my Dear Mother for the offer of a Great coat or a Blanket. I shall willingly accept one or the other of those Abr^m: has sent out, and look upon it as a mark of her kindness to me. S. Dobree lent me a Tent some days ago which I have thrown over the other and which keeps the rain out completely. Before that, the Rain came in so freely that my Bed was generally wet through of a morning, and I turned out willingly an Hour before daylight, but Luxury is the ruin of a Soldier. I have the greatest trouble to tare myself from my bed in the morning. However, I must thank him for it as it enables me to write to day which I otherwise could not have done. He offered me a Birth in his house which I was obliged to decline as it was too far out of the way in case of any alarm happening.

The Enemy have invited our Soldiers to desert. Papers printed in English, German and Portugeese have been scattered about the advanced Posts, offering to pay any Deserter the value of his Arms that brought them with him, then to pass him to his own Country or allow him to settle in the interior of France where he will be allowed to follow his trade without molestation. But they say all France is in Arms and, if we attempt to go on any further, not a Soul of us shall ever go back. I understand four or five wretches from this Division have taken the Bait. If they knew the <u>Warm climate</u> they deserve for it, I think they would have stayed all winter on these mountains before they had been hooked in that way.

Now I must answer some Queries put to me by my D^r: Mother: Curiosity led me to be introduced to these French Ladies by an Off^r: of our Reg^t: who had been taken at S^t: Sebastian and who was acquainted with them, and, I had heard when the Town was taken, of their being in the Castle and of their being very respectable and pleasant. Julia is, however, mistaken; it is not very dangerous exposing myself – at least I think so – on these Hills. I compare my Heart to a Bomb Proof* and it would require a very Powerful Battery to have the least effect on it.

Now for Master Abr^m: I thought he had read sufficiently to know that, by the Law of Nations, a Town that stands a Siege is always given to the Captors. I, however, did not take more than Molière's plays. The others were given me long after. I took with the Sanction of Law. Now, if he was found out playing any sly tricks on his

---

* Bombproof shelter.

Customers he'd get an exalted place on the sheds of the market and might have the honour of shewing his face with great advantage to the surrounding crowd. Now, if I was to do anything in that way, they would desire me to walk about my Business and not expose me to such disgrace. Such is the difference between him and I. What I have seen of his goods are of a good quality and therefore I do not think there is much danger of sentence against him. I have not received any more of the things he has sent me. I shall have now [a] plentiful supply of Clothes when the Parcels arrive. I have written to Seward at Bilbao and expect an answer every day.

Please do remember me to our good folks in London. Elizabeth must be well pleased having Ann with her. My best love to all &c:

The next natural barrier in Wellington's path was the Nivelle River. The 1/9th, as part of the force under Sir John Hope, was to advance on Urrogne and then to the Nivelle estuary at St. Jean-de-Luz, as a feint. Meanwhile, the bulk of Wellington's army would press forward on a front several miles to the south-east.

Hope's men, the 1st and 5th Divisions, encountered much lighter French resistance than the troops inland. The 1/9th, positioned on the left of Hope's line, were far enough away not to engage the French at all. After the battle they moved to Guéthary. 'Now being in quarters ... we supposed, or at least we were in hopes, that fighting and other hard fatigue was over for that season, for the enemy had taken up quarters as well as we,' wrote Hale.[4] It wasn't to be.

D[r]: Moth[r]:   Vedaste near Bayonne Nov[r]: 20th: 1813

M[r]: de S[t]: Croix has forwarded three Letters; two from my Father and one from Abram, which were longer coming from Passage to this than from Guernsey to that place, owing, I suppose, to the multiplycity of Business at Head Quarters lately.

On the 9th: the Enemy were attacked at daylight in their Position.* We had only to run down a Hill and up another. That day the point to be gained was on the left of the Enemy's Position and, from the little we could witness, there was hard fighting. We halted in front

---

* The Battle of Nivelle was actually on the 10th, although the allies moved into position late on the night of the 9th.

of a Hill that had a most <u>unhealthy</u> appearence and made ourselves as comfortable as circumstances could admit of that night.

Next morning we had the pleasure of seeing the Enemy set Fire to his huts and blow up something. This was about half past Three, and about Eight we advanced and took Possession of the Redoubt and Telegraph in front of S^t: Jean De Luz, the French having abandoned it at the time they had set the Huts on fire.

I never saw a place so difficult of access or one more likely to have given us a Passport to the gates kept by S^t: Peter. We passed by single Files through a thick underwood and, when we came to open spots, Abattis had been made and the guns of the Redoubt pointed at those spots.

We moved on to S^t: Jean de Luz. The French had attempted to burn a wooden Bridge over the Nivelle but the Inhabitants, wishing, I suppose, to court favour with the Strongest party, put out the fire and the Bridge was partly saved, but not in a state to allow the Troops to pass over it. They therefore forded it, being now low water. The Inhabitants sent early to say, if they and their property were respected, they would not quit the Town and would repair the Bridge, and, on marching through the Town, our Band playing the British Grenadiers, we had a good number of Folks to look at us, though the day was against us as it rained <u>a verse</u> and we had a tolerable drenching fording the River. We made ourselves again comfortable that night as our Baggage could not come across the Bridge and it was dangerous fording at night.

We are about a League from S^t: Jean de Luz and one and a half from Bayonne where the French are in waiting to give us a polite introduction into the Town. Our Quarters are scattered and the Roads so deep that I shall not think of running about as much, unless duty obliges me so to do.

I shall now answer my Father's Queries: After the Enemy had given way and were on the road to Irun, Col^l: Cameron endeavoured to push on to cut some of them off. I happened to be close to him and, as we were going down a lane, I got before him with about Eight or ten men and kept going on, not making the least doubt that he was following. He was ordered to halt at the same time I got in front, and he sang as loud as he could for us to do the same, but we had gained too much ground and did not hear him. The Germans and Guards were pushing on in the same direction and had not come up at the time. We halted to allow a Column of about 800 men to pass. At that time we had not above 150 men with us, and some Off[rs]: of the Guards, Germans, and us did not think it practicable to make any impression on a body of Men who had given Our Reg[t]: such a warm reception, as we acted only as their Skirmishers; each commanded his own Party.

If my Dear Father repeats all the kind things that a few Freinds are pleased to say of me, I am terribly afraid they will turn my Brain, to prevent which, however, in his next sentence, il me donne un coup de patte pour l'Oie. J'ai été tres honnète cette fois pas mime un poulet j'ai jeuné Vingt quatres heures et meme sans aller chercher aucun Butin.[*]

I assure you my Baggage was welcome. The only thing I ate from the 10th: to the 11th: was about a quarter of a pound of Biscuit.

Si notre Regiment alloit au Hommet je crois que vous auriez grand soin de la Basse cour les Poules ne servient pas premises de jucher au grand Air mais sous la clef – je suppose ceci de l'opinion qu'on paroit avoir formé de moi, mais je vais opprendre a être honnète homme, & j'espere qu'avant avoir le plaisir de vous voir je pourrai dire je suis tel.[†]

Long Orders have come out with respect to Foraging, so that it may be done honestly and Fairly, and, to prevent any surprise, the whole of the Animals of the Division go out together, escorted by a Regiment. Capt[ns]: are now allowed Two Horses or Mules, Subs One. Formerly Subs were only allowed half a one and Capt[ns]: one.[‡]

M[r]: de S[t]: Croix enclosed the Letters in a Note in which he begs I

---

[*] 'He gives me a smack about the goose. This time I was very honest, while not acting like a chicken. I fasted for twenty-four hours without looking for any loot.'

[†] 'If our Regiment was going to Hommet [a Martello tower in Castel, Guernsey, built in 1804] I think you would take great care of the barnyard. Hens are not well served roosting outdoors, but under lock and key – I suppose this must be the view you have formed of me, but I strive to be an honest man, and I hope that before I next have the pleasure of seeing you, you will be able to say that I am such.'

[‡] Wellington went to great pains to win the goodwill of the French people. 'The Discipline with regard to the protection of inhabitants and their property is much stricter than ever it was in Spain or Portugal,' explained Dent, 'which very much displeases the Soldier of those two Nations' (Dent, 44). Hale recalled that 'a general order was immediately given out, that if any man should ill-use, plunder, or defraud any of the inhabitants in any respect whatever, he should

will let him know how he can send up the things he brought for me. I sent an Answer back by one of S. Dobree's department, who will get them for me. I, at the same time, told him that, as far as [it] lay in my power, I should be glad to serve him, but that we (meaning Subs) were not in the Habit of drinking bottled wine as our means of Transport were so very limited (I might have said our Purse also but who likes to acknowledge himself a poor Wretch?), and I had made a good excuse, not at the expence of Truth.

Seward arrived yesterday from Bilbao and brought me the parcel containing two Shirts and one pair of Boots. The Other is left at Acha's. I shall have it sent to Passage by water as Seward tells me it is too large to ask any Person to bring it by hand.

There is a Report of our Advancing again if the weather continues fine, to drive Boyer* across the Adour. Bayonne itself is not fortified. There is a Citadel called S^t: Esprit the other side [of] the Adour which I understand commands the Town.

I wrote to Ferdinand some time ago. I have not heard from him lately. I suppose his Business takes up the best part of his time. Have the kindness when you write to remember me most affectionately to our Family in London, and tell Sister Anne that, though there may be some excuse for Elizabeth and Ferdinand's not writing, I shall expect to hear from her regularly. Remember me also to my D^r: Father, Julia, Abr^m, Car^l: and my Kind Freinds, particularly Uncle & Aunt W^m: & Doc^t: If things turn out as I wish, I hope to pass my Easter Holidays with you. Till then, God bless you and grant you Health and Happiness is the sincere prayer of, Dear Mother, your most Affectionate Son, P. Le Mesurier.

Having crossed the Nivelle, Wellington now had to negotiate the Nive, the river which snaked down from the Pyrenees, northwards until it met the Adour at Bayonne. 'I had determined to pass the Nive immediately after the passage of the Nivelle,' explained the duke, 'but was prevented by the bad state of the roads, and the swelling of all the rivulets occasioned by the fall of rain in the beginning of that month.'[5] The offensive was postponed until 9 December.

suffer death, or such punishment as by a general court-martial should be awarded' (Hale, 121).
* General Pierre Francois Boyer (1772–1851).

The 1/9th were to march from their quarters at Guéthary towards Bayonne, as part of Hope's corps. 'We stood to our arms about four o'clock in the morning and began to advance,' recalled Hale, 'and soon after day-light our advanced guard commenced skirmishing with the enemy's picquets; in consequence of which it was not long before our division fell in with the main body ... We continued skirmishing and advancing till we drove them within two miles of Bayonne.'[6]

Wellington's aim was for Hope to reconnoitre the Adour beyond Bayonne to see if it was traversable. Once he had surveyed the river, Hope retired. 'About seven o'clock in the evening we received orders to fall back to our former position again,' wrote Hale,' and our regiment formed the rearguard on the main road in order to cover the retreat of our wounded ... In consequence of so much rain that had fallen, the road was very bad, and so deep in some places that our hospital waggons could hardly be got along, and we were sometimes nearly half-way up our legs in a slough of dirt; and it being so very dark we were all in a miserable pickle, as it was past midnight before we could reach our quarters.'[7]

'The following morning, being the 10th, we assembled in the usual way and soon after day-light we discovered the enemy advancing upon us in all directions and in a short time our picquets were driven off their posts,' reported Hale.[8] With Hope's corps separated (the 5th Divison at Guéthary, the 1st Division miles away at St. Jean-de-Luz), Soult sent eight French divisions to overpower them. The 1/9th, in Colonel Greville's brigade, stayed in reserve, while the other two brigades of the 5th Division were sent forward to engage the enemy at Barrouillet. 'In this form we remained till towards the middle of the day,' explained Hale, 'when it was thought necessary for us to advance and relieve the second brigade, for they had suffered very much.'

Once in position, the 9th Foot found the Portuguese brigade to their left gave ground, 'in consequence of which our regiment was totally surrounded in a short time, and shots flew both front and rear. It being woody nearly all round us, we had but little knowledge what was going on only with the column we were engaged with ... but by an order from Col. Cameron, who was still in command of our regiment, we immediately turned to the right about and charged them man to man, by which we carried about four hundred prisoners on the point of the bayonet.'[9]

It was a desperate battle. The 5th Division only narrowly survived, rescued by the arrival of the 1st Division and a brigade under Lord Aylmer. Each side lost around 1,600 men. Le Mesurier was one of those killed.

*Coppy of a note addressed to Math Brock Esq.

I am sorry to have to mention poor Le Mesurier's death in this business. He received two shots in the breast, one through the heart. He died without a pang; it may be some consolation to his relations to know this.

Cameron desires me to add that in him he has lost a most gallant officer, and a worthy young Man. He is deplored by the whole corp, with whom he was deservedly a very great favourite. I had only been introduced to him three or four days before he was kill'd. Will you make this known to his friends in Cameron's name? He would have written himself but his time has been completely occupied on duty.

George Brock

Peter Le Mesurier's name appears in the Memorial Porch of the Biarritz Historical Museum (formerly an Anglican church), along with those of other soldiers who died in the campaign in the south-west of France. Had he survived for just a few more months, he would have seen the end of the Peninsular War.

While Wellington was invading France from the south, Russian, Austrian and Prussian forces advanced from the north-east and by 31 March had forced the surrender of Paris. Napoleon agreed to abdicate, and on 17 April Soult and Wellington concluded an armistice.

Of course, that was not the end of the story. Exiled to the island of Elba, Napoleon escaped to France, raised a new army and declared himself emperor once more. The allies brought an end to his ambitions at Waterloo.

* Presumably Lieutenant George Brock to his brother Matthew. Their sister, Amelia, was Lieutenant-Colonel Cameron's wife. The Brocks were a Guernsey family. This note is written in a different hand to the rest of the letters.

Notes

The Le Mesurier Family

1 H. H. Peveril Le Mesurier 291–4
2 Moullin, 'Plans and Details of Les Vieux Beaucamps' 79–80

Life in the 9th Foot

1 Hale, 47

1 Corunna and Vigo

1 *Cobbett's Weekly Political Register*, 24 September 1808
2 Oman, I, 491
3 Oman, I, 498
4 Surtees, 75
5 Moore, II, 283
6 Surtees, 77
7 Moore, II, 284
8 Surtees, 79
9 Moore, II, 286
10 Moore, II, 381
11 Surtees, 79–80
12 Surtees, 89
13 Harris, 85
14 Gavin, xiv
15 Surtees, 95

2 Walcheren

1 Hale, 38
2 Gomm, 118
3 Hale, 41
4 Harris, 115
5 Gavin, xvii
6 Hale, 46

3 Gibraltar and Malaga

1 PRO/WO 31/287

4 Guernsey and Canterbury

1 Hale, 51–52
2 Hale, 56
3 Dent, 25
4 Hale 6–7

5 Portugal

1 Grattan, 140

6 Ciudad Rodrigo and Badajoz

1 Hale, 70–1
2 Gomm, 250
3 Bell, 23
4 Surtees, 139 & 142
5 Blakeney, 264

6 Bell, 28
7 Surtees, 147
8 Surtees, 149
9 Oman, V, 281
10 Bell, 66
11 Oman, V, 301
12 Gomm, 271

7 Salamanca and the Occupation of Madrid

1 Hale, 90

8 The Siege of Burgos

1 Gomm, 287
2 Hale, 92
3 Gomm, 289
4 Hale, 93
5 Hale, 94–95
6 Gomm, 290
7 Bell, 59
8 Gomm, 291
9 Surtees, 186–187
10 Bell, 63
11 Hale, 100–101

9 Vitoria and San Sebastian

1 Dent, 33
2 Gomm, 301
3 Hale, 102

4 Hale, 103
5 Hale, 104
6 Dent, 35
7 Dent, 35
8 Hale, 106
9 Gomm, 305
10 Dent, 37
11 Gomm, 305
12 Bell, 75
13 Dent, 39
14 Hale, 109
15 Hale, 111
16 Gomm, 311
17 Hale, 111
18 Hale, 112
19 Gomm, 319–20
20 Hale, 114
21 Dent, 41

10 The Bidassoa, Nivelle and the Nive

1 Blakeney, 311
2 Dent, 42
3 Bell, 96
4 Hale, 121
5 *London Gazette*, 30 December 1813
6 Hale, 121
7 Hale, 122
8 Hale, 122
9 Hale, 123–4

Bibliography

Unless otherwise stated the place of publication is London.

Manuscript Sources

Priaulx Library, Guernsey
Letter from Peter Paul Dobree to George Pryme, 27 August 1811.

Public Record Office (PRO)
WO 31/252, 31/258, and 31/287 – Office of the Commander-in-Chief: Memoranda and Papers. Letters relating to Le Mesurier's original commission and promotion.

Royal Norfolk Regimental Museum, Norwich (RNRM)
45.1.1 Cameron's Account of Attack on Convent.
45.1.2 Letter from John Cameron to Colin Campbell, 24 March 1836.
45.2 Cameron's Account of the Battles of Rolica and Vimeiro.
45.4 Colin Campbell's Journal.
45.9 Letter from Cameron to William Napier (?), 7 December 1836.
45.9.1 Cameron's Account of Attack on Convent.

Printed Sources

Anon., *The Whim: A Periodical Paper by a Society of Gentleman.* Canterbury: Rouse, Kirby & Lawrence, 1810–11.
Arthur, Captain Sir George Compton, *The Story of the Household Cavalry.* Constable, 1909.
Beatson, Major-General F. C. Beatson, *Wellington: The Bidassoa and the Nivelle.* Arnold, 1931.
Bell, Major-General Sir George, *Rough Notes of an Old Soldier.* Staplehurst: Spellmount, 1991.
Berry, William, *The History of the Island of Guernsey.* Longman et al., 1815.
Blakeney, Robert, *A Boy in the Peninsular War.* Murray, 1899.

Bibliography

Bonnard, Brian, *Alderney from Old Photographs*. Stroud: Amberley, 2013.

Brett-James, Antony, *Wellington at War*. Macmillan, 1961.

Brett-James, Antony, *Life in Wellington's Army*. Allen and Unwin, 1979.

Carey, Edith F., 'Peter Le Mesurier, Governor of Alderney, 1793–1803.' *Report and Transactions of La Société Guernesiaise*, Vol. X. Pt.I., 1926.

Carr, Sir John, *Descriptive Travels in the Southern and Eastern Parts of Spain and the Balearic Isles in the Year 1809*. Sherwood et al. 1811.

Chartrand, Rene, *Spanish Guerrillas in the Peninsular War*. Oxford: Osprey, 2004.

Chatterton, E. Keble, *The Old East Indiamen*. Werner Laurie, 1914.

Davies, D. W., *Sir John Moore's Peninsular Campaign 1808–1809*. The Hague: Martinus Nijhoff, 1974.

De Garis, Marie, *Folklore of Guernsey*. Guernsey: Guernsey Press, 1986.

Delavoye, Alexander, *Life of Thomas Graham, Lord Lynedoch*. Richardson, 1880.

Dent, William (compiled by Leonard W. Woodford), *A Young Surgeon in Wellington's Army*. Old Woking: Unwin, 1976.

De Quincey, Thomas, *Autobiographic Sketches*. Edinburgh: James Hogg and London: R. Groombridge, 1853.

Duncan, Jonathan, *The History of Guernsey*. Longmans, 1841.

Dunn-Pattison, R. P., *Napoleon's Marshals*. Methuen, 1909.

Forbes, Archibald, *Battles of the Nineteenth Century*. Cassell, 1896–97.

Fortescue, J. W., *A History of the British Army*. Macmillan, 1899–1930.

Gavin, William, 'The Diary of William Gavin.' *Offprint from the Highland Light Infantry Chronicle*, 1920–21.

Glover, Gareth, *From Corunna to Waterloo*. Greenhill, 2007.

Glover, Michael, *Wellington's Army*. Newton Abbot: David & Charles, 1977.

Glover, Michael, *The Peninsular War*. Penguin, 2001.

Gomm, Sir William Maynard (edited by Francis Culling Carr-Gomm), *Letters and Journals of Field-Marshal Sir William Maynard Gomm, G.C.B., Commander-in-Chief of India, Constable of the Tower of London ... from 1799 to Waterloo, 1815*. Murray, 1881.

Grant, James, *British Battles on Land and Sea*. Cassell, 1897.

Grattan, William, *Adventures with the Connaught Rangers 1809–1814*. Arnold, 1902.

Green, John, *The Vicissitudes of a Soldier's Life*. Louth, 1827.

Guernsey Society, *The Guernsey Farmhouse: a Survey by Members of the Guernsey Society*. De La Rue, 1963.

Hale, James, *Journal of James Hale, late Sergeant in the Ninth Regiment of Foot*. Cirencester: Watkins, 1826.

Harris, Benjamin (edited by Christopher Hibbert), *The Recollections of Rifleman Harris*. Century, 1985.

Jacob, John, *Annals of some of the British Norman Isles constituting the Bailiwick of Guernsey*. Paris: J. Smith, 1830.

Howard, Martin, *Walcheren 1809*. Barnsley: Pen & Sword, 2012.

Jones, John, *Journal of the Sieges carried on by the Army under the Duke of Wellington*. 2nd Edition. Egerton, 1827.

Le Mesurier, H. H. Peveril, 'Notes on the Armorial China of some of the Guernsey

Families.' *Reports and Transactions of La Société Guernesiaise*, Vol. XII.Pt.III, 1935.

Le Mesurier, Hubert, 'The Le Mesuriers who lived at Les Beauchamps.' *Quarterly Review of the Guernsey Society*, Spring 1959.

Le Mesurier, Hubert, 'Stories about Les Beaucamps.' *Quarterly Review of the Guernsey Society*, Autumn 1959.

Le Mesurier-Foster, Ray, *The Rough Index to the Le Mesurier Family*. www.guernsey-society.org.uk. 2010.

Loraine Petre, F., *The History of the Norfolk Regiment*. Norwich: Jarrolds, N.d.

MacCulloch, Sir Edgar, *Guernsey Folk Lore*. Elliot Stock, 1903.

McCormack, John, *The Guernsey House*. Chichester: Phillimore, 1980.

Moore, Sir John (edited by Major-General Sir John Frederick Maurice), *The Diary of Sir John Moore*. Arnold, 1904.

Moullin, E. B., 'The Old House of Les Beaucamps, Castel.' *Quarterly Review of the Guernsey Society*, Spring 1955.

Moullin, E. B., 'Plans and Details of Les Vieux Beaucamps, Castel.' *Quarterly Review of the Guernsey Society*, Winter 1957.

Batty, Robert, *Campaign of the left wing of the Allied Army, in the Western Pyrenees and South of France, in 1813–14*. Murray, 1823.

Musteen, Jason R., *Nelson's Refuge: Gibraltar in the Age of Napoleon*. Annapolis: Naval Institute Press, 2011.

Neale, Adam, *Letters from Portugal and Spain*. Phillips, 1809.

Newcome, Johnny (pseud. for David Roberts), *The Military Adventures of Johnny Newcome*. Methuen, 1904.

Oman, Sir Charles, *A History of the Peninsular War*. Greenhill, 1995.

Plowden, Alison, *Caroline and Charlotte: Regency Scandals*. Stroud, Sutton, 2005.

Riley, J. P., *Napoleon and the World War of 1813*. Cass, 2000.

Ross, Michael, *The Reluctant King: Joseph Bonaparte*. Sidgwick & Jackson, 1976.

Shadwell, Lawrence, *The Life of Colin Campbell, Lord Clyde*. Blackwood, 1881.

Summerville, Christopher, *March of Death: Sir John Moore's Retreat to Corunna, 1808–09*. Greenhill, 2003.

Surtees, William, *Twenty-five years in the Rifle Brigade*. Greenhill, 1996.

Tupper, Ferdinand Brock, *Family Records*. Guernsey: Barbet and London: Baldwin & Cradock, 1835.

Warren, Samuel, *A Letter to the Queen on a Late Court Martial*. Blackwood, 1850.

Wellington, Duke of (edited by John Gurwood), *The Dispatches of Field Marshal the Duke of Wellington: during his various campaigns in India, Denmark, Portugal, Spain, the Low Countries, and France*. Cambridge: Cambridge University Press, 2010.

Williams, William, *England's battles by Sea and Land, from the Commencement of the French Revolution*. London Printing and Publishing Company (1854–59).

Index